WOMEN IN GAME OF THRONES

Power, Conformity and Resistance

Valerie Estelle Frankel

McFarland & Company, Inc., Publishers

Jefferson, North Carolina

Library of Congress Cataloguing-in-Publication Data

Frankel, Valerie Estelle.
    Women in Game of thrones : power, conformity and
resistance / Valerie Estelle Frankel.
        p.   cm.
    Includes bibliographical references and index.

    ISBN 978-0-7864-9416-3 (softcover : acid free paper) ∞
    ISBN 978-1-4766-1554-7 (ebook)

    1. Game of thrones (Television program) 2.   Women on
television.   3. Feminism on television.   I. Title.
PN1992.77.G35F73 2014
791.45'72—dc23   2014010532

British Library cataloguing data are available

On the cover: Lena Headey as Cersei Lannister in *Game of
Thrones*, 2013 (HBO/Photofest)

Printed in the United States of America

McFarland & Company, Inc., Publishers
  Box 611, Jefferson, North Carolina 28640
    www.mcfarlandpub.com

Women in
Game of Thrones

ALSO BY VALERIE ESTELLE FRANKEL

Buffy and the Heroine's Journey: Vampire Slayer as Feminine Chosen One (McFarland, 2012)

From Girl to Goddess: The Heroine's Journey through Myth and Legend (McFarland, 2010)

EDITED BY VALERIE ESTELLE FRANKEL

Teaching with Harry Potter: Essays on Classroom Wizardry from Elementary School to College (McFarland, 2013)

Acknowledgments

With grateful thanks to Yonatan Bryant, Matthew Diamond, Steve Frankel, Matt Gottlieb, and Ben Leitner for discussions, debate, and all things *Game of Thrones*.

Table of Contents

Table of Contents

Introduction

Game of Thrones and its treatment of women is currently one of the most hotly debated issues in popular culture. Certainly there is a spectrum of strong women, from Brienne to Daenerys. Some viewers give the flimsier characters a free pass as "products of their historical era," while others find the show problematic but watch it despite its flaws. The question is, is *Game of Thrones* presenting a feminist statement? Or just pandering to men with its degraded, underdressed prostitutes in increasingly sensationalized scenes?

Emilia Clarke, who plays Daenerys, summarizes fans' warring attitudes quite well: "The world we're describing is not the world we're living in today. In my mind, it's loosely based around medieval times, where women weren't even close to being thought of as equal to men. When you put it into perspective and look at what these women have accomplished and what they are capable of doing against all odds, I definitely think it's empowering." She adds, "You turn on the television at any point, and nine out of ten times, you're going to see more naked women than naked men. I cannot wait for the day when that is very different" (Keveney).

The evidence suggests that it isn't "just a boys' show." In fact, women account for 42 percent, or about two million, of the show's 4.8 million viewers. Furthermore, women have about 50 percent of the online conversations about *Game of Thrones* ("Shocker (Not): Women Like *Game of Thrones*"). Executive producers David Benioff and D.B. Weiss are often asked their views on the women's roles (especially the nude ones) on the show. Weiss responds: "I think there's a mistaken notion fantasy is a boys' club and aimed more at teenage boys. These books are aimed at adults and had, if anything, more strong female characters than male. Television is such a great place to fill that gap that seems to have opened up in film, where I don't think you see the strength and depth of female characters" (Keveney).

George R.R. Martin, author of the original book series, considers himself a feminist, with female characters as vibrant and expressive as the male ones: "To me, being a feminist is about treating men and women the same," he says. "I regard men and women as all human—yes there are differences, but many of those differences are created by the culture that we live in, whether it's the medieval culture of Westeros, or 21st century Western culture" (Salter). Most fans acclaim Martin for his three-dimensional female characters. Even a hated figure like Cersei is still a relatable person.

However, on the show, the characters are more likely to be forced into traditional archetypes; Brienne's painful backstory and horror at killing vanishes, leaving her a conventional warrior woman. Robb's television wife is a trite career woman who "doesn't need a man to get by." The archetypes have a deeper problem as well: Strong characters are portrayed with classically masculine characteristics, and weak characters with feminine ones. Thus the women must reject their feminine side to operate in the men's sphere. For every female character demonstrating power, there also seems to be an accompanying weakness. Cersei and Catelyn act from emotion and they generally lose at politics. Brienne keeps losing her employers after picking unlucky sides. Talisa is killed. Arya, a child, wields power through her disguises and rejection of her identity. Daenerys begins the story raped and abused, before she falls in love with that very rapist.

Certainly, there's a spectrum of female characters. However, the number of characters who resort to sex to get ahead or abandon all trace of womanhood as a path to power leaves very few women playing the game of thrones in their own right, and even fewer who enjoy being female. As behavioral models go, most of these are sadly lacking.

Despite these disturbing twists, the actresses of *Game of Thrones* are enthusiastic about their roles. Lena Headey (Cersei) notes: "I think the women in *Game of Thrones* are fascinating, admirable, frightening" (Keveney). Michelle Fairley (Catelyn) adds:

> The women do not come over as victims. [They] seem to be in control of their own destinies. There is a lot of sex in it because that's the nature of the world they live in, the time they live in, which could be said about today and the way women in the media use their sexuality to further their careers. But if they're the ones controlling it and guiding it, is that sexist? [Keveney].

Gwendoline Christie (Brienne) believes the show's massive success with women lies in its approach to rounded female characters. "It has women being really badass, it has women being Machiavellian, being scheming, women being brilliant and women being incredibly strong, physically, mentally and wearing some really incredible gowns," she explains (qtd. in "Stars Turn Out").

This book looks at issues of feminism and empowerment character by character, examining through their archetypes how they conform to traditional roles and how they break out as individuals. A glance at similar characters in history is included, to show how much they are or aren't products of their times; Martin's characters are largely based on medieval figures, especially those in the War of the Roses. While this book focuses on the more popular and widespread show through the currently completed third season, it includes details, quotes, and a few minor book characters for purposes of comparison or analysis. The issues appearing in the series reflect issues today. Examining the tropes of fantasy and history reveals much about modern viewers and their understandings of femininity.

PART I

Controversial Issues in the Series

Gratuitous Sex?

HBO shows, especially the histories and historical retellings, are famous for nudity and explicit sex. They are, as one critic notes, "populated by dehistoricized male characters who have magnificent bodies, engage in energetic sex and commit brutal and spectacular violence. They present the erotic spectacle of female bodies being sexually abused and the violent spectacle of male bodies being physically abused" (Glynn 161). The sex and violence are combined in the case of the women, and both are usually presented to titillate. Torture turns sexual even when it isn't meant to be, and the women are controlled, subjugated before they are killed.

Violence against women is common onscreen, as it provokes a visceral terror in both genders.

> As slasher director Dario Argento puts it, "I like women, especially beautiful ones. If they have a good face and figure, I would much prefer to watch them being murdered than an ugly girl or a man." Brian De Palma elaborates: "Women in peril work better in the suspense genre. It all goes back to the *Perils of Pauline*.... If you have a haunted house and you have a woman walking around with a candelabrum, you fear more for her than you would for a husky man." Or Hitchcock, during the filming of *The Birds:* "I always believe in following the advice of the playwright Sardou. He said 'Torture the women!' The trouble today is that we don't torture women enough" [Clover 234].

The bodies are also unrealistically presented: "History in these dramas has been populated with people who are clean, buff, and toned and who have sex at the drop of a period hat. Modern hair gels, breast implants and teeth whitening agents anachronistically exist" (Glynn 161). *Game of Thrones,* the television adaptation, is no exception.

While a few interesting character moments result from new conversations and jokes, the majority of original scenes in seasons one and two are the ones with prostitutes. Ros, the red-headed whore, adopts the roles of several different prostitutes in the books. Littlefinger's brothel also appears more. As such, season one criticism revolved around the naked women in scenes that stop the plot dead and thus seem unnecessary to story or character development. "When there's a naked woman on the screen, people start making judgments about it," Esmé Bianco (Ros) said. "I've been over here [in Los Angeles] since *Game of Thrones* came out, so I don't know how different the reaction has been in Europe, where people are a lot more tolerant of nudity on screen. People [here] see a pair of breasts, and they forget that there's a story going on."

"One of the reasons I wanted to do this with HBO is that I wanted to keep the sex," George R.R. Martin acknowledges, as he considers many of those moments central to the story (Hibberd, "EW Interview: George R.R. Martin"). However, is it too much, even for cable? Many scenes, from Renly and Loras's relationship (with new wife Margaery eager to join in) to Daenerys's sex lesson, were suggested in the books and seen explicitly in the show. Likewise, book–Osha impresses Theon with her spearwork, and show–Osha seduces him. Are the naked women scattered about King's Landing aiding in telling a great story or are they simply unnecessary?

In "*Game of Thrones:* Making Sense of All the Sex," critic Scott Meslow notes that the series "is set in a world in which sex is the primary means by which women can assert their power…. It's by design that virtually all the women in the series can be divided into two categories: noblewomen and prostitutes. For women without money or a bloodline to protect them, sex is the greatest means of survival." Yet, historically, there were shopwomen, tavernkeepers, servants, and crafters, older women and young children. True, noblewomen were traded like property, and only widows like Catelyn or Cersei generally managed to lead armies or become regents. But certainly there were many interactions with dressed women doing more than being bought and sold.

[Producer David] Benioff is particularly rankled that the criticism sometimes suggests that the show is more sexualized than the books. "That's just patently untrue," he said. "I think that people, because they're seeing things on screen, you're actually seeing someone's body, so it's much more in your

6

face than when you're reading it on the page." He cited a specific example from the fifth novel, *A Dance with Dragons:* a sex dance with full female and male nudity. "That scene would never been on that show. It couldn't be. And there are scenes, graphic sexual scenes, with 14-year-olds in the books, which would have us all thrown in prison, justifiably so. So we, actually, I think, if anything, shy away from some of the more sexual material. That's the only criticism, I think, that I would get defensive about" [Arthur].

The books may be more sexual, but the show's nudity is more sexist: Female characters spend too much time stripping in order to manipulate the male characters. Whether the Red Priestess asks her fanatical devotee Stannis to give her a monstrous pregnancy or Margaery Tyrell tries seducing her gay husband since she's expected to have royal heirs, women only know how to rule with their bodies, not their wits. And when they use their wits and distract the idiot soldiers with their cleverness, it's still a seduction scene.

The prostitutes are probably the most criticized aspect of the television adaptation. TV writer and academic Myles McNutt of *Cultural Learnings* invented the word "sexposition" to describe the show's frequent expository speeches delivered by or to naked women who otherwise have no effect on the plot. The most unnecessary scene to most viewers is the one where Littlefinger directs two prostitutes to perform while he ruminates about power and love and pleasing men. The producers admitted it was unnecessary, adding, "We wrote that as an audition scene, never thinking we'd shoot it," but when they saw Littlefinger's acting, which was "strange and compelling," they were very impressed (Mitchell). Many critics have strong opinions on the scene's inclusion: McNutt adds, "I like the idea that Littlefinger is using some of his own strategies for tricking/deceiving men like Ned in his advice, but any real symbolism is lost amidst the moaning." Mary McNamara, in "HBO, You're Busted," notes, "The upper frontals got so gratuitous—two women teaching themselves the tricks of prostitution while a male character, fully clothed, muses about his personal history and definition of power— that fans took to Twitter to complain." Rhiannon, the critic at *Feminist Fiction,* points out that the naked women desensitize the viewers:

> The scene doesn't say that Westeros is cruel, or that Littlefinger is a jerk, although both of those things are true in this moment too. It simply says that naked, faux-lesbian women are there, in the background, to entertain the *viewer* while all the boring exposition stuff is going on. Far from high-

lighting how cruel and misogynistic Westeros is, this abundance of female nudity actually lowers the shock-value of the world due to overexposure. Should the viewer care that Joffrey is stripping Sansa naked in front of the court, when such things are just par for the course? ["Sexposition and Exploitation"].

"I don't know why sex and violence get highlighted so much," says producer D.B. Weiss. "You don't hear people talking about gratuitous punchlines and gratuitous politics: It's all about what belongs in any given scene. We put in the show what we think belongs in the show" (Arthur). Surely exploiting women and displaying them as objects should be filed differently than characters using too many punchlines. However, it must be conceded that the producers heeded complaints and dialed back the prostitute "sexposition" in favor of plot-relevant, amorous sex between couples like Robb and Talisa, and Jon and Ygritte. As Meslow concludes, "In the end, it's up to each viewer to decide whether this much explicit content is necessary, or worth sticking around for."

Rape

The frequent rapes and attempted rapes, even more frequent in the books, also generate a great deal of controversy. Viewers and readers can accept that rapes and unwanted arranged marriages were common in such times, and that scenes like the Dothraki violently attacking the Lazareen and abusing the women are realistic. It's true that many women were raped in the Middle Ages, especially in wartime, so the subject is presented with historical accuracy. But the question is, how else is the subject treated? Rape as entertainment and titillation appears around the world in a truly disturbing current of violence.

Critical representations of the harsh reality of sexual violence, as in feminist films such as *Dust* and *Cruel Embrace,* are particularly pertinent in the context of systematic rape of women in wars. Feminists have disclosed the frequent use of rape as a weapon in war (cf Brownmiller 1975). At the time of writing this chapter, news was reported about rape camps in Bosnia, about enforced pregnancies and the Catholic interdiction on abortion even in those extreme circumstances. Most horrifying of all, it is purported that some rapes were filmed on video and distributed as pornography for the soldiers [Smelik 192].

By contrast, "most feminist films about sexual violence give a lucid analysis of the predicaments and contradictions of women's experiences in a male-dominated culture, without the fetishism, voyeurism and sadism of traditional Hollywood cinema." Feminist films don't treat rape as entertainment but as a violent, traumatic experience from which the victims must recover and discover the way to peace. "On the contrary, they evoke a deep sympathy with the plight of the female victims" (Smelik 90–91).

Game of Thrones, book and show, is caught between these examples. As the essay "Power and Feminism in Westeros" reflects, rape is condemned in both:

> There's an enormous amount of violence against women in *A Song of Ice and Fire,* and its portrayal is uniformly negative. It is always uncomfortable rather than titillating. Rape and sexual violence, both from "protectors" and from strangers, are persistent threats to all the female characters. Robert Baratheon drunkenly rapes Cersei; when she tells him he's hurt her, he blames it on alcohol. Sansa, Arya, and Brienne all experience verbal threats of sexual violence from a wide variety of men. This omnipresent threat in these women's lives creates what amounts to an environment of sexual oppression. That this circumstance is rarely remarked upon by the characters shows just how entrenched it is in the culture [Spector 185].

The Dothraki consider rape an acceptable practice and the Ironmen believe "The Drowned God had made them to reave and rape, to carve out kingdoms and write their names in fire and blood and song" (II.169). When Daenerys sees the Dothraki killing and raping a peaceful village girl, she is horrified—no amount of conforming to Dothraki ways will make this acceptable to her. Ser Jorah tells her, "You have a gentle heart, but you do not understand. Those men have shed blood for the *khal.* Now they claim their reward" (I.668). Likewise, one of Dany's maids tells her the men "do this girl honor" (I.670). Daenerys fights this cultural imperative and demands protection for the women. However, it backfires. Mirri Maz Duur betrays her out of revenge, and one girl (in the books) is later raped and murdered by Drogo's warlord. Dany has failed to save them.

With entire cultures committing to this misogynistic violence, the practice gains a type of legitimacy.

Indeed, what of the sexuality of most of the female characters in the series? Those who aren't raped outright at some point in the story must live with the knowledge that such sexual degradation always exists as a very real possibility. One argument against such brutal content, and it's a compelling one, is that the sexual humiliation of women in *A Song of Ice and Fire* is just too cavalier, too omnipresent—that it overwhelms other aspects of the books. How would male readers react to an epic story written by a woman where virtually every chapter features a man being violently assaulted? [Hartinger 164].

Other rapes are treated as expected threats of wartime, in the Battle of Blackwater or along the Kingsroad. Women are expected to travel with protectors, while men are assumed to be savages during the time of unrest.

In the books, these acts are common but also reviled—in Westeros, they're evil, unforgivable acts. Spousal rape repels the better male characters and several want to kill the perpetrators, even kings, to protect the queens. King Robert regrets his rapes of Cersei, though they continue, and Jaime is desperate to protect Queen Rhaella, even from Mad King Aerys. Rapists are condemned to the Wall for life imprisonment or castrated—most earth cultures today don't punish rape so harshly. How the men in charge treat these acts is an important part of the books: Stannis castrates men under his command for raping wildling women, indicating a rigid justice even for women not under his protection. Davos is disgusted when Salladhor demands Queen Cersei and refuses to make it a condition. Jaime executes one of the Mountain's men who tries to rape a serving maid (IV.446). He counsels his servant to be kind to her if she's willing to be his lover. Tyrion refuses to consummate his marriage to Sansa because he knows she's young and unwilling. On the show, less time is spent on punishments, so it's not as evident that rape is a terrible crime.

Of course, the individual leaders are often corrupt. Victarion Greyjoy, Theon's uncle, hates his brother Euron for raping and impregnating his third wife. Victarion responds by beating her to death in order to cleanse himself of the taint of dishonor, and he blames Euron for the loss. Bronn, a brute and disloyal sellsword, tells a lady as he steals her birthright that he'll pass her around the garrison if any of them will have her, as he puts it (IV.688–89). When Theon takes Winterfell in the books, the kennel master's daughter Palla is raped, and he whips the rapists to show his fairness. Later, however, Theon threatens Palla to make her father serve him. Tywin arranges marriages for Cersei and Sansa, against the women's wishes. Most disturbing of the patriarchs is Viserys Targaryen, who tells Daenerys, "I would let his whole tribe fuck you, all forty thousand men and horses too, if that's what it took" ("Winter Is Coming," 1.1).

Similarly, Jon Snow has heard that Craster "was a kinslayer, liar, raper, and craven, and hinted that he trafficked with slavers and demons" (II.355). Rape is one of his many unsavory acts, including incestuous rape, but he is a necessary ally. To preserve their relationship with him, Lord Mormont orders the Night's Watch not to touch his wives (who also happen to be his daughters). On their return trip, when the order's discipline breaks down, one of the first things the chaos spawns is the rape of those women, who previously had been considered sacrosanct. These actions mark the men as traitors and apt targets for the mysterious Others.

Using rape to create a character's backstory is problematic because it reduces the character to the violent act itself, rather than a person. In other series, Red Sonja or Lisbeth Salander become embodied female rage and damage more than fully formed individuals. Echoing this tradition, Gilly is a victimized female, and her entire story arc as she offers herself to her rescuer Sam reflects this backstory. Likewise, Mirri Maz Duur was raped, so she takes revenge on the Dothraki. It becomes unclear whether she's meant to be a just person or an evil one, a wise advisor or a crafty trickster—violence was done to her, so she lashes out, even against Daenerys who showed her kindness.

The two greatest monsters in the series, Gregor Clegane, the Mountain That Rides, and Ramsay Bolton, bastard lord of the Dreadfort, are both known for rape and savagery. Gregor's appearances have been trimmed on the show, but in the books, he begins a campaign of rape and murder through the Riverlands during Robb's war there. When the Targaryens fell, Clegane raped Princess Elia and murdered her children with a savagery that permanently taints his reputation. Even Tywin Lannister, who uses Clegane for his dirtier jobs and rarely justifies himself to anyone, tells Tyrion, "The rape … even you will not accuse me of giving that command, I would hope" (III.719).

Ramsay's brutality appears in season three as he tortures Theon. (In the books, these scenes appear as flashbacks when Theon reappears in book five.) Ramsay is also involved in a book two subplot in which he seizes a widow in the North, forcibly weds her, and then locks her in a tower where she starves. He kills his legitimate brother, leaving himself as sole heir. By the time he appears in book five, he is a reviled figure, even more so when readers see his savagery toward women. "When Ramsay catches them he rapes them, flays them, feeds their corpses to his dogs, and brings their skins back to the Dreadfort as trophies. If they have given him good sport, he slits their throats before he skins them. Elsewise, t'other way around" (V.423). In fact, Ramsay comes by his brutality from his father, who participates in the Red Wedding and whose men chop off Jaime's hand in the show. Ramsay tells Theon, "I shouldn't make jokes. My mother taught me not to throw stones at cripples. But my father taught me, aim for their head" (3.10).

Daenerys's own rape on the show (though not in the books) is one of the most problematic changes. The female conqueror and heroic mother of dragons was once a rape victim who grew to love her rapist. Meslow adds:

> Daenerys Targaryen was the primary victim of Westeros' lopsided sexual politics in [the first] episode: She was nakedly appraised and traded off like an animal by her brother, Viserys, then raped by her brutish new husband, Khal Drogo. ("The Kingsroad" features another scene of Drogo callously raping Daenerys, which raises disturbing questions about just how much sexual violence she's been subjected to since her wedding night.) It's worth noting that all of the sex [in *Game of Thrones*' first episode] has consisted of a man taking a woman from behind while she's on her hands and knees. There's something animalistic about the ways in which the men treat women in *Game of Thrones* in general, and sex is the most obvious signifier.

In the book, Drogo is kinder to Daenerys. Yes, the only word of her language he knows is "no," but by making the word a question and gently seducing her until she says "yes" on their wedding night, the message is far different. Daenerys has never had a choice about anything, thanks to her vicious brother. Under Drogo's protection, beginning from their wedding night, she evolves into an outspoken khaleesi. She asks her attendant for sex lessons and seduces Drogo so they conceive a child. But in the book, though she complains of her brother "selling" her to Drogo, she doesn't fall in love with her rapist, just a mysterious foreigner.

On the show, Daenerys is sobbing and miserable, clearly desperate to escape the terrifying stranger. In the second episode, she stares despairingly at her dragon eggs instead of her husband. These scenes are titillating with full nudity and no lasting trauma seen, from Dany and Drogo's early encounters to Joffrey with a pair of prostitutes (though the latter grows increasingly violent and disturbing).

By contrast, Brienne and Sansa's fully clothed near-rapes focus more on the emotional pain of the ordeal. In "The Old Gods and the New," (2.6), Sansa is nearly raped. After being abandoned by Joffrey and rescued by the Hound, she sobs to Shae in her room that she doesn't understand how anyone could do such a thing. She sounds both childish and terrified. As she struggles through nightmares, the audience relives her terror with her. This scene is presented as horrifying without nudity or ambiguous emotions. It also serves to show the extent to which law and decency have broken down in the Capitol: The common people hate the Lannisters enough to riot and turn savage. They also tear the High Septon to pieces, declaring a war on their religion as well as their king.

In the same scene in the book, the unattractive Lollys, a lady of the court, is raped "half a hundred times" and gets pregnant as a result. Her eligibility for marriage, as her family attempts to foist her on uninterested lords and considers naming her child Tywin, is a subject of humor, not pathos. This is a far more problematic instance, as she is dismissed and ignored.

"Walk of Punishment" (3.3), deals with rape of many sorts. Even Theon is nearly raped during his escape attempt, the first male rape or attempted rape shown on the series. His experience is momentary before his persecutor is slain, and its repercussions are not dealt with onscreen. It becomes just one of many of the tortures Theon undergoes. In the dungeons, he's later set upon by naked women he shows no interest in, as he begs for escape. He's finally castrated, undergoing a horrific bodily invasion at the hands of his captor.

Ser Jorah points out in this episode that the Unsullied do not kill civilians or rape innocent women, unlike other soldiers. They have been castrated of their male urges and also their selfish urges to be a perfect fighting force, completely obedient to the will of Daenerys. On the other hand, they have gained this status by their own forced slavery and castration, to say nothing of the babies they killed during training.

After purchasing them, Dany asks Missandei if she's willing to go to war where she could be killed. Missandei replies that all men must die, and Dany reminds her that they are not men. This conversation seems to allude to rape—the fate of women in war, especially female slaves, but not men. Dany makes it clear that she realizes what she is risking for herself and the other innocents.

In a comic counterpoint to these more grisly scenes, Tyrion buys Podrick Payne time with three prostitutes as a reward. Two are fully frontally nude and the third does provocative acrobatics. Pod returns to the castle strutting—the prostitutes appeared pleased with him and have refunded Tyrion's money. Fascinated, Tyrion and Bronn ask him for details, so they can take "copious notes." A deeper meaning here is the prostitutes' message to Tyrion: A year before, Joffrey tortured two prostitutes and sent them back to Tyrion as a message. Shy, stammering Pod is one of the gentlest characters on the series. He pleased them, in all likelihood because he's self-effacing and kind rather than cruel or selfish. In this exchange, the women show what they want for a single scene amongst so many of pain and terror.

A truly chilling moment is Brienne's attempted rape, as the men haul her off into the darkness and she screams with rage. In the book, Jaime suggests she distance herself as much as possible, as he does when forced to do awful things. His suggestion on the show that she think of Renly is repeated from the book, but his flippant tone is new and far more offensive. Jaime manages to save her by appealing to the men's greed, but moments later, his own hand is chopped off. This is a rape of a sort, crippling him and permanently depriving him of power. With his hand gone, Jaime cannot perform any of the masculine acts of his life, from swordplay to cutting his meat. Jaime's trauma is referenced in his nearly every scene, while Brienne's goes largely unmentioned. It even seems to change his character more than hers.

When a character is raped to make an impact on the male characters' story arc, the women are cast as disposable casualties who exist only to affect the men, like when Tywin has a score of his guards rape his son's peasant wife to teach Tyrion a lesson. This type of writing trivializes violence against women and focuses on how it affects the men, not the women. Lyanna Stark's possibly consensual carrying-off is the ultimate example of this, since her "rape," as the men call it, began Robert's Rebellion. King Robert is still obsessed with Lyanna, over a dozen years after her death. He tells Ned, "What Aerys did to your brother Brandon was unspeakable. The way your lord father died, that was unspeakable. And Rhaegar ... how many times do you think he raped your sister? How many hundreds of times?" (I.112–13). Rhaegar's wife, Elia of Dorne, was raped and killed when the Lannisters took King's Landing. Her brothers, the current rulers of Dorne, have never forgotten this and still long to avenge her death,

In a scene unique to the show, Tyrion sends Joffrey two prostitutes. When Joffrey's offered this "gift," he looks momentarily terrified, unable to deal with adult women, only terrified Sansa. He refuses to let them touch him. Devilishly winding his crossbow and ignoring the prostitutes' pleas, Joffrey demands that one woman torture the other and then report to Tyrion "to show him what you've done," as Joffrey says (2.4). It is a scene of Joffrey torturing those of lower status than himself to send a message to a fellow man, emphasizing the women's unimportance. "It was a savage, disturbing scene of escalation and punishment and served as a reminder that Ros is a pawn in a larger game of power," Ros's actress said.

> No matter where any of the characters think they've gotten to in terms of power, there's always somebody that's willing to beat them down. It's the one time that we see Ros where her sex appeal does nothing for her and doesn't get her out of that situation. It's not about her being a prostitute; it's about her being just another person that Joffrey is going to stomp on [Lacob, "*Game of Thrones*' Esmé Bianco"].

Though this is a significant message, it's lost in the scene, which is more about performance, power, and titillation than it is a cry for the women to find power in Westeros.

Similarly, Roose Bolton casually tells the story of Ramsay's conception:

> I was hunting a fox along the Weeping Water when I chanced upon a mill and saw a young woman washing clothes in the stream. The old miller had gotten himself a new young wife, a girl not half his age. She was a tall, willowy creature, very healthy-looking. Long legs and small firm breasts, like two ripe plums. Pretty, in a common sort of way. The moment that I set eyes on her I wanted her. Such was my due. The maesters will tell you that King Jaehaerys abolished the lord's right to the first night to appease his shrewish queen, but where the old gods rule, old customs linger [...]. So I had him hanged, and claimed my rights beneath the tree where he was swaying. If truth be told, the wench was hardly worth the rope. The fox escaped as well,

and on our way back to the Dreadfort my favorite courser came up lame, so all in all it was a dismal day [V.429].

With rape leading to the birth of Ramsay Bolton, "The characters acknowledge an argument that Martin's been building for us all along: rape produces damage that lingers beyond a single act, a single victim. It can produce monsters that contribute to the destabilization of entire societies" (Rosenberg 26).

Male Gaze

Ginia Bellafante in her often-quoted *New York Times* article on *Game of Thrones* claims that fantasy is written for men and (apparently) romance and sex scenes are for women. She explains:

> The true perversion, though, is the sense you get that all of this illicitness has been tossed in as a little something for the ladies, out of a justifiable fear, perhaps, that no woman alive would watch otherwise. While I do not doubt that there are women in the world who read books like Mr. Martin's, I can honestly say that I have never met a single woman who has stood up in indignation at her book club and refused to read the latest from Lorrie Moore unless everyone agreed to *The Hobbit* first. *Game of Thrones* is boy fiction patronizingly turned out to reach the population's other half.

Admittedly, some fantasy epics like Tolkien's star mostly male characters. However, there are thousands of female fantasy authors from Anne Rice and Charlaine Harris to Marion Zimmer Bradley and Ursula K. LeGuin. There are women writing about women's issues, addressing race and other social issues, and crafting high Tolkienesque fantasy. Calling epic fantasy a genre for men is unfair and inaccurate.

Further, the *Game of Thrones* sex scenes are biased towards men and do not appear designed to appeal to women. The *Saturday Night Live* sketch where a teenage boy is humorously revealed as the co-producer seems far more fitting.

It isn't that more female body parts are shown than male body parts (though they are). It's that the men are treated as characters and controllers of the scene, while the women range from exploited to ignored barely-people. In his essay on the nude in European painting, John Berger observes, "Men act and women appear. Men look at women.

Women watch themselves being looked at" (qtd. in Smelik 10). Though the art has evolved, the motif has not. Kate Arthur in "9 Ways *Game of Thrones* Is Actually Feminist" comments:

> There's a Skinemax edge that creeps into *Game of Thrones* once in a while that at best cheapens the show, and at worst advances the persistent idea that women's naked bodies—even in the best of storytelling—are garnishes. While the show aspires to lure viewers who consume the best, smartest television, it also panders to the *True Blood* audience drunkenly yelling "boobs!" from the back row.

Laura Mulvey pioneered the study of gender-bias in cinematic gaze, explaining: "There are three different looks associated with cinema: that of the camera as it records the pro-filmic event, that of the audience as it watches the final product, and that of the characters at each other within the screen illusion." However, all three display significant sexism on *Game of Thrones,* as with much other media. Cameras focus on female body parts, showing viewers what they're expected to watch. As Mulvey describes gaze in film:

> At first glance, the cinema would seem to be remote from the undercover world of the surreptitious observation of an unknowing and unwilling victim. What is seen on the screen is so manifestly shown. But the mass of mainstream film, and the conventions within which it has consciously evolved, portray a hermetically sealed world which unwinds magically, indifferent to the presence of the audience, producing for them a sense of separation and playing on their voyeuristic fantasy.... Although the film is really being shown, is there to be seen, conditions of screening and narrative conventions give the spectator an illusion of looking in on a private world.

Long, lingering pans over a woman's body place viewers in the mind of a male main character and emphasize a woman as love or lust interest. Woman becomes an object being viewed, not a viewer, while the viewer learns to surrender her identity and identify as a straight man. Thus all the population must identify with the standards of straight men. Such film techniques are seen in many movies from Marilyn Monroe's entrance in *Some Like It Hot* to the stripteases and flirtation in *Charlie's Angels.* Some shows parody this as *Scary Movie* features repeated ripping clothes scenes and *Naked Gun 33⅓* shows a camera panning up a woman's legs, then knees, then more legs, for quite some time. Scarlett Johansson in *Avengers* and *Iron Man 2* and most Jessica Alba movies and shows include extensive shots over their bodies.

Certainly, *Game of Thrones* takes us into private bedrooms and tents, sharing with us many moments that in Martin's book stop at the tent door. On the television, the intimacy of the point of view is lost, and sex scenes are common with minor characters like Ros as well as major ones. However, it's the power roles of the sex scenes that are at issue here.

Mulvey identifies two forms of pleasure in visual media: pleasure in admiring another person and using the sight for sexual stimulation and identifying with the image seen.

> In a world ordered by sexual imbalance, pleasure in looking has been split between active/male and passive/female. The determining male gaze projects its fantasy onto the female figure, which is styled accordingly. In their traditional exhibitionist role women are simultaneously looked at and displayed, with their appearance coded for strong visual and erotic impact so that they can be said to connote to-be-looked-at-ness.

Mulvey adds that men, as controllers of the patriarchal structure, are made uncomfortable by being the object of the gaze, so they are instead cast as the gazers. This split appears several times, as Littlefinger directs his own porn show between two strippers in his brothel and Joffrey does something similar in his chamber, while displaying his own savagery. In both scenes, the women are minor characters, naked prostitutes designed to be watched, who aren't significant to the story. The more important male characters don't strip or participate in the sex scene; they instead order the women to put on artificial performances, while the men watch and judge them. Esmé Bianco (Ros) thinks that the objectification of women in these situations need not reflect on her: "Objectivity is almost a choice you make," she said. "As a burlesque performer, I didn't choose to be objectified. I'm entertaining people, and people can choose to see me as an object because I'm naked, but I don't choose to see myself like that … I hold the power" (Lacob, "*Game of Thrones*' Esmé Bianco"). She may hold the power in her mind, but viewers are encouraged to see the women as bodies rather than characters.

Other scenes in this vein include Melisandre stripping and giving birth while Davos watches, Margery stripping and trying to seduce Renly, Osha stripping for Bran's guards, and Sansa undressing while Tyrion peeks through a screen. Even powerful Daenerys rises from her bathtub to display herself for Daario, like a reward. Though these are private moments, we the audience are invited to watch the women strip and the men admire. The technique of "fragmentation" is often seen, focusing on isolated body parts. In three seasons, there are no scenes where a man strips for the admiration of a clothed woman. Even Lancel Lannister's brief scene as Cersei's kept lover lacks nudity, performance, or degradation. When Melisandre ties a helpless Gendry to the bed, the camera alternates between his face and a point-of-view shot over his shoulder at her naked upper body. Even in this situation, with active woman and passive, subordinate man, the camera angle is male.

Most sex scenes are heterosexual, with male and female body parts displayed for viewers. However, the men are shown full body, as powerful characters acting on women rather than passive sex slaves. While focus on women's body parts is often very close, panning slowly over the body like a pair of staring eyes, female gaze is often more distant with a focus on the entire body, acknowledging the man, not just as a potential lover but also as a specimen of manliness and power male viewers want to emulate.

> As the spectator identifies with the main male protagonist, he projects his look onto that of his like, his screen surrogate, so that the power of the male protagonist as he controls events coincides with the active power of the erotic look, both giving a satisfying sense of omnipotence. A male movie star's glamorous characteristics are thus not those of the erotic object of the gaze, but those of the more perfect, more completely, more powerful ideal ego conceived in the original moment of recognition in front of the mirror. The character in the story can make things happen and control events better than the subject/spectator, just as the image in the mirror was more in control of motor coordination [Mulvey].

Spectators, presumably male ones, get to identify with Littlefinger or Joffrey, the princes of their own particular spheres who can do anything they wish to the prostitutes. The power is theirs. Even men who are designed as attractive subjects to attract a female gaze, like Daario Naharis, are active characters who make important decisions. Thus male heterosexual viewers empathize with them even as other viewers admire their physiques. In her essay on gender in slasher films, Carol J. Clover notes:

> Some critics have wondered whether the female viewer, faced with the screen image of a masochistic/narcissistic female, might not rather elect to "betray her sex and identify with the masculine point of view." The reverse ques-

tion—whether men might not also, on occasion, elect to betray their sex and identify with screen females—has scarcely been asked, presumably on the assumption that men's interests are well served by the traditional patterns of cinematic representation. Then too there is the matter of the "male gaze." As E. Ann Kaplan sums it up: "Within the film text itself, men gaze at women, who become objects of the gaze; the spectator, in turn, is made to identify with this male gaze, and to objectify the women on the screen; and the camera's original 'gaze' comes into play in the very act of filming" [235].

Thus viewers are "made to" identify with men and "against" women. All the gender-biases stripping only exacerbates these feelings.

Brienne's bathtub scene is set apart, when she shares a large pool with Jaime in season three. When Jaime flippantly remarks that with Renly dead and his arm maimed, Brienne isn't much of a protector, she stands in rage. Her body is not displayed to the camera, only to Jaime. The scene is built as a moment of honesty between characters, with no seduction on either side. However, the episode's writer notes:

> For Brienne, there's this amazing, empowering moment, where she owns her ... I don't know the word ... her womanness. That moment where she stands before him, naked, defiant, when he's challenging her on her protection of him and Renly. And then that look on Jaime's face when he's looking at her before him. Really powerful stuff [Cogman, "Season 3 Interview"].

Being naked is weakened femininity on the show, generally speaking, and Brienne acts more from anger than a desire to show off her body. Brienne and Daenerys a few episodes later shouldn't have to strip for men to show their "womanness"—male characters don't strip to show their manliness.

In cinema, female gaze shows up on occasion: Daniel Craig's famous shirtless and small swim trunks scene in *Casino Royale* has become a popular image for the James Bond franchise. Angel and Spike are frequently shown mostly naked and even tied up by villains on *Buffy the Vampire Slayer*, which subverts most gender tropes. The *Avengers* franchise features many shirtless men disheveled, working out, and occasionally spied on by females, from Thor's mudwrestling scene to pans over Captain America boxing and the basically naked Bruce Banner.

Some viewers note that there's certainly male nudity on *Game of Thrones*: An article in *Gloss Magazine* notes: "It is chock full of naked man butt! Jon Snow, Jamie Lannister, Robb Stark, Khal Drogo, and Sir Loras and the dudes he bangs are all prime examples of the top choice man meat this show regularly presents to the female gaze" (Peck). Another critic notes, "*Game of Thrones'* Season 3 also seemed to have a higher diversity of nudity, with a notable influx of male backsides and even a few flashes of male full-frontal" (Noble). Kit Harington, who plays Jon Snow, adds, "There are female fans who enjoy the show for nudity too, who show up to Comic-Con screaming and make you feel like a rock star. I understand, looking at Nikolaj [Coster-Waldau (Jaime)]. He's like a demigod; it's ridiculous" (Hill). Certainly some male bodies are shown. But it's also a matter of attitude. As Mary McNamara notes in "HBO, You're Busted!" these shows are terribly slanted:

> Although there is male nudity—men occasionally, though not always, appear shirtless and/or bottomless when they are having sex with women—there are no male brothels, no scenes of clothed women, or men for that matter, sitting around chatting in a room filled with naked men…. For all their many functions, women's bodies are not props and prostitution is not something that should be regularly relegated to atmosphere.

The men are successfully having their way with women rather than being degraded in houses of prostitution or coercion. None are forced to strip for a woman's viewing. *Game of Thrones* with its prostitutes of course takes its place among many other HBO and Starz shows for cable. "No one can beat HBO for hookers—the pole dancers of *The Sopranos*, Al Swearengen's Gem Saloon on *Deadwood*, the record-breaking female nudity of *Rome*, and now, *Boardwalk Empire*. HBO has a higher population of prostitutes per capita than Amsterdam or Charlie Sheen's Christmas card list," McNamara adds. All of these shows are known for the sex, all of which appeals to the male gaze.

Episode 1 of *The Borgias* contains several sex scenes. In the first, a woman is shown gazing at herself in a mirror during the act, emphasizing herself as an object of gaze. Later the new pope slips into his ward's room to watch her naked and flagellating herself at his orders before he seduces her. Later she has sex with another man—he is fully clothed; she is naked and soon murdered. As the episode begins and ends with men's conspiracies, it's clearly established as a man's world.

On *The Tudors,* Henry and his best friend Charles "seduce, cast aside, or send women running back to their husbands. They are heterosexual supermen" (Glynn 168). Granted, the first episode focuses on the women's smiling faces as well as interlocked body parts—having affairs is portrayed as something the women want as much as the men, for it frees them from oppressive husbands and fathers. Still, the men are the choosers and controllers.

> *The Tudors* resonates with the present in its depiction of a country struggling for strength and security. England's dynamic nature is presented as bound up with the king's forceful virility and militaristic aggression as he propels his country towards a better future, a reclamation of Western masculinity under threat by weakness on the international stage [Glynn 169].

It's a man's world, and a manly show within that world. Thus viewers are encouraged to empathize with the powerful men once more.

However, the presentation of nudity sometimes differs. As an interviewer discusses with Anna Paquin, female star of *True Blood*:

> *Michael Martin:* It's a sexy show. But what's interesting to me is that the guy playing your brother is the one who's gratuitously topless and naked, kind of like the women in '80s horror movies.
> *Anna Paquin:* We take his clothes off a lot. As the season goes on, the nudity gets shared around, but in the first couple of episodes, he carries the brunt of that.
> *Michael Martin:* What did you and the other women in the cast think of the guy playing the naked-bimbo role? Payback?
> *Anna Paquin:* It is kind of funny. It is a very sexy show. All of us girls are running around in shorts that barely cover our behinds. Yeah, he's naked a lot, but when you have a body like that ... I mean Ryan [Kwanten] has, in all fairness, a ridiculously nice physique, so I don't think he minds too much [M. Martin].

Paquin describes co-star Kwanten's physique in a way that encourages female fans to look, while discussing his appearances as naked eye-candy on the show. At the beginning of *True Blood's* season three, Sookie gazes lingeringly at a fully naked Eric Northman, who even invites her to look, asking, "See anything you like?" He ends the sixth season gloriously, frontally nude, with a slow camera pan in. *True Blood,* unlike the others, was based on a series of mystery-romances aimed at female readers, a likely motivation for the show's outreach toward females.

HBO's *Sex and the City* is the most female-driven of the shows. As such, each episode focuses on relationships and relationship problems. The female point of view is key, as Carrie provides the narration. While many issues and taboos are discussed that don't normally appear in mainstream television, body parts aren't terribly prevalent. The female characters, however, spend much of their time admiring men's physiques and discussing them. Sex scenes generally focus on the female main characters' faces, inviting viewers to empathize with them rather than exploit their bodies. As such, this show is quite unusual in the world of cable.

Fake Lesbian Scenes

The books have a homosexual relationship between Loras and Renly, shown much more explicitly on the show. On the show, Loras finds another male relationship afterwards as well. In medieval Europe, male-male or female-female relationships existed, but they were not conducted as modern gay or lesbian couples, conforming to modern stereotypes. Thus Renly's "rainbow guard" and status as the best-dressed man at court seem excessively modern. The television scenes, where Loras shaves Renly and Jaime calls Loras a "curly-haired little girl" likewise feel anachronistic. A homosexual relationship would have been more like Achilles and Patrocles—knight and squire or king and favored courtier. Some of the book's suggestive comments are more fitting for the time, as Tyrion notes: "Varys had suggested the woman to him; in former days, she had run Lord Renly's household in the city, which had given her a great deal of practice at being blind, deaf and mute" (III.655). Loras publicly admits only that he and Renly "prayed" together the night he was killed, a likely euphemism for sex (III.760). Nonetheless, Jaime humorously isn't fooled: "Now sheathe your bloody sword, or I'll take it from you and shove it up some place even Renly never found," he tells Loras (III.698).

Female-female relationships in medieval Europe were largely conducted behind closed doors away from male chroniclers, who often believed only men were sexual enough to initiate any sort of relationship. (When Benedetta Carlini, an abbess of Pescia, was discovered to have had a long-term sexual relationship with a nun under her supervision, she was certified as possessed, the only explanation her male examiners could conceive.) In *Game of Thrones,* there are no long-term female-female sexual relationships or clearly identified lesbian characters, even in the books. This is not surprising, as most relationships between females are subordinated and given less story time than male-male or male-female relationships. A few all-female sex scenes exist, but they are problematic enough to be open to criticism.

The two prostitutes exploring each other at Littlefinger's direction, and later Joffrey's, certainly have no interest in each other or in their male spectator. This performance is meant to titillate the men. Hollywood persists in scenes with attractive straight women making out with each other because they are so terribly sexual, as shown in the films *Cruel Intentions, Wild Things,* and *The Royal Tenenbaums.* Shows like *Friends, LA Law, Ally McBeal, Heroes, How I Met Your Mother, Gossip Girl,* and *Desperate Housewives* show specific one-time encounters, generally heavily hyped to improve their ratings. This has become known as the "Sweeps Week Lesbian Kiss" because it happens so regularly across so many shows. The women aren't portrayed as being sincerely interested in each other or planning to date women, but they kiss, presumably for the enjoyment of the male heterosexual audience.

Daenerys' "sex lesson" from the prostitute Doreah is a similar performance for the camera, with straddling and grinding. In the book, they have dinner together in the privacy of the tent, and later Daenerys reflects on skills she's acquired from what appears to have been only a verbal consultation.

While Daenerys appears to only be attracted to men (judging by her thoughts in the books), she has a series of additional book-encounters with handmaiden Irri. Daenerys shares her bed with alternating servant women after Drogo's death. (In medieval times, with cloth and heating expensive, this was a common practice.) In the third book, Ser Jorah kisses her, and that kiss awakens the "dragon," as Daenerys thinks of it. Daenerys is attracted to Jorah but resists having an affair with him. She thinks of him as an advisor rather than a true love and soulmate. That night, she begins touching herself, with her maid Irri curled beside her.

> The handmaid put a hand on her breast, then bent to take a nipple in her mouth. Her other hand drifted down across the soft curve of belly, through the mound of fine silvery-gold hair, and went to work between Dany's thighs. It was no more than a few moments until her legs twisted and her breasts heaved and her whole body shuddered. She screamed then. Or perhaps that was Drogon. Irri never said a thing, only curled back up and went back to sleep the instant the thing was done [III.324–325].

The following night, Daenerys politely tells Irri she's not comfortable doing that, though Irri protests it's an honor to pleasure the khaleesi. The relationship is master-servant, not erotic or romantic—Daenerys wants a man, and Irri's kisses "tasted of duty" (III.993). Daenerys is not who Irri desires either. Daenerys is even consciously aware that Irri is a substitute for the men she cannot have. In the fifth book, she calls upon Irri once again to act as the bodily substitute for the sellsword Daario Naharis, for whom Dany lusts:

> That night she could not sleep but turned and twisted restlessly in her bed. She even went so far as to summon Irri, hoping her caresses might help ease her way to rest, but after a short while she pushed the Dothraki girl away. Irri was sweet and soft and willing, but she was not Daario [305].

These scenes emphasize Daenerys's interest in specifically heterosexual sex.

In book four, Cersei has a sex scene with her best friend, Taena Merryweather. The woman is a "dark," "exotic" Myrish woman with whom Cersei exchanges many confidences (IV.150). Cersei, succumbing to paranoia and nightmares, has Taena share her bed so she won't be alone. One night, a bit drunk, Cersei stumbles into bed and wonders "what it would feel like to kiss another woman…. She wondered what it would feel like to suckle on those breasts, to lay the Myrish woman on her back and push her legs apart and use her as a man would use her …" (IV.685).

Cersei specifically wants to be the man in their sexual encounter; this is about dominance rather than affection or attraction. Cersei pinches Taena's nipple to wake her and squeezes until Taena cries, "You're hurting me." The queen then asserts her authority: "I am the queen. I mean to claim my rights." Taena reacts with enthusiasm.

> "Please," the Myrish woman said, "go on, my queen. Do as you will with me. I'm yours." But it was no good. She could not feel it, whatever Robert felt on the nights he took her. There was no pleasure in it, not for her [IV.692].

After, Cersei rejects Taena before Taena can pleasure Cersei in turn. Cersei thinks several times of Robert and not at all of Jaime, probably because Robert would dominate her with violence and pain to feel like a king—this is what she's seeking, not the true love she experiences with her twin. She later smirks gleefully, "Without her valiant brother, our

25

little queen [Margaery] is next to naked" (IV.684). She wants to make other women vulnerable as men have made her. This proves sadly ironic when she falls into the clutches of the High Septon.

Race

> Another major problem with the show is race. All of the major characters in the show are white. The minor characters of color who exist in the show are Otherized: basically, presented as exotic, evil, or helpless. (The only exceptions I can think of are Missandei, Talisa, and Grey Worm.) There is a gross "white savior" aspect to one of the major subplots which was especially apparent in last week's season finale.

As Luz Delfondo notes above in "Why More Feminists Should Watch *Game of Thrones*," the series' racial diversity is problematic. Daenerys, apparently "the little white girl adventuring amongst the brown people" in Slaver's Bay, makes many viewers uncomfortable in "Mhysa" (3.10). The brown-skinned slaves raise her to the skies, calling her "mother" in the trope of the "great white savior." She has proclaimed them free, and they could not have freed themselves without her help. Now she has come to be their messiah and teach them her superior ways.

The postcolonial feminist philosopher Gayatri Spivak warns that when people from one country try to help those in another, they run the risk of infantilizing them, doubting that the locals will ever manage to right the wrongs and save themselves. The saviors become oppressors, perpetually treating their subjects as dependent and childlike. Thus "we reproduce and consolidate what can only be called feudalism" (qtd. in Goguen 210).

In the book, Daenerys has a vision of this scene in the House of the Undying, emphasizing it as her destiny:

> Ten thousand slaves lifted bloodstained hands as she raced by on her silver, riding like the wind. "Mother!" they cried. "Mother, mother!" They were reaching for her, touching her, tugging at her cloak, the hem of her skirt, her foot, her leg, her breast. They wanted her, needed her, the fire, the life, and Daenerys gasped and opened her arms to give herself to them [II.707].

She names herself the freer of slaves, and sets up a society on that basis. However, the slaves of the books are mixed: people of the Dothraki, and Free Cities and even the race of the Ghiscari slaveowners as well as the dark-skinned Summer Isles (III.314). The image thus isn't so color-coded.

In the show, the scene was filmed in Morocco, with the crowd made of entirely of locals. Martin comments:

> Slavery in the ancient world, and slavery in the medieval world, was not race-based. You could lose a war if you were a Spartan, and if you lost a war you could end up a slave in Athens, or vice versa. You could get in debt, and wind up a slave. And that's what I tried to depict, in my books, that kind of slavery.
>
> So the people that Dany frees in the slaver cities are of many different ethnicities, and that's been fairly explicit in the books. But of course when David [Benioff] and Dan [Weiss] and his crew are filming that scene, they are filming it in Morocco, and they put out a call for 800 extras. That's a lot of extras. They hired the people who turned up [Anders].

Many fans compare Dany's adventures to a metaphor for colonialism, like that seen in *The Man Who Would Be King, Avatar, Indiana Jones, Tarzan, John Carter of Mars, The Last of the Mohicans,* and *The Lost World.* In such stories, the local way of life is usually depicted as savage and backwards, with the white ruler showing them a better way. Upon visiting Slaver's Bay, Ser Barristan trains knights among the locals while Daenerys appoints local children as pages and loathes native dress. Daenerys is determined to end the barbarity of the fighting pits, but is shown to be naïve as the former gladiators and former slaves beg to return to their old way of life and the terrorist attacks against Daenerys's regime escalate. Martin notes that some fans compare it to "our current misadventures in Afghanistan and Iraq" but that he is not making such a direct parallel, adding, "I've said many times I don't like thinly disguised allegory, but certain scenes do resonate over time" (Pasick).

However, the "white savior" appears earlier as well: The Dothraki "savages" live on the plains, raiding and riding as they wish before Daenerys appears. Their rituals are alien, as Daenerys consumes an entire raw horse heart, and eats horse and dog meat. Her chorus of handmaids prattle "it is known" about all their religious customs, implying they are fact. Daenerys ignores them often. Even the lessons she learns among them are problematic:

> The idea of the "noble savage"—the notion that being a despised other always endows you with great dignity and wisdom—is just another stereotype. It's

a well-intentioned one, but it's almost as limiting as the others. When minority or outcast characters exist in a story solely to teach lessons to members of the majority, it's just one more way of seeing everything from the majority point of view [Hartinger 160].

The different Dothraki khals and their followers are also not clearly differentiated. The cities of Slaver's Bay are slightly unalike, but none have the variation seen between cities in Westeros, like King's Landing and Dragonstone.

Among the Dothraki, Daenerys takes on some of their traditions like dress, but refuses to retire to Dosh Khaleen, the city of Dothraki crones. Instead, she insists on ruling the khalasar, and most of the people leave since she is imposing her world's customs on theirs. No female khals are shown in the series, but instead the crones rule in a different way. The book notes, "Even the mightiest of *khals* bowed to the wisdom and authority of the *dosh khaleen*" (I.492). As Daenerys refuses this role and commands that Drogo's bloodriders become hers, they all quietly refuse her. She manages to keep only the sick and old remnants of the people, and she does it through the magic of Westeros and Old Valyria—waking her dragons—rather than learning their traditions and becoming one of the Dothraki. She keeps them as warriors and even advisors, but she's determined to lead them across the sea they fear and use them to conquer her homeland.

Prophecy suggests that she will one day conquer all the Dothraki. In the house of the Undying, she has a vision of "a line of naked crones" shivering before her under their home by the Mother of Mountains (II.707). Quaithe, Daenerys's magical advisor, tells her to return to what she was: "To go north, you must go south. To reach the west, you must go east. To go forward you must go back, and to touch the light you must pass beneath the shadow" (II.426). In book five, she leaves the cities of Slaver's Bay and returns to the grasslands to meet the Dothraki tribes once again. As such, she may impose all her teachings and lead them to Westeros at last, validating her culture as superior.

The people of Westeros (basically England) are white, as are the wildlings. The southernmost of the seven kingdoms, Dorne, has people from a different background who are more Spanish–Middle Eastern in culture. Dornish characters will arrive in King's Landing in season four, played by Chilean actor Pedro Pascal (Prince Oberyn Martell) and partly

Indian Indira Varma as his lover. Those from the Summer Islands are played by African-American actors (Xaro, Salladhor Saan, and Missandei are basically the only characters with this origin, but more could appear). Far-off Yi Ti has not been seen, nor have its people, but it appears to represent China, as the continent of Sothoryos is Africa. The cities of Slaver's Bay echo Carthage, and are filmed in Morocco, with mostly Moroccan actors.

The continent of Essos varies: Talisa comes from Volantis, with her exotic olive skin, but Braavos, a former slave colony, echoes historical Venice with a mixture of races. Pale Varys was born in Lys. Shae comes from Lorath, most cryptic of the cities. The look of Old Valyria, from which the Free Cities of Essos derive, is supposed to be Daenerys's look—silver-gold hair and purple eyes (in the books) or white hair on the show. Little of the free cities has been seen after Daenerys's wedding to Drogo in Pentos—a few characters have so far been representative.

Of course, the cultures are not one-to-one representations of their real-world counterparts. Martin notes, "Dothraki are partially based on the Huns and the Mongols, some extent the steppe tribes like the Alvars and Magyars. I put in a few elements of the Amerindian plains tribes and those peoples, and then I threw in some purely fantasy elements. It's fantasy" (Anders). Their color reflects this background, though Jason Momoa (Drogo) hails from Hawaii.

It's realistic that the equivalent of medieval England has few non-whites visiting—those who are there are treated as exotic foreigners, from the Summer Islands dignitary seen in the books to Talisa the healer. However, with few non-white characters, their treatment becomes representative of their race, making disturbing commentary.

Giving Robb and Tyrion exotic foreign girlfriends from Volantis emphasizes their sexual prowess, as they are able to "satisfy" exotic women. Likewise, Podrick pleases even the expert courtesan who can perform the Meereenese knot, and Jon surprises and pleases the experienced wildling Ygritte. However, Talisa's "color change" from the books accompanies heightened cruelty. In the online post "*Game of Thrones and Violence Against Women of Color*," the author writes:

> The grotesque and unnecessary violence against Talisa was particularly disturbing due to her status as one of the few people of color on the show. *Game of Thrones* stars an almost entirely white cast, and an even smaller

subset of the people of color on the show are women. Even more troubling is the fact that almost every single one of these women of color have been subject to graphic, often sexualized, violence not originally present in the text.

In the books, Talisa's equivalent white character from Westeros is not present at the Red Wedding. She survives, not pregnant, and her family affiliation with the Lannisters is restored. Talisa, pregnant, is stabbed repeatedly in the belly, an image of particular violence against women. She dies in front of Robb, heightening their tragedy. The aforementioned post notes, "I assume that the showrunners made her pregnant in order to add another layer of tragedy to the already explosive scene, but the real effect was to further create a world in which women of color are subject to increasingly disturbing and repulsive forms of violence."

Daenerys's two Dothraki handmaids, the other non-white women in the show, remain as part of her entourage in the books as she conquers Slaver's Bay. Doreah from Pentos dies in the desert, but Irri and Jhiqui are an ever-present part of the story, as are Daenerys's three bloodriders. Granted, the show streamlines characters as it has far too many to handle. Missandei becomes a more useful guide to Slaver's Bay, so she is kept and the Dothraki women eliminated. However, the non-white women surrounding Daenerys are thus reduced.

> Jhiqui is not mentioned after the season 1 finale, and it is assumed that she abandoned Dany and fled with the rest of the khalasar that turned against Dany when Drogo died. Irri was betrayed and violently killed by another (white) handmaid of Dany, Doreah, who then abandons Dany.... Irri's death in itself is not extremely violent in terms of *Game of Thrones*, where people are murdered with shocking frequency. What makes it significant though is the fact that at the time of her death she was the only woman of color on the show ["*Game of Thrones* and Violence Against Women of Color"].

Irri's death was filmed but cut for time (and thus appears in the DVD extras). However, her offscreen sacrifice certainly seems a prelude to Talisa's brutal onscreen death. Both characters fail to break out of supporting roles to Daenerys and Robb respectively. While Missandei never embarks on an independent character arc to date, it is hoped she may do so in the future.

Independent Action versus Acting for Others

The chart below demonstrates another problem for the female characters: Almost all of them act in service to men. Most characters appearing in the show are listed, though a few soldiers, servants, and scions of various houses have been trimmed. Major characters are in bold (determined by the number of episodes in which they appeared).

A definition seems necessary on "characters who live in relation to others." These characters don't just love another person—that other person and his or her agenda and well-being is their entire purpose in the story, the only window viewers have to their life. Most or all conversations are about this other character, most or all screen time is spent worrying about what this other character thinks about their actions. Melisandre aids Stannis (at least ostensibly); Catelyn nurtures Robb and Bran (and to a much lesser extent, her other children and Tully relations); Brienne guards Renly, Jaime, and Catelyn; and so forth.

At other times, a character's entire storyline exists to affect another: While Ygritte may have had a life before Jon Snow, in the series she's never seen outside his presence or talking with others about anything except him. Thus too many women spend every appearance in show and book relating to, seducing, and otherwise completely consumed with obsession for men. Joffrey's sister Myrcella, sent to Dorne for a season two alliance-marriage, is a pawn fought over by Cersei, Tyrion, and the nobles of Dorne, while she barely speaks a handful of lines, even in the book. Margaery and Cersei have frequent spats, but at the heart of them is Margaery's influence over Joffrey. Sansa's every scene is pacifying Joffrey or dealing with a lecherous Littlefinger. A strong young woman like Meera Reed who spends all her time fussing over Bran and her brother is discarding her own agenda to care for her world's dominant gender.

If we apply the Bechdel Test, this series is in trouble. The test (named for comic strip creator Alison Bechdel) insists that a film or show must meet the following criteria:

1. It includes at least two women
2. who have at least one conversation
3. about something other than a man or men

Agendas on *Game of Thrones*

	Males		Females	
Independent Characters Following their Own Path				
INDEPENDENT: Acting for their own agendas and playing the Game of Thrones without confining their influence to a single character.	**Stannis, Robert, Renly, Tyrion, Littlefinger, Varys, Joffrey, Robb, Tywin, Viserys, Theon,** Illyrio Mopatis, Mance Rayder, Balon Greyjoy		**Daenerys,** Yara, Lady Olenna	
INDEPENDENT: Refusing to play, entering self-imposed exile	**Jon, Ned, Bran, Sam, Jaime,** Sandor Clegane, Beric Dondarrion		**Arya**	
Characters in Relation to Others	Men toward Men	Men toward Women	Women toward Men	Women toward Women
Protectors and Bodyguards	Hodor—Bran Bronn—Tyrion Kingsguard—Joffrey Jory Cassel—Ned	**Jorah—Dany Barristan—Dany** Bloodriders—Dany Grey Worm—Dany RodrikCassel—Catelyn Yoren—Arya	**Brienne—Renly & Jaime** Meera—Bran Osha—Bran	Shae—**Sansa** **Brienne—Catelyn** (Both spend much more time serving their men)
Lovers	**Loras—Renly**	**Drogo—Dany** Lancel—Cersei Daario Naharis—Dany	**Ygritte—Jon, Sansa—Joffrey, Margaery—Renly & Joffrey Melisandre—Stannis Shae—Tyrion** Gilly—Sam Talisa—Robb Selyse—Stannis Ros—many Prostitutes—many	

				Catelyn—Bran & Robb Cersei—Joffrey Lysa—Robin	
Parents				**Catelyn—Bran & Robb** **Cersei—Joffrey** Lysa—Robin	
Magicians and Seers	Thoros of Myr—Beric Dondarrion				Mirri Maz Duur—Dany Quaithe—Dany
Sidekicks, Servants, and Liege Lords in Service to Others		**Sam—Jon** **Davos—Stannis** Pod—Tyrion Ilyn Payne—Joffrey Brynden Tully—Robb Edmure Tully—Robb Kevan Lannister—Tywin Lannister Salladhor Saan—Stannis Various knights	**Pycelle—Cersei** Qyburn—Cersei Gendry—Arya Hot Pie—Arya		Doreah—Dany Irri—Dany Jhiqui—Dany Missandei—Dany
Mentors		**Commander Mormont—Jon** **Maester Luwin—Bran** Qhorin Halfhand—Jon Jojen—Bran Benjen Stark—Jon Maester Aemon—Jon	Syrio Forel—Arya Jaqen H'ghar—Arya	Old Nan—Bran	
Dependents (Children who obey adults or big siblings)		Rickon—Bran, Tommen—Joffrey	Robin—Lysa	Shireen—Davros, Myrcella—various	
Obstacles (Characters who only function as villains for other characters)		Janos Slynt, Walder Frey, Gregor Clegane, Rickard Karstark, Craster, Locke, Roose Bolton, Ramsay Snow, Allister Thorne, Various knights	Pyat Pree, Xaro, Slavers of Astapor & Sellswords—Dany		

Phrased in such cut and dry terms, it's hard to think of any in the show. Even Brienne's plea to fight for Catelyn is a result of King Renly's death. Sisters Arya and Sansa fight about Joffrey while sisters Catelyn and Lysa fight about Tyrion and little Robin. Shae protects Sansa, but all their talks focus on the men menacing the younger girl, from Joffrey to Littlefinger. The book series likely has a few Bechdel scenes in that many thousand pages, but offhand, only the sex scene between Daenerys and her handmaid comes to mind (yes, really). And even then, she's thinking of Ser Jorah.

The Bechdel test articulates the principle that fictional women should form bonds of sisterhood and work as a team, rather than competing over men and quarreling like Cersei and Margaery. Unfortunately, there is little female-female friendship, teamwork, or even interaction. In the books as well as the show, male relationships with women or other men are paramount.

In the eighties, a male writer conducted a survey to see how a thousand different people defined femininity. Men of middle age and older, those most invested in the patriarchal tradition, defined femininity as related to men—women were most womanly while being admired by and attractive to men or during heterosexual sex. Male interviewees of any age didn't think of women as feminine while giving birth or nurturing children, only in relation to themselves. Without men, women appear to fade from sight. By contrast, masculinity is often defined by relation with its own gender—working or being a man among men (Walker 35–36). This problematic viewpoint likewise appears in *Game of Thrones* as the women relate only to men, while the men interact with other men and play political games as well as interacting with the women.

A few of these were hard to place—filing Drogo as only Dany's lover would certainly insult him, but that's his role in the story—not to lay waste to the countryside but to change Dany as a person. How the characters function in the story is key: The pirate Salladhor Saan wants independence, but all his dealings are with Stannis and Davos, and outside of their tale he doesn't appear. Sansa's every conversation seems to be about Joffrey, hating him and escaping him perhaps, but this is still a life in relation to his. Her conversation with Cersei on her new adulthood is likewise all about Joffrey and marriage. No fathers appear on the chart, as devoted fathers like Davos and Ned still spend more story time on politics, whereas the mothers focus every scene on the child.

What does all this prove? four independent female characters (Dany, Arya, Yara, Lady Olenna) appear to be pursuing their own path without relation to others, either to rule or find a destiny free of the chaos, compared to 21 independent male characters, major and minor. Every other female character, and there are many, lives to serve someone and put his (usually *his*) interests ahead of hers. Those following their own agendas like Melisandre or Margaery still ostensibly serve a man, and there are no scenes in which they reveal more independent agendas. Thus 16 dependent female characters spend their time worrying about the man on whom they focus all attention.

The number of female relationships of any sort, even friendships, is minimal in the series. Only a handful of female characters—Dany's handmaidens and mysterious mentors—devote themselves to another female. (Shae's protectiveness towards Sansa—not part of the books— is the one exception, but Shae's relationship with Tyrion is more central to her employment and status. Likewise, Catelyn and Brienne spend almost no scenes together.) Without Daenerys, these numbers would be far more skewed.

Certainly, in this feudal society, we have many male characters exerting themselves on behalf of a lord or other male character. But the numbers are terribly unbalanced. Nowhere is there a relationship of two women in any category without a man being at the center of it—Dany's women, like Shae, advise their mistress on how to relate to the men around her in every conversation. Catelyn never has a private talk with either daughter on any subject, save Sansa's episode one plea to wed Joffrey. Catelyn's one mission for Brienne concerns guarding Jaime.

In several ways, women's status as Other is emphasized: Several characters go disguised as boys or men and it's a surprise that they're female. These include Brienne's helmet-doffing and Arya's revelation to Gendry. This emphasizes that male is "normal" and female is "unusual" or "surprising." Far more males (including main characters, secondary characters, and nameless soldiers) die in the series, reinforcing the concept that the females are unique in a male world.

> The presence of woman is an indispensable element of spectacle in normal narrative film, yet her visual presence tends to work against the development

of the story line, to freeze the flow of action in moments of erotic contemplation. This alien presence then has to be integrated into cohesion with the narrative. As Budd Boetticher has put it: "What counts is what the heroine provokes, or rather what she represents. She is the one, or rather the love or fear she inspires in the hero, or else the concern he feels for her, who makes him act the way he does. In herself the woman has not the slightest importance" [Mulvey].

This mode of criticism might seem unfair for *Game of Thrones* since many female main characters, especially Arya and Daenerys, drive the plot. However, they are a significant minority. Far more women follow the Boetticher path above and exist only to influence the story's men. Daenerys stands out as an independent female acting for herself, with women and men in service to her. D.B. Weiss notes: "There are plenty of opportunities for young women to be scared, abused, and terrorized in film and television, but there are virtually no roles that let them step into the fire—literally or otherwise—and come out the other side reborn as a leader and a warrior with an otherworldly poise and strength" (qtd. in Cogman, *Inside HBO's* Game 155).

While several male characters embark on the classic Chosen One arc, dying or nearly dying, only to be reborn more powerfully with new wisdom and power (Bran, Jon, Davos, Theon, Mance Rayder, Beric Dondarrion, Victarion Greyjoy, Jon Connington, and arguably others), only Daenerys fulfills this among the women.

Of course, there are great moments of power and agency: Sansa leads the women in prayer during the Battle of Blackwater. Shae beats Tyrion in a drinking game, revealing that she's nothing like he expected. Catelyn faces down an angry Lord Karstark and demands his obedience. Arya's every moment sparkles. But far too many women spend all their time in the story in service to a man instead of themselves.

PART II

Exploring Archetypes and Tropes

Female Archetypes

Martin explains, "I wanted to present my female characters in great diversity, even in a society as sexist and patriarchal as the Seven Kingdoms of Westeros. Women would find different roles and different personalities, so women with different talents would find ways to work with it in a society according to who they are" ("A Very Long Interview"). At the same time, he notes that fantasy series fail when writers stray into writing in stereotypes. "Some women hate the female characters," he says. "But importantly they hate them as people, because of things that they've done, not because the character is underdeveloped" (Salter). Certainly, the show streamlines backstories and dialogue, while the books have thousands of pages to present such things. However, the show often removes the ambiguity that makes some of Martin's characters so compelling. Arya is no longer seen killing innocents, nor is Cersei. Melisandre is more violent and opportunistic, more eager to exploit her sexuality, even with pawns like Gendry. As such, Melisandre becomes a classic femme fatale, Arya a classic action girl or Amazon with far less nuance.

Archetypes are not far removed from stereotypes: the wise old mentor, the witch, the damsel in distress. Carl Jung pioneered this theory of psychology, analyzing how these images appear in dreams, myth, and religion, all representing parts of the self. Martin's seven new gods are archetypes in this fashion: the Maiden, Mother, and Crone triad popular in much of world mythology along with the Father, Warrior, Smith, and mysterious Stranger.

The universality of archetypes helps them speak instantly to readers and watchers, but makes them the opposite of believable, beloved people.

The better characters subvert or break out of these roles: Book Asha is not just a brash pirate queen but also a responsible leader, worried daughter, and eager lover. Book Sansa and Margaery appear to be helpless marriage pawns, but both develop schemes and secrets as they forge covert alliances. On the show, characters are more clearly pigeonholed: Catelyn's advice turns more emotional as she becomes Robb's worried traditional mother and Jon's evil stepmother, who once prayed for him to die. Yara the pirate only interacts with her hidebound father and brother, leaving behind her sympathy for her mad mother or capable command of her loyal men.

Seeing how the show characters conform or break from the popular archetypes proves valuable in discovering which ones are unnatural or wooden and which are fully formed. Toni Wolff, longtime mistress of Carl Jung, described four main female archetypes: Mother, Hetaera, Amazon, and Medium.

Wolff's Archetypes

	As creator	*As destroyer*	*Power*	*Animus*
Amazon	Competitor, hard worker, builder	Fighter and death-dealer	Man's world of war and intellect	Father
Hetaera	Inspiratrice, lover, enabler	Femme fatale	Woman's world of relationships and self-knowledge	Lover
Mother	Nurturer, protector, teacher	Devouring mother	Life, birth, and creation	Son
Medium	Seer, magician, wisewoman	Deceiver and distorter of the future	Death, rebirth, and the future	Wiseman

The Amazon is the virgin warrior—Brienne, Arya, some of the wildling women. While the Amazon, like Artemis from Greek myth, may take occasional lovers, she has no permanent consort considering herself fiercely independent and complete in herself. By contrast, the Hetaera or sacred lover always acts on behalf of her consort. She is his lover or soulmate, image of perfection or muse, or on the dark side, femme fatale. The Mother likewise acts in the world on behalf of her child, not herself. There is the guide and guardian as mother, or on the dark side, the overpowering, smothering, infantilizing mother: Catelyn on the one side, Cersei and Lysa on the other. All three are widows, emphasizing their role as sole protectors of their children and heirs.

Each role has her classic Animus, her male counterpart who completes her or whom she exists to complete: As the mother lives and acts for her child, the hetaera for her lover, these are the more dependent figures. They are Anima women, women who exist to be the female counterpart for someone, as Ygritte connects Jon with wildling spirituality or Shae teaches Tyrion love. An Anima often molds herself to be what the man most wants, as Margaery fondles Joffrey's crossbow and speaks lovingly of the excitement of killing. By contrast, the Amazon may begin as a "Daddy's girl," but she's known for her independence, as is the Medium, who is often said to relate predominantly to the universe.

The Medium or Medial Woman is the most enigmatic of these figures. She is the prophetess, sage, witch, or sorceress. Molton and Sikes, authors of the primary work on Toni Wolff's archetypes, explain, "She is both a puzzle to herself and a mystery to those she encounters. In contrast to the other types, her primary relationship is to the other, the unknown, to God or gods" (225). She is Melisandre, Mirri Maz Duur, Quaithe—the advisors and mystics dispensing cryptic advice.

Each has the capability to bring salvation, death, or sometimes both: Just as Martin's characters behave ambiguously, straddling lines between hero and villain, characters can cross the lines between creator and destroyer or even between categories of archetypes. Arya is sometimes protector, sometimes killer, just as Melisandre can be lover and mystic. "A woman's self-nurture includes an invitation for her to explore and integrate all four of the types into her awareness and understanding, one by one, over time" (Molton and Sikes 295). A fully formed character does this, slipping out of her cookie-cutter role to embody many through her life. Daenerys, more than any other character, can be seen taking all the positions, growing from victim-princess into war leader, lover, and mother of slaves, all while having mystic visions of the future.

Most *Game of Thrones* females fit better in a single box. Further, they're all gender-coded. As the prolific blogger Rhiannon notes in *Feminist Fiction*, the strong warrior women are coded masculine, while the mothers and lovers are coded feminine. (The mediums, traditionally somewhat androgynous, are comparatively minor characters in the story.) While the masculine characters like Arya win throughout their adventures, the feminized characters are drooping victims:

Masculine characters are all about overt strength and fighting the system directly. They are outspoken and bold, can fight, do not flinch at the sight of blood, and are capable of killing.

Feminine characters, on the other hand, are softer. They fight using smiles and kind words and manipulations. They are often concerned with marriage and motherhood, and tend to keep their true opinions to themselves. They are often, although not always, somewhat naive and romantic ["*Game of Thrones*: Not the Women They Were Before"].

It could be argued that all female archetypes fall into Wolff's four roles or into Rhiannon's gender split. For the sake of clarity, characters in this book are further divided into other popular tropes: the helpless damsel, warrior woman as lover, career woman, trickster, and crafty grandmother.

The Strong Females

Westeros is full of strong women. Most fans immediately mention Daenerys, Arya, and Brienne, with some adding Catelyn, Cersei, and Melisandre. Certainly, in different ways, all these women are strong. Less-seen characters are just as strong: Ygritte and Osha, the wildlings; Theon's sister Yara; Robb's healer-bride Talisa; Meera Reed with her net and frog spear. Lady Olenna scolds the most powerful men and negotiates with the lords of Westeros. Even Daenerys might find her intimidating. But such strength is problematic in its own way: As Sophia McDougall notes in her essay on the "strong women" trope:

> What happens when one tries to fit other iconic male heroes into an imaginary "Strong Male Character" box? A few fit reasonably well, but many look cramped and bewildered in there. They're not used to this kind of confinement, poor things. They're used to being interesting across more than one axis and in more than two dimensions.... The ones that fit in most neatly— are usually the most *boring*. He-Man, Superman (sorry). The Lone Ranger. Jack Ryan, perhaps. Forgotten square-jawed heroes of forgotten pulp novels and the Boy's Own Paper. If Strong-Male-Character compatibility was the primary criterion of writing heroes, our fiction would be a lot poorer. But it's within this claustrophobic little box that we expect our heroines to live out their lives [McDougall].

"Strong women" are frequently written with no other personality besides that strength. Carina Chocano comments in her similar essay that "strong woman" refers to the old-fashioned "strong, silent type," rather than a character with "blubbering, dithering, neuroticism, anxiety, melancholy or any other character flaw or weakness that makes a character unpredictable and human" (2). In fact, these latter characteristics are often found in fictional men, because it's these weaknesses that make characters interesting. Beloved three-dimensional characters like Sherlock Holmes or Bilbo Baggins are known for quirks and flaws as well as triumphs.

This applies in *Game of Thrones,* where Ned, Theon, and Robb are torn between ambition, vengeance and family loyalty. Littlefinger and Varys's past humiliations fuel their present ambitions. Sam is terribly afraid, but buries that fear to save Gilly. Gilly, by contrast, identifies herself as a mother desperate to protect her child, and never wavers from that role. Likewise, Meera, Osha, Olenna, and Margaery are barely fleshed out characters who play a single part repeatedly. There are some one-note "strong male characters." But they're people like Stannis, terribly unlikable, or Yoren and Beric Dondarrion, well-meaning but limited in their story arcs.

On the show, Brienne, Meera, and Yara have no backstories at all. They're like fantasy game characters thrown into the mix: Meera Reed. Mission: defend brother and Bran. Weapons: spear and net. Hit points: as follows. Book characters like Chella, daughter of Cheyk, who prides herself on collecting ears from the enemy (one of Tyrion's recruits among the Hill Clans), have even less personality: Like the women of Bear Island, they are simple warrior women mixed among the men, with no more than their names to differentiate them. (By contrast, Tyrion keeps two male hill clan leaders around for some time.) Even characters like Melisandre aren't seen displaying Theon's angst or conflict: She has a mission to serve her god and Stannis, so that's what she'll do. Even in her book's point of view scene, she's calm and certain.

Brienne gets a backstory and becomes a point-of-view character in the fourth book. Lyanna Stark has hobbies. Osha has religion. Rhiannon of *Feminist Fiction* sees the books containing far more nuance than the show:

> One of the strengths of *A Song of Ice and Fire* is its willingness to play with and subvert fantasy narrative tropes, especially with its female characters. The warrior woman is also a naive romantic who has never killed a soul.

The scrappy young girl becomes an emotionally damaged child hell-bent on revenge…. Characters resist simple categorization. *Game of Thrones'* inability to understand this is one of its biggest flaws. Although the show has created some wonderful moments and built on some of the book's less developed characters (like Shae) in compelling and interesting ways, it often falls back on the desire to fit female characters neatly into the categories that the book defies ["*Game of Thrones*: Not the Women They Were Before"].

Brienne and Arya, the masculinized characters, are delightfully strong, mouthy, assertive, and self-reliant. They will battle anyone who talks down to them or threatens their weaker sidekicks. But as such they also become predictable, more cardboard than multifaceted. They become the classic archetypes "who are tough, cold, terse, taciturn and prone to scowling and not saying goodbye when they hang up the phone," as Carina Chocano puts it in her *New York Times* article—outlines rather than people (1). Emotional woman are weak; stoic women are powerful. "Feminist film theory has yet to explore and work through anger, which for women continues to be, as it has been historically, the most unacceptable of all emotions," notes critic Tania Modleski (qtd. in Smelik 90). The feminized women are too "nice," while only the masculinized characters can display masculinized anger. Chocano adds:

> "Strong female character" is one of those shorthand memes that has leached into the cultural groundwater and spawned all kinds of cinematic clichés: alpha professionals whose laserlike focus on career advancement has turned them into grim, celibate automatons; robotic, lone-wolf, ascetic action heroines whose monomaniacal devotion to their crime-fighting makes them lean and cranky and very impatient; murderous 20-something comic-book sales-girls who dream of one day sidekicking for a superhero; avenging brides; poker-faced assassins; and gloomy ninjas with commitment issues. It has resulted in characters like Natalie Portman's in *No Strings Attached*, who does everything in her power to avoid commitment, even with a guy she's actually in love with; or Lisbeth Salander in Stieg Larsson's Millennium trilogy; or pretty much every character Jodie Foster has played since *Nell* or, possibly, *Freaky Friday* [1].

Thus Arya, Yara, and Brienne completely reject their femininity. All three are determined to be men in a man's world, from featureless clothing to strength on the battlefield. In one episode, Arya even dismissively comments that "most girls are stupid" (2.7). This hardly marks her as the height of feminist power. Chocano adds that "what we think of as 'virtuous,' or culturally sanctioned, socially acceptable behavior now, in women as in men, is the ability to play down qualities that have been traditionally considered feminine and play up the qualities that have traditionally been considered masculine" (3). In essence, "strong female characters" are female characters with no gender at all. When women have power, they are treated as unusual exceptions to the gender divide. Thus the girl learns that being masculine is superior.

A better role model for girls would be someone who acts like them and doesn't dismiss them as useless. Women who loathe being women and spend all their time convincing others they're not just as good as (or better than!) men, they basically *are* men, are strong. But they make problematic feminist icons.

Daenerys is more multifaceted and conflicted as she makes painful choices. In her book scenes, she's uncertain, conflicted, and occasionally panicked. By season three of the show, she's become a delightfully powerful warrior. However, her inner turmoil from the book's point of view scenes has faded. We see the externally confident woman who leads the Unsullied and treats with the sellswords, but no moments of uncertainty or distraction, besides her attraction to Daario. As she grows in power, she's in danger of becoming this trope herself.

The Warrior Woman Archetype

Warrior women like Xena and Wonder Woman in scanty armor, skilled with sword and bow, are a common trope in fantasy. Éowyn, Honor Harington, She-Ra, Mu Lan, Sarah Connor, Princess Leia. Westeros sees this archetype as well, not only with Brienne, Ygritte, Meera, Osha, Yara, and Arya, but in their country's history. Nymeria was a warrior queen who conquered Dorne with ten thousand ships; the laws of Dorne represent female primogeniture as a result, and Arya names her wolf for her. Arya's hero is Visenya the Dragonrider, who, with her brother and sister, conquered Westeros. However, these characters appear so far back in the history of Westeros that they have become legend.

In fact, the warrior woman is more than fantasy, even in our world. A few lady knights existed in the middle ages: In 1149, the women of the town of Tortosa fought in its defense. The men considered surrendering, "which the Women hearing of, to prevent the disaster threatening their City, themselves, and Children, put on men's Clothes, and by a resolute sally, forced the Moors to raise the Siege" (Ashmole). Raymond Berenger, count of Barcelona, heard of their valor and founded the Order of the Hatchet, which offered exemption from all taxes and precedence over men in public assemblies. In England between 1358 and 1488, 68 ladies were appointed to the Garter. The Italian Order of the glorious Saint Mary granted the rank of *militissa* to women, and the Low Countries had several orders of *Chevaliéres*.

Far more women warriors were never formally knighted, but served as soldiers and commanders around the world, even in patriarchal Europe. Warrior nuns were growing so numerous in the fifteenth century that the popes began issuing decrees against women in combat ... decrees that formed the basis for Joan of Arc's execution (Jones 154). Julienne du Guesdin of Brittany defended her convent against an English captain and tossed three men to their deaths from the battlements. Renee de Bourbon reformed convents at the head of an army (Salmonson 171). Nuns battled in the Crusades in full armor. Around the same time, Italian *cavalieresses* rode to battle and directed naval attacks in Venice. In fact, the queen is the most powerful chess piece to honor Caterina Sforza, who defended the Castle of Saint Angelo (Jones 181). Queens and princesses across Europe led armies to defend or capture territory.

At a royal tourney to honor King Henri II and his mistress, Diane de Poitiers, one knight broke an amazing number of lances. When the king requested an interview, the knight lifted a helm to reveal a woman: Louise Labe, sporting the motto *Belle a Soi*—beautiful to oneself (Prioleau 174). Her father, a rich merchant, allowed her to take lessons beside her brothers, so she learned fighting and writing. Wearing a doublet and plumed beret, Louise lived as she chose. She wed a wealthy, older rope-maker who funded her dazzling literary salons, where she debuted her charming, sometimes erotic poetry—all proclamations of female equality. Her friends called her the tenth muse and "France's greatest lyric poet" (Prioleau 175). A 1348 chronicle describes forty or fifty women "in divided tunics" jousting on "excellent chargers" at a tournament (qtd. in Salmonson 120). Agnes Hotot likewise fought in a fourteenth century tourney in her ill father's place. When she won her bout, "she loosened the stay of her helmet, let down her hair, and disclosed her bosom" so her opponent would know a woman had conquered him (qtd. in Salmonson 119).

In 1428, a 16-year-old peasant named Jehanne convinced the Dauphin of France to put her in charge of his army of six thousand. She vowed that the angels had come to her and given her this holy mission: She could reclaim Orleans from the English and have him crowned at Riems. In July 1429 she succeeded in her goal and Charles VII of France was indeed crowned in the Cathedral of Reims. In May 1430 Joan of Arc, as she became known, was captured by French nobles who feared her influence over the king and sold her to the English. She was charged in an ecclesiastical court with heresy, blasphemy, idolatry, and sorcery, and finally burned at the stake in May 1431. In those days, it was not unusual for female soldiers to fight alongside the men, from the thirty women wounded in the Battle of Amiens to the female soldiers who followed Johannes Huss of Bohemia. For this reason, it was not terribly unusual for Charles to have accepted Jehanne as commander (Jones 174–75).

Great ladies, as protectors of their lands and estates, led armies in war even without formal investiture of knighthood. Often they would fight on behalf of a young son or captured husband, wearing full armor and leading charges on the field. Upper-class women most often fulfilled command functions rather than engaging in hand-to-hand combat and were seldom wounded ("Martial and Physical Arts"). While the medieval world saw isolated female pirates, mercenary captains, and brave peasant girls seeking individual glory, these ladies, without military titles or honors, could and did change the face of history.

In this tradition, "Lady Brienne" appears not to have been formally knighted. There is no thought of calling her "Ser." "Brienne's enough ... I'm no lady," she adds (2.3). Many medieval women made a similar choice, at least ostensibly defending their lands in the absence of a man. The Breton wars of succession were fought between Jeanne of Penthièvre and Jeanne of Flanders, both of whom led their armies in person. The latter lady conducted the defense of her castle in Montfort, even encouraging her women to "cut their skirts and take their safety in their own hands." She led a raid on the enemy camp, burning tents and supplies, after which she became known as "Jeanne la Flamme" (Newark 113–21). She roused the village in a man's armor.

The countess of Montfort was there in full armour, mounted on a swift horse and riding through the town, street by street, urging the people to defend the town well. She made the women of the town, ladies and others, dismantle the carriageways and carry the stones to the battlements for throwing at their enemies. And she had bombards and pots full of quick lime brought to keep the enemy busy [Froissart, qtd. in Jones 170].

In a different tradition, Arya's brother gives her a sword and her father arranges for dueling lessons, both historical anachronisms. Of the few known female duelists, most only fought as curiosities and performers when the real age of dueling had long passed. Eighteenth century duelists included Mademoiselle La Maupin, La Maillard, Mademoiselle de Guignes, Mademoiselle d'Aiguillon, Mademoiselle Leverrier, Lady Almeria Braddock, Mrs. Elphinstone, Comptesse de Polignac and Marquise de Nesle.

There have been numerous anecdotes of female duelists, pirates, and warriors from that period: Mary Read, Anne Bonny, Catalina de Erauso, Long Meg, and so on ("Martial and Physical Arts"). The Germans had laws for how female duelists should comport themselves. One form of duel, specifically used for rape cases as well as other offenses, had the man standing in a pit with the woman swinging a stone at him (Jones 166).

In the seventeenth and eighteenth centuries, several woman-on-woman duels were recorded, generally over a man. However, some women stood up for themselves against the other gender. In the seventeenth century, a French cavalry officer rudely moved into the home of the Countess de Saint-Belmont and planned to remain there. When he ignored the countess' annoyed note, she sent another signed "Chevalier de Saint-Belmont," challenging him to a duel. She showed up in men's clothes, rapidly disarmed him, and said, "You thought, monsieur, that you were fighting the Chevalier de Saint-Belmont, but you are mistaken. I am *Madam* Saint-Belmont. I return you your sword, monsieur, and politely beg you to pay proper respect to any request made by a lady in future" (Baldrick 170). Madame de Chauteau-Gay, usually seen riding horseback with kilted skirts and a man's wide-brimmed hat, challenged her lover's captain to a duel over some mistreatment the lover had suffered. Though the officer brought two friends to the duel, Madame de Chauteau-Gay bravely battled all three, though they defeated and killed her (Jones 167).

Dona Catalina de Erauso of Spain became a soldier of fortune in Peru, dueling with sword, knife, and pistol. Called "the Nun Ensign," she strutted through Europe as a cavalier, and the pope gave her special dispensation to wear men's clothes (Salmonson 82). In Potosí, Peru, a pair of swashbuckling female lovers. Doña Ana Lezama de Urinza (an orphan) and Doña Eustaquia de Sonza (a rich heiress), modeled themselves after her life. They engaged in street duels dressed as a pair of caballeros (knights) and were known as the Valiant Ladies of Potosí as well as a celebrated pair of lovers (Salmonson 258). Mademoiselle Leverrier challenged the man who had jilted her to a pistol duel. Though he chivalrously fired his pistol in the air, she responded by shooting him in the face (Baldrick 173–74). Mlle. De Maupin of Paris dueled with many professionals, often battling three at a time. Though she was arrested for dueling unlawfully, King Louis decreed that the law applied only to men and pardoned her (Salmonson 176–77).

Arya learns dueling from Syrio Forel of Braavos, and then later earns help from the Faceless Man Jaqen H'ghar, who offers her passage to Braavos and training with the Faceless Men. Venice (the inspiration for Braavos) was famous for its male duelists and assassins, but female versions were unheard of. At the same time, however, a few Venetian women led mercenary armies as Condottieri of Venice, like Bona Lombardi and Onerata Rodiana. Simone de Beauvoir mentions Hippolyta Foramenti, who led a company of noblewomen during the siege of Pavia, Girolamo Riario's heroic wife and leader, and the Sienese women who marshaled three thousand female troops. Arya may discover her path as a female warlord and mercenary captain, or she may hide in their ranks as an assassin.

The Warrior: Arya and Brienne

The strongest women (in some ways) are Arya and Brienne, extolled by all the critics who laud the show's feminist virtues. In the books, the pair have other sisters-in-arms. Pretty Maris the sellsword is "six feet tall and earless, with a slit nose" (V.569). Arya's hero is Visenya Targaryen, "a great warrior" and dragon rider with "a Valyrian steel sword she called Dark Sister" (2.7).

"Stout, grey-haired Maege Mormont, dressed in mail like a man, told Robb bluntly that he was young enough to be her grandson, and had no business giving her commands ... but as it happened, she had a granddaughter she would be willing to have him marry" (I.54). The "liege lord" of Bear Island is a mother as well as warrior, and here we see her fulfilling both roles. Her oldest is granted the right to be part of Robb's personal guard when she demands it. The other ladies of Bear Island are equally independent. The youngest, ten-year-old Lyanna, writes a sassy letter to Stannis saying, "Bear Island will only bow to the King in the North, who must be a Stark" (V.52). With Maege's brother commanding the Wall and her nephew exiled, she and her daughters are their house's only leaders. Under such circumstances, it was acknowledged, especially in earlier times, that a woman might fight to protect her interests.

The warrior women are second-wave feminism's ideal: career-focused and completely independent without spouse or children, equal to "the boys," immune to love or softer emotions. As discussed, however, these women have all cast aside all traces of femininity to compete with men and thrive in a man's world.

> While the books series presents a huge range of dynamic and well-developed female characters, the show writers seem determined to edit the story so that all stereotypically feminine women seem weak and worthy of disdain. Girls, like Arya, who fight to throw off femininity and become "one of the boys," are the only ones who are really strong or worthy of respect [Rhiannon, "Are 'Most Women Stupid?'"].

As heroine's journey scholar Maureen Murdock explains, many modern women begin this way, androgynous in business suits and determined to compete with men in the workplace. Only as they mature do they quest "to fully embrace their feminine nature, learning how to value themselves as women and to heal the deep wound of the feminine" (3).

Arya is clearly miserable in her role as a girl. She can outshoot Bran, but she's chided for her untidiness and is never as perfect as demure Sansa. She continues as an anticonformist through her journey. When she practices swordplay with Mycah the butcher's boy, trying out the sword Jon gave her out of love, she is punished. Arya, already transgressing against her gender and class rules, stands up to Prince Joffrey, the spoiled heir to the patriarchy. However, Mycah is killed, and Nymeria will be slaughtered unless Arya parts with her forever. Arya chases Nymeria into the woods and the powerful direwolf, named for a warrior queen of Westeros, journeys into the wilderness to rage and savage men. She is part of Arya, only allowed to become a powerful killer far from the civilized world.

In King's Landing, Arya trains with Syrio Forel in her own type of "dancing" and "needlework"—a parody of feminine activity. In Braavos, swordfighting is meant to be quick and light, depending on a small frame. For the first time, Arya's interests are encouraged, and her girl's body is actually an advantage. Syrio notes that her being "skinny as the shaft of a spear" will mean she's harder to hit. Likewise, Arya's being left-handed (another sign of nonconformity) is "good" as it will make her enemies "more awkward" (I.224). When she corrects his use of "boy" to address her, he says, "Boy, girl ... you are a sword, that is all" (I.224). Syrio is the first person to dismiss her gender as irrelevant to her goals; only training matters. As she babbles "Master Syrio says ..." at every meal, she's becoming truly happy in her element. "She's always up to something. There's never a dull moment," her actress Maisie Williams notes (qtd. in Cogman, *Inside HBO's* Game 58).

When she escapes the palace, Arya manages well on the streets, catching pigeons and bartering them in the books. "She's a complete tomboy. She doesn't do what people expect her to do," says actress Williams. "She's quite naive in a sense. She doesn't realize swordfighting is dangerous and kills people. It just looks cool and fun" (Keveney). After her father's execution, Yoren disguises her as the boy Arry, warning her that revealing her true gender will mean rape and death. Being female is cast as terrible vulnerability—only boys will survive. At the same time, her boyishness proves an advantage here, and she's encouraged in all ways to become one of the all-male crowd. Only as Tywin's page is her female identity revealed. Working for him, Arya tiptoes carefully as each revelation, from literacy and high birth to northern origins moves Tywin closer to discovering her secret.

She befriends Gendry and Hot Pie. The latter, as a baker, has the feminized traits as Arya has the masculine ones. Her offhand comment that most girls are stupid shows how little she wants to be one of them (2.7). On seeing Melisandre, she notes, "I don't like that woman," and one of the brotherhood responds, "That's because you're a girl" (3.6). It would be more accurate to say "a girl *who never spends time with girls.*" In fact, Arya is responding to the fact that the Red Priestess is dangerous and has captured her friend; the brother is wrong to consider this simple jealousy for the priestess's beauty. As Arya fires arrows at a dummy's "Face, tits, balls," noting, "I hit them right where I wanted to," Arya becomes a killer, though one who will strike out at both genders. Cersei is on her list right beside Joffrey.

> The razing of worldview and reconstruction of perspective happen quite literally for Arya. She reacts to her trauma by abandoning her identity and reinventing herself from the roots up no less than ten times, assuming identities ranging from her wolf Nymeria, into whose skin she can slip, to Arry, an orphan boy and street urchin, to Beth, the blind beggar who ultimately carries out her first assassination for the Faceless Men. In this case, the measure is also practical, as she is the heir of a noble house, easily recognized and relentlessly hunted [Cole 80].
>
> Disguises are a necessity for a young woman constantly in danger of being imprisoned, raped, or killed—particularly one who is of use as a political pawn. But a disguise can also be a tool with which a character can remake herself. At first, it seems that Arya's disguises—her new identities—are molded by others.... Even so, her willingness to throw off her gender demonstrates her understanding of the workings of power in her world. She can do things as a boy that would be denied her as a girl [Spector 177].

All her power came from her former identity as a marriageable pawn (Sansa keeps this identity as the Tyrells and Lannisters fight over her, the last known heir to the North). In the later books, an imposter Arya is introduced. The actual Arya and her blood of kings is not needed, only a brunette in a gray cloak.

Artemis girls are active, stubborn, career-driven, and independent. They feel strongly for causes and want to explore new territory. An Artemis woman pursues her own course. "In her affinity for the wilderness and undomesticated nature, Artemis is the archetype responsible for the at-oneness with themselves and with nature felt by some women" (Bolen 51). Arya becomes one with nature as she wanders through the forests alone and dreams of her solitary wolf Nymeria, who becomes a savage and slayer of men. While Sansa's Lady is killed, leaving her a weak shell of herself, Arya's wolf thrives independently at one with the wilderness. "She has been known to bring down aurochs all by herself, that no trap or snare can hold her, that she fears neither steel nor fire, slays any wolf that tries to mount her, and devours no other flesh but man" (IV.373). As such, she's a strong mirror for Arya herself. As she travels, Arya's mission is vengeance, a quest both family-based and personal. She's determined to go her own way, with no one knowing of her identity.

"Show me how—I want to be able to do it too," she tells Jaquen.

"If you would learn you must come with me.... The girl has many names on her lips: Cersei, Joffrey, Tywin Lannister, Illyn Payne, the Hound. [In the book, she doesn't repeat Tywin's name, and she has several more minor characters on her list.] Names to offer the red god. She could offer them all … one by one."

"I want to but I can't. I need to find my brother and mother … and my sister" ["Valar Morghulis," 2.10].

At the Red Wedding, she gets close, but arrives moments too late. Nonetheless, she kills to avenge her family, and gradually becomes a killer in truth. Whether or not she becomes a Faceless Man and commits to their lifestyle, Melisandre is correct: She becomes a killer. Martin notes:

> The whole thing of the child soldier is a fascinating construct. We have this picture of children [as] so sweet and innocent. I think some of the recent history in Africa and some of the longer history have shown that under the right circumstances, they can become just as dangerous as men, and in some ways more dangerous. On some level, it's almost a game to them [Anders].

As she trains, far from the Game of Thrones other characters play, she loses her identity piece by piece: her friends, her Needle, her quest for vengeance as some of her enemies perish by other means. Without her family or role in society, Arya can be who she wishes. Every critic on the Internet agrees that she's an 11-year-old girl "more badass than basically every adult character combined" (Sackler). However, she becomes more like the Faceless Men, a shadow vanished from the world rather than a player like Cersei or Daenerys.

Jean Shinoda Bolen, author of several books on female archetypes, describes the Artemis woman, the virgin as warrior woman. "On the one hand, she rescues women and feminist values from the patriarchy, which devalues or oppresses both. On the other, with her intense focus on goals she can also require that a woman sacrifice and devalue what has traditionally been considered feminine" (71). Arya loses her femininity first as her fine dresses are stolen her first night alone. After this, her high birth and all her family members vanish, until she is isolated, with nothing but her fierceness. According to Pearson, traditional males are Warriors and Seekers, while traditional females are Caregivers and Lovers. It's notable that men in Westeros are more of the first category, but women in Westeros are completely polarized: Female questors and fighters have no relationships as Arya and Brienne strike out alone, rejecting the temptations of love or family. This dichotomy appears in real life as well. Famous feminist Adrienne Rich comments:

> We have tended either to become our bodies—blindly, slavishly, in obedience to male theories about us—or to try to exist in spite of them.... Many women see any appeal to the physical as a denial of mind. We have been perceived for too many centuries as pure Nature, exploited and raped like the earth and the solar system; small wonder if we now long to become Culture: pure spirit, mind. Yet it is precisely this culture and its political institutions which have split us off from itself [285].

While Brienne appoints herself a protector of women (Catelyn and her daughters), she rejects everything feminine in herself. While she serves Renly devotedly, Renly is completely unattainable (he's married, above her station, and indifferent to women). Brienne's fixation on someone she'll never have could be seen as defensive: She need never make her feelings known and never be hurt. All her life, she's been despised for her height, her skill at swordplay, her "ugliness" (often referenced in the books). When younger, she told her suitors she would only marry a man who could best her in combat. No one did, but all insulted her and called her unwomanly and freakish. The warrior woman "takes little time for a social life. Her relationships are mostly impersonal" (Molton and Sikes 189). Further, these women conform fully to the masculine sphere. "Insofar as the armor shields them from their own feminine feelings and their soft side, these women tend to become alienated from their own creativity, from healthy relationships with men, and from the spontaneity and vitality of living in the moment" (Leonard 17).

Her elderly father, possibly even more supportive than Ned Stark, allows his only child to swear her sword to Renly's court and go adventuring instead of fulfilling her duties as heir. When Lord Bolton's men hold her, her father offers a fair ransom. In turn, Brienne feels guilty that she can't be a proper heir to him. She calls herself "the freakish one, not fit to be a son *or* daughter" (IV.672).

However, most men are her adversaries, and she treats them as such. "All my life men like you've sneered at me, and all my life I've been knocking men like you into the dust," she tells Jaime Lannister (2.8). Bolton's men see her as a pawn because of her gender, and they attempt to rape her, then finally hurl her into a bear pit to watch her die for their entertainment. (She manages to hold her own with a wooden sword before Jaime aids her.) Weiss comments, "Gwendoline Christie is fantastic. She so perfectly embodies the kind of wounded strength the character requires. And she's been training. She will kick your ass" (Lacob, "*Game of Thrones*' Creative Gurus").

Rhiannon of *Feminist Fiction* notes that the book character has a bit more nuance. "She has a strong sense of honor, is fairly naive about how the world will work, is very romantic like Sansa, and has never killed a single person. When she finally does kill somebody, it's a huge emotional moment for her, and not one that she's proud of. In the show, on the other hand, she kills in the second season without blinking." Thus she goes from a woman who is a warrior to the stoic warrior woman trope. "It is as though the writers have taken the 'soft' feminine bits out of her in order to make her more neatly fit our *expectations* of what a fighting woman would be like" ("*Game of Thrones*: Not the Women They Were Before").

In book and show, she's a woman in service to others, spending much more time defending Jaime than Catelyn. She also needs Jaime to rescue her multiple times. Of course, on book and show, Brienne's never spent much time with women, deliberately placing herself on the men's battlefield instead.

She isn't seen having friendships or other relationships with women in the series, with one exception. Brienne tells Catelyn, "I could serve you if you would have me. You have courage. Not battle courage perhaps, but, I don't know, a woman's kind of courage" (2.5). However, she and Catelyn have almost no time together before Brienne sets out with Jaime on a near-impossible quest to keep him alive and trade him for Catelyn's daughters.

Jaime is first depicted as a figure of selfishness and cruelty, willing to betray his oaths of loyalty to two kings, cuckold the royal throne with his twin sister, and push a boy to his intended death.

Brienne of Tarth: Your crimes are past forgiveness, Kingslayer.
Jaime Lannister: Why do you hate me so much? Have I ever harmed you?

> *Brienne of Tarth:* You've harmed others—those you were sworn to protect, the weak, the innocent ["The Prince of Winterfell," 2.8].

The warrior woman's sense of justice is often absolute. "In this perspective, not only is an action either all bad or all good, but the person who does such a thing is too" (Bolen 70). Maisie Williams (Arya) notes that her character has a similar mindset. "Everything in her world in black and white" (qtd. in Cogman *Inside HBO's Game* 58). Only by learning empathy and moral complexity can the warrior amend this worldview. On the show, Brienne's more stoic and a bit harsher than her book counterpart, though it's a nice scene at the end of season two when she takes time to bury the murdered women they come across. Brienne is the only true knight of the series, determined to protect the innocent and champion the helpless.

> Christie says she's thrilled that her ultrabutch warrior woman, Brienne, is a new kind of female action hero, breaking ground in a genre best known for damsels in distress. "If you look at Madonna, she challenged traditional concepts of femininity in a man's world," she says. "Powerful women like her provide the heartbeat for Brienne" [Hill].

Her character is very strong and certainly female, but her dislike for her own sex, like Arya's, makes her a problematic feminist icon. She devotes herself to Catelyn and her daughters, but barely ever has a conversation with them, or any other female.

In turn, "the man who sees in Artemis admired qualities that are undeveloped in himself is usually drawn to her strength of will and independent spirit" (Bolen 63). Jaime is drawn to Brienne because she's all he isn't. She worked for her sword skill and position; none of it was given to her because of her birth, gender, or beauty. Brienne's inflexible defense of morality rubs off on Jaime until he too becomes a protector of the innocent (Brienne herself and the Stark girls). In her time with Jaime, however, Brienne changes as well. She learns to see the world as more complex. Jaime is not the treacherous kingslayer she had thought, as he acted to protect his family and people. When she and the audience learn more about him, unexpected complexities are revealed.

"You know, when you have actors with that kind of chemistry, it brings a dynamic to the relationship that I didn't see when I was writing it. Romance isn't the right word ... but there's definitely a ... I don't know how to put it. A tension, a sensuality that isn't necessarily on the page," writer Bryan Cogman notes. "We had some crew members who are insisting the two of them end up together! But it is a love story of sorts, not a conventional one by any means ..." ("Season 3 Interview").

Brienne is an Artemis figure for whom a "relationship with a man is through a role of being competitor or that of a comrade and rival who makes no personal demands" (Molton and Sikes 208). Still, it is a relationship, one filled with a growing respect and trust. They develop a buddy-cop relationship as their goals temporarily align—to keep Jaime safe and return him to King's Landing. Though Brienne acts aloof and Jaime callous and expedient, they begin to care for each other and give sympathetic advice:

> *Jaime Lannister:* When we make camp tonight, you'll be raped. More than once. None of these men have ever been with a noblewomen. You'd be wise not to resist.
> *Brienne of Tarth:* Would I?
> *Jaime Lannister:* They'll knock your teeth out.
> *Brienne of Tarth:* You think I care about my teeth?
> *Jaime Lannister:* No, I don't think you care about your teeth. If you fight them, they will kill you, do you understand? I'm the prisoner of value, not you ["Walk of Punishment," 3.3].

The attempted rape is a disturbing moment in Brienne's arc—the men who capture them don't care about Brienne's mission or loyalty to the Starks. She's female and noble, and that's all that matters. Likewise, Jaime is maimed on a whim, rather than in some complex political maneuver. Brienne's near-rape occurs off-camera with her horrified screams and Jaime's disgusted rage; it's not a prurient moment, unlike Daenerys's relations with Drogo. In this scene, she's a helpless woman like any other, much as she wishes to be treated as a man. It is Jaime who saves her with eloquence, though he only buys her a temporary reprieve. Like Jaime, Brienne begins to discover a world of warring loyalties, until finally she must choose between betraying her friend and betraying an innocent.

The Bodyguard: Osha and Meera

Osha and Meera are additional warrior women, though their mission of guarding Bran and Rickon gives them less story arc. Osha the wildling woman, a seer of a sort, has ancient wisdom and knows the White Walkers are returning. She is the one to deliver the famous message that Robb and his bannermen are riding the wrong way—the real conflict lies North of the Wall, not among the five kings. Beyond this though, she has little insight to offer. She is not Bran's tutor in the ways of Northern magic, only his protector.

Osha's backstory appears in "The Bear and the Maiden Fair" (3.7). She and a wildling were in love, but he turned into a wight and she had to burn down their hut to kill him before he strangled her. Now she scoffs at the concept that tragedies happen for a reason and refuses to return to the Wall. This remains nearly her only piece of advice.

She is also not precisely sexual—she's never seen in a voluntary romance. In her first independent act of the show, Osha strips for Theon, seduces him, and escapes with Bran and Rickon.

> *Osha:* There are other ways to serve, my prince.
> *Theon:* Like what?
> *Osha:* We know things, the free people … savage things ["The Old Gods and the New," 2.6].

She opens her blouse, and then drops her dress. Hands coyly over her breasts, she asks for freedom in exchange for sex. Theon agrees if she "serves" him well. On the way, she kisses a guard to distract him, and then slits his throat. In the book, she earns Theon's trust without seduction. As such, her seduction as a means of escape (when she's a fully capable warrior) weakens her, making the point that women must use their feminine wiles as tools rather than other skills. Martin comments that Natalia Tena has truly reimagined his Osha.

> Who is a pretty minor character in the books, has a one-note personality, is really there to advance the plot, and fulfill certain plotpoints. And Natalia Tena made it such an interesting and vibrant, alive character, and much different. Natalia is much younger and much more attractive than my Osha, who was ten, fifteen years older, weathered, leathery … [Anders].

Show Osha is notably different, but less independent, not more.

Both Meera and Osha are the protectors for the seers and dreamers of the story. Though female, Meera is presented as somewhat asexual, functioning as a defender for the young men and allowing them to grow spiritually instead of learning warfare.

When Meera and Jojen Reed arrive, Osha threatens an unarmed

Jojen, and then Meera threatens her in turn. As a warrior and scholar pair, the siblings are much like Osha and Bran. Nonetheless, Osha reacts to them with hostility.

> *Osha:* He should be ashamed, your brother, needing you to protect him.
> *Meera:* Where's the shame in that?
> *Osha:* Any boy his age, who needs his sister to protect him, is gonna find himself needing lots of protection.
> *Meera:* Some people will always need help. That doesn't mean they're not worth protecting ["Dark Wings, Dark Words," 3.2].

Despite her words, Osha has made the choice to protect Bran and Rickon, both helpless on the battlefield. In wildling society, men and women both fight; her comments are not meant to show sexism but instead the need for everyone to know self-defense. (It's unclear what happens to crippled wildlings in the north, but they live in desperate conditions and only warriors have been shown.)

A medieval family like the Reeds would not typically have trained the daughter as a warrior and the boy as a seer and scholar, not with a child of each gender available. But in Westeros, Meera is the better warrior with a "woven net," "long bronze knife," "old iron greathelm," and "wicked frog spear" (II.328). Like Brienne, she's allowed to train as a warrior and then go questing, presumably with her father's blessing.

The Reeds' quarrel with Osha doesn't take place in the books, as Meera and Jojen arrive earlier to pay fealty to the Starks, halfway through the second volume. After they help Bran, Rickon, and Osha escape River-run, they divide forces, with Rickon and Osha journeying into the wilderness and Meera and Jojen heading north with Bran and Hodor, similar to the end of season three. Having them all travel together on the show emphasizes that the two women basically fill the same role, more archetypes than fully realized women.

Meera and Osha's squabbling on the trip is more painful, making the point that any powerful women, like Cersei and Margaery, must hate each other on sight, even if they have similar goals. Friendship between women is very rare in the series, compared with male-male or male-female bonds. As Osha and Meera quarrel, they're squabbling over the series' men, especially Bran, adding another layer of clichéd gender behavior. Bran, the one with higher reason, demands they make peace. Of course, both women emphasize their protective goals and determination to protect their charge. While they lack a great deal of nuance and characterization, they are both the "strong warrior women" found throughout the series—capable, loyal, and fearless.

The Pirate: Asha/Yara

Asha Greyjoy (called Yara Greyjoy on the show to avoid confusion with the wildling Osha) is a pirate captain and war captain, commanding thirty longships and conquering the Northern castle of Deepwood Motte. Of course, back home she's the lady of the Iron Islands, possibly her father's heir (though Ironmen expect a male lord). Her actress Gemma Whelan says, "Yara is strong, fierce and proud of who she is ... wearing her exceptionally empowering, leather thigh-high boots" (qtd. in Cogman, *Inside HBO's* Game 127).

Readers first meet her from Theon's point of view, as he ignores all the evidence to dismiss the woman in front of him as one he can use sexually and then discard. Instead, she has become more the man of the family than Theon has. Just as he always was in Winterfell, he's been upstaged.

> Theon finds that while he's been gone, his cocky sister has become the hard young man of the Iron Islands. Yara doesn't just sexually one-up her swaggering little brother (in a scene that plays like an outtake from a particularly filthy Shakespeare comedy); she usurps his place at his father's side. Yara has commanded men and killed them; unlike Theon, she would never wear jewels she hadn't "paid the iron price" for—i.e., liberated from fresh corpses she's made. When the Iron Islands eventually head to war, Balon tells a sputtering, incredulous Theon that Yara will command a fleet of 30 ships. Theon will get one. Its name? *The Sea Bitch.* "We thought she'd be perfect for you," his sister smirks [Rastogi].

In the books, Theon gives it this name as a compliment to Asha, as he ignorantly flirts with her. Both hold a message to Theon that a strong woman will be commanding his destiny, though his book gesture is to honor his ship with a woman he means to seduce and discard. He values his first ship little more than he values his female conquests.

When Asha reveals who she is, Theon has no recourse but to cringe before her trickery. He has been taken in completely, has boasted of how he will take his place as heir and marry off his useless sister, as he thinks.

Benioff comments: "Gemma [Whelan] and Alfie [Allen] make an insanely good pair of siblings. We could make a whole series about the Greyjoys" (Lacob, "*Game of Thrones*' Creative Gurus").

Asha responds in turn: In the books, she pretends to be vulnerable as well as sassy, wheedling with Theon not to seduce her because she's married and pregnant. He selfishly persists. However, she later reveals that her axe is her husband, and her dagger her sweet suckling babe. As she shows off with them at their father's table, she proves she's more man than Theon is.

By the end of season three, their father has given up all interest in his velvet-dressed son. Hearing he's been castrated is the final blow.

> *Balon Greyjoy:* Theon disobeyed my orders. The boy is a fool. He cannot further the Greyjoy line. I will not give up the lands I have seized, the strongholds I have taken. Get this away from me.
> *Yara Greyjoy:* He's your son.
> *Balon Greyjoy:* Son? He's not a man any more.
> *Yara Greyjoy:* He's your son. He's my brother. He's a Greyjoy.
> *Balon Greyjoy:* Watch yourself. I've made my decision.
> *Yara Greyjoy:* And I've made mine. I'm going to pick the fastest ship in our fleet. I'm going to choose the 50 best killers on the Iron Islands. I'm going to sail up the Narrow Sea all the way to the Weeping Water. I'm going to march on the Dreadfort. I'm going to find my little brother and I'm going to bring him home ["Mhysa," 3.10].

Yara, who has never been a man, places more value on her brother and less on his manliness. She resolves to begin a war if that's what it takes to reclaim him. Since this conversation never takes place in the books, many fans are eager to see Theon's sister battle for him on the show. It's notable that she flat-out defies her family patriarch here, something that almost no one of either gender does on *Game of Thrones*.

The warrior woman sometimes has a sensitive side, especially for protecting vulnerable family members. Yara shows love for family here, as she does in her last goodbye to Theon. She recalls cuddling him as a baby and plaintively says, "Don't die so far from the sea." Though Theon's defied her, threatened to marry her off or send her to the Silent Sisters, though she thinks herself a more fitting heir than he is, she still reaches out to save him. He ignores her as he always does.

Yara is also notable as one of the very few adult females who never strips onscreen, for any reason (to date). In the fifth book, she considers offering Stannis her "fair young body" (V.336), but decides not to—she values herself too highly. As such, she contrasts with many more feminized females (in the worst, most stereotyped sense). Tyrion often notes that Cersei would barter her body for all sorts of rewards, and Arianne of Dorne uses herself as a bribe. Osha, Margaery, Gilly, and Shae are just as problematic.

At the same time, the Warrior Woman archetype occasionally has relationships. She may start out enamored of a fellow warrior, as Eowyn is of Aragorn, but this relationship rarely lasts.

> The warrior's lover may compete with her and feel jealous of her success. But even if they remain in accord, they are too similar. Neither brings the melding of opposites who join in a perfect relationship as animus and anima. She may regard him fondly, even love him, but he offers her no potential for growth. Each constantly mirrors the other, offering support and acceptance, but no change [Frankel, *From Girl to Goddess* 208].

Thus the warrior woman seeks out "the sensitive scholar who represents the missing side of the warrior woman's personality" (Frankel, *From Girl to Goddess* 209). He is gentle and spiritual where she is physical and aggressive. Like Eowyn's final choice, Faramir, he guides her to a higher level of wisdom. Axe-wielding Asha has such a gentle, even feminized lover in book five: "Qarl the maid," so called for his lack of beard. She likes the feel of his "smooth, soft skin" (V.336). When Qarl makes love with her, he calls her his queen. She in turn calls him a "beardless boy," and adds that her husband will put him in a dress (V.335). Asha genuinely loves Qarl, her subordinate, whom she takes as a paramour to please herself rather than acting to please one of the story's men. As such, she's an unusually independent and developed female ... despite her single viewpoint chapter in book four and solitary three in book five.

Historically, some women were fierce pirates, while ladies defended their holdings on the seas. Three female captains fought in the Danish Battle of Bravalla: Webiorg, Wisna, and Hetha. They battled with swords and armor to defend their king. The Gothic princess Alvilda of Sweden took to the seas when her father promised her to Prince Alf of Denmark against her will. She sailed with an all-female crew, confined to oars and hand weapons in the twelfth century. She captured ships and harried trade until Prince Alf was sent to battle the pirates. When her ship was finally boarded and she was escorted to the prince, she removed her helm to his astonishment. Reputedly, he proposed on the spot (Jones 166).

Jeanne de Clisson, the fourteenth-century "Lioness of Brittany," sailed her Black Fleet during the Hundred Years' War, battling the ships of King Philip VI. After the king executed her husband, she marauded in the English Channel for thirteen years, attacking French ships. According to some reports, Jeanne personally decapitated prisoners with an axe and tossed their bodies into the sea. She finally retired and remarried in 1356, returning to France for the rest of her life.

The Irish "Pirate Queen" Grace O'Malley (actually named Grainne Ni Maille) was said to have buried nine tons of treasure along the Irish coast. Her father trained her in land and sea warfare, preparing her to prey on Spanish and English fleets. She gave birth at sea and led a battle a few days later, pistol in either hand. She had such a fierce reputation that Queen Elizabeth was urged by her advisors not to send the navy against the "pirate queen," though the queen eventually made peace with Grace and welcomed her to court. Upon meeting her, Queen Elizabeth released her son and brother from captivity and granted Grace a stipend. Grace continued piracy through her sixties.

Other famed lady pirates were the infamous Lady Killgrew of Cornwall and Maria Lindsey of Plymouth, who fought in a captured officer's uniform. Anne Dieu le Veut was another pirate heroine. When her husband Captain Laurent de Graffe was smashed by a cannonball, she, the ship's "lucky charm," sprang into action and took command.

Anne Bonney and Mary Read were the ocean's most famous pirate partners. Anne got hired as a pirate by stealing a ship and murdering its crew. In the service of Calico Jack, she met Mary, a widow and veteran sailor on a man-of-war (thanks to creative cross-dressing). They marauded for three years (reputedly as lovers), and when captured, both women pled pregnancy to avoid execution, cleverly balancing their gender roles to achieve the maximum freedom.

The Career Woman: Talisa

Medieval female physicians were rare but not unheard of. Trotula of Salermo studied at Italy's famed medical school during the eleventh century, and she authored the groundbreaking medical book *The Diseases of Women*. In sixth century France, the former Queen Radegund founded the monastery of Saint Croix at Poitiers, complete with a hospital and medical training for the 200 nuns. Marie Colinet of Berne was a German traveling doctor and surgeon around 1580. She invented a technique of removing metal shrapnel from a patient with a magnet, but her husband was given the credit. Thus Talisa Maegyr, traveling physician, fits into medieval history as well as the world of Westeros.

In the books, Robb's wife is named Jeyne Westerling. She's a submissive ninny and her family are Lannister bannermen. Jeyne is an awkward fifteen-year-old, "a pretty enough child" but "not a girl to lose a kingdom for" (IV.944). Robb falls for her because he's so overcome by grief on hearing of Bran and Rickon's deaths that he allows the girl to "comfort him." When his honor kicks in belatedly the next morning, he offers to marry her to restore her honor, though his honor as a king in a marriage alliance with the Freys is forfeit. Trapped in a situation with no good choices, he decides to protect another person's honor above his own. All this is revealed to Catelyn after the fact and not witnessed by the readers.

However, the Westerling family in the book remain loyal to the Lannisters. Jeyne's mother doses her with contraceptives each day, so she never falls pregnant with Robb's child; Robb dies at the Red Wedding without an heir. In return, the Lannisters pardon and reward the Westerlings. (Jeyne does not accompany her husband, as it's feared her presence will offend the Freys.) Jeyne, who truly loved her husband and wanted to bear his child, is left with only tragedy. Even those who conform to the system have no chance of a happy ever after.

As love scenes for the character were written with a more complex and exotic backstory, Martin suggested a new name for Robb's new wife. Talisa Maegyr, a healer from the Free City of Volantis, leaves behind a world of slavery and privilege to become a saver of lives. She notes that after a slave saved her little brother, "I decided two things that day. I would not waste my years planning dances and masquerades with the other noble ladies. And when I came of age I would never live in a slave city again" (2.8).

In "The Old Gods and the New" (2.6), Talisa seems polite to King Robb but hardly desperate for a man. She gradually falls in love with

Robb and then marries him at the end of season two. She's very much a career woman; she's seen healing the Lannister hostages even after becoming queen. She dresses simply and practically, in contrast to Margaery when she campaigns with King Renly. As an independent woman of no house, one who gave up her birthright to follow her chosen path, she's unlike anyone that the sheltered Robb has ever met.

Robb in turn grew up as Winterfell's heir, one of the top ten most eligible men in Westeros. He's used to noblewomen and their mothers flinging themselves at him, but here at last is a woman who's complete in herself, who feels free to contradict or ignore him. He's captivated.

However, Robb taints his reputation as king and engineers his own downfall through this imprudent marriage. In the books, he's grief-struck and impetuous, stuck far from home—on the show, his mother and bannermen don't spend much time dissuading him. The match is presented in unrealistically contemporary terms, with Robb and his mother speaking of following his heart. Christopher Orr of *The Atlantic* notes,

> In changing the match from one made for honor—in the book Robb marries Jeyne because he feels duty-bound to do so after sleeping with her in a moment of weakness—to one made for love, they give the relationship a somewhat jarringly modern feel ["*Game of Thrones*: A Feminist Episode"].

A king, or even the heir to Winterfell, would not expect to wed a foreign healer, however enticing, and would certainly not break his royal word and alliance for such a whim—marrying for love rather than family alliance is a modern notion in the western world. His choice of Talisa is problematic in other ways:

> It was refreshing to see the show present a romantic love scene for the very first time, rather than the general exploitative nudity we see every week. But Talisa's speech, just before Robb jumps her, creates a new context for their relationship which makes me distinctly uncomfortable: he's attracted to her because she's not like other women.... She's "not like other girls," strong and confident and willing to speak out of turn to the king. In isolation, this is not a bad thing. Some women are like that. But when her entire worth, the entire reason she is worthy of Robb's affection, is that she bucks the trend and is unlike regular, silly, simpering women (like the poor unnamed, unknown Frey girl, who might not be so keen on being married to a stranger either) ... that has unfortunate implications for the series' view on women as a whole [Rhiannon, "Are 'Most Women Stupid?'"].

Not every woman has the money and temerity to leave her country, family, and heritage behind forever. It's like Arya's "girls are stupid" comment, suggesting that the independent, unfeminine warrior women are "right" and everyone else is "wrong": An imitation male lifestyle is not just a valid choice, it's the only choice. Like Arya, Talisa seems to strut around saying, "I am a strong female." Shouldn't there be other paths to power? Not in Westeros.

Many viewers watching the pair travel to the Red Wedding guessed at the inevitable tragedy that would follow. In fact, Lothar Frey stabs Talisa repeatedly in the belly, creating a moment of violence that's "deeply sexualized; moments before she was stabbed seven times in the stomach, she and Robb shared a tender moment to discuss what they would name the son she was carrying" ("*Game of Thrones* and Violence Against Women of Color"). Robb and Talisa are punished by the patriarchy and the old order, Walder Frey, for their interracial marriage between a lord and an independent foreign woman. The twist here is truly disturbing.

The Warrior-Anima

The more remote and unreal the personal mother is, the more deeply will the son's yearning for her clutch at his soul, awakening that primordial and eternal image of the mother for whose sake everything that embraces, protects, nourishes, and helps assumes maternal form, from the Alma Mater of the university or the personification of cities, countries, sciences and ideals [Jung 112].

Jon, who never knew his mother, embraces Ygritte as his teacher, first lover, and confidante as she tests his loyalty. To King Robert as well, dead Lyanna means more to him than his famously beautiful living wife. Lyanna represents a perfect world in which he could have love and family, peace and security, all shattered when Rhaegar Targaryen stole her away. In her name, he dedicates himself to battle: "As long as men can carry off the women that other men love, there will be wars of honor—not to mention generation upon generation of women raging under the burden of thwarted sexual and romantic desires" (Rosenberg 18). These women are more than an influence on their men. They remain the female voices echoing in their heads and hearts—the voice of the internal feminine.

In ancient myth and legend, the hero usually encounters a heroine who represents the wildness and magic of nature, who draws him into the forest and teaches him about the unseen realm. This is not necessarily a romance—Galadriel performs this role for Frodo and the white doe performs it for Harry Potter. The Lady of the Lake offers Arthur protection as a shadowy figure whom he never directly meets. In this meeting of opposites, masculine and feminine, physical and spiritual, the woman represents the growing magic inside the hero.

This is the Anima, the female archetype that is all things—mother, sister, lover, guardian, guide, all whispering within the man. Jung explains that the more primitive, simplest stage is a biological attraction. The next stage of understanding is romantic love as the man relates to the woman as individual. Next the physical transmutes to spiritual and she becomes more guardian than lover. In the highest stage, the man sees the Anima as a catalyst to higher wisdom.

Men of Westeros, cut off from much of the world's softer side, are seeking connection with femininity. Thus, several of them fixate on finding this perfect partner who will bring them love together with higher wisdom. The warrior woman, one of the boys yet not, is an ideal target for this kind of affection. She in turn is only seen through the man's perspective, in the books and even on the show. Thus she appears to have no identity aside from her relation to her men.

YGRITTE

Ygritte is a warrior woman, but a different archetype from Brienne and Arya. Technically, she has the brashness, aggression, and sexual experience that code her as masculine. Nonetheless, she's not fighting for duty or honor but love. Rose Leslie (Ygritte) describes Jon, noting, "The love she has for him dominates everything. He changes her values" (de Graeve). Unlike Yara, Arya, and Brienne, her entire plot involves acting on behalf of another, as Meera and Osha do for Bran.

In fact the character only exists to influence Jon Snow. As such, she's his Anima, the character who teaches a male character about emotion and intuition. She represents his first weakening on the Black Brothers' path: He freezes when he sees the wildling he's about to kill is a woman, and in the book, she reminds him of Arya. He spares her life, then lets her escape when ordered to execute her. Her role in the story is to humanize the wildlings, and provide temptation as she wheedles him to join them. "Ygritte is brash, aggressive, funny, and fiercely protective of everything she holds dear. She is willing to risk everything to for what she cares about, but even more so to defend her freedom," notes Jenna Sackler on *Feminists at Large*.

Ygritte abandons her loyalty to the wildlings and insists Jon abandon his to the Night's Watch: "I'm your woman now, Jon Snow. You're going to be loyal to your woman" (3.6). Her loyalty is treated as unimportant and transient in the story, while Jon's oath to the Night's Watch torments him. In the story, her identity as wildling warrior is thus secondary.

In their relationship, in many ways, Ygritte is "the man"—older and more sexually experienced. "For the unschooled kitchen maid, the animus [male match] is a powerful prince, but for the warrior woman, the ideal mate is gentle and intuitive" (Frankel, *Girl to Goddess* 31). Jon may seem a powerful warrior, but at times, he's an uncertain teenager, who grew up more than a bit isolated. In the wildlings' camp, Jon is called a girl for his smooth cheeks and a eunuch when he refuses Ygritte. He is the one worried about an illegitimate child, in a reversal of traditional gender roles. "Why did he feel like some blushing maid," he asks himself (III.206). In their secret cave, she is the one to initiate him into sex. He in turn concentrates on her pleasure, rather than his own. Bryan Cogman, writer of the episode "Kissed by Fire," notes, "Ha! Yeah. I think Rose Leslie blushed a bit [upon reading the script].... But, yeah, it was nice to write a love scene in which the man was ... er, 'there' for his lady" (Cogman, "Inside Season 3").

As the story progresses, Ygritte's plot arc is coded as feminine. She is the one to nearly plummet from the Wall, and Jon is the hero-man who saves her. Beyond the Wall, she is terribly naïve, as she thinks a windmill is a castle and Jon responds with amused condescension, noting that she'd faint at the sight of Winterfell. He's surprised she's unaware of history—that six wildling attempts on the Wall have all failed and that her next one will as well. The pair even speculate about how she'd look in a silk dress.

Ygritte instead is Jon's inspiration and connection with the natural world as she keeps him alive long enough for him to integrate with the wildlings. She also shows him a world of romantic freedom. With her, he can escape the laws of Westeros and the Black Brothers, while she ignores what would be proper for a castle-bred lady. Ygritte's favorite line is, "You know nothing, Jon Snow," and she becomes his guide to the ways of the wildlings and life in the North. She also seems to suggest he fundamentally doesn't understand the wildling way of life. By the fifth book, he's still thinking of her and what she told him: "*You know nothing, Jon Snow.* He had learned though, and Ygritte had been his teacher" (V.464). As Jon grows to understand the wildlings as sympathetic people, he's increasingly torn.

Rose Leslie notes that Ygritte suffers just as much when they part: "She's devastated that Jon left her—had several conversations with Kit about these two characters who are madly in love with each other. Ygritte was convinced Jon would become part of the tribe and form a team together" (de Graeve). This leaves Ygritte as the scorned woman; the man has the power in their relationship and he chooses his friends and honor over her.

She takes her "strong woman's revenge" by shooting him, but she fails to keep Jon. Her plot arc has ended and she has failed. Her actress adds, "It's that devastation that he has betrayed her—it's horrible in episode 9 when he leaves on a horse, and it hits her there and then— 'He's not gonna get away with this! I'm going to hunt him down and hurt him!'" (de Graeve). Though she leaves scars on him, she fails in this as well.

DALLA AND VAL

Mance Rayder's wife and sister-in-law (from the books) are independent wildling women, significantly different from Ygritte. Mance Rayder introduces Dalla saying, "Treat her like you would any queen, she is carrying my child." He also introduces her sister Val, adding, "Young Jarl beside her is her latest pet" (III.99). In an intriguing gender reversal, the wildling woman has a "mistress" of a sort.

Dalla is little seen as a character. Presumably she does act as Mance Rayder's queen, though traditional marriage isn't a wildling tradition. The concept may come from Mance, who was once a black brother. Though Val and presumably Dalla are warrior women, they are prized by the Westerosi for their status as brides—Val becomes known as "the wildling princess" as knights compete for the status of wedding her.

When Jon recruits her for missions, he must do so stealthily as her marriage status makes her too valuable to risk.

By the fifth book, Val shows her teeth. She is a defiant, tough, loving wildling woman much like Ygritte. Jon Snow says of her, "If you force her to marry a man she does not want, she is like to slit his throat on their wedding night" (V.54). Val in turn notes that Jon is welcome in her bed: "Once he's been gelded, keeping those vows will come much easier for him" (V.703). Despite her strength, most of her scenes revolve around discussions of her marital status.

In a jarring turn for modern readers, Val and Ygritte are both determined to be wed through abduction—there's no other way they'll willingly respect their future husbands. Some ancient tribes on earth prided themselves on this type of marriage: "Taking his wife by force, the warrior proves he is able to annex the riches of others and burst through the bounds of the destiny assigned to him at birth." He thus establishes himself as a powerful warrior (de Beauvoir 83).

As such, Ygritte's and Val's acceptance of being carried off seems problematic. Still, the women have their own way of understanding the custom. "I'd sooner be stolen by a strong man than be given t' some weakling by my father," Ygritte notes (III.558). When Jon challenges her, pointing out he could be brutal or cruel, she responds that she'd cut his throat in his sleep. She adds, "A man can own a woman or a man can own a knife, but no man can own both" (III.559). In fact, Jon with his medieval approach is missing the thought process behind the wildling tradition of bride-stealing: The men do not own their brides. They win them through the theft, but if they make the women unhappy, the women will go elsewhere. Compared to Westeros with its binding marriage to possible brutes and rapists, the wildling way is more enlightened.

Ygritte's refusal to wed anyone who isn't strong enough to carry her off sounds like rape on the surface, but is actually a reference to ancient European traditions. Brunhilde, the Valkyrie warrior woman, lies waiting for the strongest hero to penetrate her defenses and carry her off. However, unlike Sleeping Beauty, she creates the test herself. "Valuing herself highly, she tests the heroes, lying in a ring of flame that only the greatest can penetrate" (Frankel, *Girl to Goddess* 30). In her ancient epic, she's guarded by mountains, a ring of fire, and heavy armor, all designed to test the hero with the challenge she has created. In the medieval retelling called the *Nibelungenlied,* she shuts herself in a high tower to test her suitors with tournaments and games of skill. As the prize, she is also the judge, and occasionally the executioner. Red Sonja, in her film, notes, "No man may have me, unless he's beaten me in a fair fight," and Brienne says nearly the same thing in her youth. As the wildlings put it, "The suitor risks a savage beating if he is caught by the woman's kin, and worse than that if she herself finds him unworthy" (V.901).

This archetype of the tough woman willing to barter herself in marriage is seen repeatedly in the series: Arianne, princess of Dorne, is eager to make a marriage alliance with a strong kingdom and its heir. She also dreams of being carried off by force. When she was a younger maiden, traveling, she recalls, "I sat beside the well and pretended that some robber knight had brought me here to have his way with me ... a tall hard man with black eyes and a widow's peak" (IV.425). Though she romanticizes being carried off, and bribes rescuers with her hand in marriage, she resolves, "I want a consort with teeth" (IV.849).

Lyanna Stark

"That's Lyanna, my father's sister. King Robert was supposed to marry her, but Rhaegar Targaryen kidnapped her. Robert started a war to win her back, he killed Rhaegar, but she died anyway," Bran explains succinctly (1.10).

Archetypally, Lyanna appears to belong beside Ygritte and the wildling women who seek strong men to carry them off. She was tough as Arya, known for her riding and eager to carry a sword if she'd been allowed. Ned thinks that Lyanna heavily resembled Arya, in temperament as well as looks. Harwin of Winterfell mentions that Lyanna rode very well, just as Arya does, and Lord Bolton calls Lyanna "half-horse" (III.235). She was brought up with the Stark devotion to duty and the old ways, a champion of justice and protector of the weak. Nonetheless, she apparently fell for Rhaegar and ran away with him, sacrificing all responsibility to create a war with their torrid affair.

At the Tourney of Harrenhal, Lyanna reportedly found a young Howland Reed, Meera and Jojen's father, being bullied by three teenage squires. She roared, "That's my father's man you're kicking" and attacked them with a tourney sword. "The she-wolf" (as the Reeds and others called her) may have been that tourney's mystery knight called the

"Knight of the Laughing Tree" (a heart tree) who defeated the three squires' knights. When the defeated trio sought to ransom back their arms, the knight insisted that the squires' lords teach them courtesy. At the tourney's end, Prince Rhaegar shocked the attendees by crowning Lyanna the Queen of Love and Beauty rather than his wife, Elia of Dorne. If he guessed Lyanna was the mystery knight, he may have been impressed by her fighting skills and sense of justice, not just her beauty. At that moment, "all the smiles died" (I.631).

Some time after, Rhaegar kidnapped Lyanna. Lyanna's betrothed, Robert Baratheon, considered this rape, though other accounts suggest love. Lyanna's feelings for Robert appear to have been lukewarm, observing that with his many bastards Robert wouldn't be faithful to her. She said, "Love is sweet, dearest Ned, but it cannot change a man's nature" (I.379). By contrast, Robert's love for Lyanna, still present over a decade later, is an idealized love. "Do you want to know the horrible truth? I can't even remember what she looked like. All I know is that she was the one thing I ever wanted. Someone took her from me and seven kingdoms couldn't fill the hole she left behind," Robert tells Cersei (1.5). Robert insists on visiting her tomb on arriving at Winterfell, shaming Cersei in public with his disregard. Ned observes that Robert only saw her beauty, not the boldness and strength of will that defined her personality. Lyanna's death instilled in Robert a great hatred of the Targaryens, and he sends assassins after Daenerys in Lyanna's memory.

Lyanna's father and brother, along with their friends and companions, died challenging the Targaryens for her. When Robert and Ned were condemned as well, Robert's Rebellion began. Robert finally slew Rhaegar at the Trident, with the rebellion immortalized by its final scene: two men fighting over a woman.

As if she hadn't caused enough death, Ned rode to the Tower of Joy where Rhaegar had brought Lyanna, and his companions died battling three knights of the Kingsguard. (Their presence and Lyanna's death amid fever and blood suggests that she birthed Rhaegar's child, possibly Jon Snow.) Lyanna's Targaryen son would be a focus point for rebellion and bloodshed if his identity was revealed; thus Ned insists the child is his own and tells no one the truth. Jon in turn becomes a source of family strife between Ned and Catelyn. Once again, the idealized Lyanna (as Ned keeps the vow to his dying sister with all his honor) causes pain to those still living. Even Ned's memories of her are fanciful, as he envisions gusts of blue roses and a haunting "Promise me, Ned," rather than their day-to-day activities.

Though her early life is characterized by brashness, fairness, and physical skill, Lyanna's function in the story is romanticized and feminine. She exists completely to influence the men's actions through their love for her. This echoes the comic books' "women in refrigerators" trope of a heroine who is violently murdered only to affect the hero. This term, coined by writer Gail Simone, describes "the use of the death or injury of women characters as a plot device to stir the male hero into action" (Booker 261). Women who only affect the men with their existence are considered the weakest of characters, an example of women who have no purpose or importance in their own lives. They are not superheroes, only fragile girlfriends and lovers.

Cersei reveals to Ned that Robert's love for dead Lyanna over herself made her eager to betray him with her brother Jaime. Thus Lyanna inspired not just Robert's Rebellion, but the War of the Five Kingdoms that followed. Lyanna's feelings in the first war (in which her lover's family killed her own) are unknown (as yet) and she is dead for the War of the Five Kingdoms. As such, she becomes a pawn in history, as the battles are fought for her idealized self, not her actual person.

While Robert and Ned adored Lyanna, Rhaegar too loved her more than his wife Elia of Dorne. Elia in turn was murdered when the Lannisters took King's Landing in Robert's Rebellion. Gregor "The Mountain" Clegane raped and murdered her and killed her young children. This legacy has led to a Dornish hatred of the Lannisters and all they rule. As Elia's brothers and Lyanna's brothers continue to fight and die for them, and as their family and lovers go to war for their sakes, they are the perfect example of women who only existed to influence the story's men. Both deceased, their legacy continues as men still battle in their names.

The Feminized Females

Many critics comment that weak females were a product of medieval times and thus proper to depict in the series. Certainly the

Sansa or Cersei type was common—the innocent maid dreaming of marriage or the scheming wife and widow with little real power. However, there were other medieval tropes barely seen. For instance, almost no middle class, poor, or elderly women appear—only highborn children and middle-aged ruling ladies. In history, midwives were often the advisors for their communities. Many women gained powerful roles in the clergy (a role we may see in book six through Tyene Sand). And the herbwomen were often the community healers, a role now taken by male maesters.

Further, Martin did not write historical fiction, but fantasy—the Maesters of the Citadel could have been a group that admitted women. The Black Brothers could have had an order of Black Sisters. Female wargs haven't been seen, only male ones. Only the Faceless *Men* (oddly) seem to go for gender equality. Since their face-switching likely involves cross-gender action, they're in a very ambiguous place already. And of the red priests, the females seem to have disturbingly exploitative sex magic and birth magic in their job descriptions; the men do not.

Many women in medieval times through the present day disguised themselves as men to operate in their world with increased agency. Mary Anne Doane, author of *Femme Fatales: Feminism, Film Theory, Psychoanalysis,* notes, "The idea seems to be this: It is understandable that women would want to be men, for everyone wants to be elsewhere than in the feminine position. What is not understandable within the given terms is why a woman might flaunt her femininity, produce herself as an excess of femininity" (6).

Such a women with this excess of femininity is Cersei, who dresses in elaborate silken gowns, goes on and on about how she should have been born a man, and seduces various men around her. The femme fatale often flaunts her femininity and powerlessness ... until she strikes. Worse yet are the powerless prostitutes, embodying feminine sexuality and nudity like a performance—in fact, many times they are asked to pretend for a spectator like Littlefinger or Joffrey. This emphasizes that the feminine role *is* a performance; women in society must become the characters men expect. Simone de Beauvoir explains:

> One is not born, but rather becomes, woman. No biological, psychic, or economic destiny defines the figure that the human female takes on in society; it is civilization as a whole that elaborates this intermediary product between the male and the eunuch that is called feminine [283].

Margaery's self-conscious performances as benefactor of poor orphans and admired subject of a royal wedding, Gilly's reliance on the less-than-capable Sam to build fires for her in the wilderness, Daenerys's line that she's "only a young girl and unused to the ways of war, but ..." are all artificial, meant to influence the men around them. "Womanliness is a mask which can be worn or removed" as the woman deliberately uses her own body as a disguise (Doane 6). Melisandre, the mysterious femme fatale, cultivates her sensuality, teasing and provoking Stannis, Davos, and Gendry, even as she hides her true motives. Ygritte and Sansa also act as the mystery woman. Ygritte comes from a mindset terribly different than Jon's, while Sansa masks her true emotions before everyone. Both are hyper-aware of their roles as love interests, and they identify themselves as belonging to this man or that.

Betty Friedan warns that traditional or "'normal' femininity is achieved, however, only insofar as the woman finally renounces all active goals of her own, all her own 'originality' to identify and fulfill herself through the activities and goals of husband or son" (189). Friedan notes that young men must decide on life paths; women need not—they all must become mothers. So Catelyn, Lysa, and Cersei play the game of thrones on behalf of their sons, all the while succumbing to clichéd irrationality. This irrationality and emotionalism are coded feminine. Film analyst Carol J. Clover explains, "Angry displays of force may belong to the male, but crying, cowering, screaming, fainting, trembling, begging for mercy belong to the female. Abject terror, in short, is gendered feminine" (240). "In traditional societies, men are socialized to be Warriors and women Caregivers," another analyst notes (Pearson 96). The women find themselves in service to men, for indeed, that's the classic female role.

There's also a total lack of sisterhood among these women, particularly the mother figures. Catelyn is distant and cold towards Talisa, and never seen interacting with Arya (and barely with Sansa). Cersei is nasty towards Sansa and vicious towards Margaery. Lysa threatens Catelyn, Melisandre threatens Arya. Mirri Maz Duur schemes against Daenerys. This is particularly cruel, as the mother is the one to validate the maiden's growth and teach her to become a mother herself.

Martin's novella "The Princess and the Queen" (set in distant history) epitomizes female rivalry. Dowager Queen Alicent refuses to surrender the throne to her stepdaughter Rhaenyra and battles on behalf of her son Aegon, though he initially has no interest in ruling. Like Lysa or Cersei, she proves an aggressive widow, determined to solidify her claim. The story emphasizes the women's long-term rivalry, beginning at a factionalized ball at which Rhaenyra wears Targaryen black and red, while the queen wears green, color-coding their factions thereafter. This female-female conflict leads to the decline of the dragons, which die out soon after many are slaughtered in the civil war. As such, female greed and grasping behavior is shown to destroy much of Westeros.

All these portrayals of femininity are problematic, with rivalries, emotionalism, and political ineptness; nonetheless, the gratuitous sex scenes pose the biggest problem. Male characters gain power with swords or political maneuvering, women gain power by stripping. It's a bad message. The strongest female characters with the most agency—Brienne, Arya, Yara, and Catelyn Stark—keep their clothes on at all times. (Sadly, Brienne amends this in the bathtub of season three, but she and Jaime make it quite clear to each other that this isn't that kind of moment.) As Daenerys grows into a liberated khaleesi, she too stays dressed for the most part.

Daenerys makes equally flawed emotional decisions, hoping that the sorceress she saved from rape will respond to kindness, but she misjudges the depth of the woman's rage and her family dies. In all these women's attempt to rule, they "lose," from Cersei's attempts to take the upper hand with Tyrion to Daenerys's shaky grip on her slave city of Meereen. Her sympathy for slaves and hostages there keeps her from returning death with death and keeps her from flying to Westeros. Both, while in character, are unwise political maneuvers. Granted, they're in a harsh world where everyone seems to die rather than win, but it's disappointing that the women lose because of their soft feminine emotions.

If women trying to be men and women succumbing to weak feminine stereotypes are excluded, there are no positive female main characters in the series. (This point is arguable, of course, and many feminized or masculinized women display great moments of cleverness, strength, and agency.) Some see the stripping Red Priestess as feminist, others an offensive parody. Sansa and Catelyn have many supportive fans and many enemies calling them the weakest characters on the show. The author of the blog Feminists-at-Large writes:

Whether it is having her brother father her children to protect the Lannister bloodline or seducing key informants and strategic assets, Cersei firmly believes (as she tells young Sansa Stark) that "a woman's weapon is between her legs." She regularly defies the commands of her father, her husband the king, and all of the men on the Small Council. The lioness of Lannister embodies feminism—even though she is a villain, through and through—because despite her life of luxury and privilege, she is not afraid to get her hands dirty to achieve her goals, nor does she allow any man to dictate her actions [Sackler].

This paragraph seems problematic: Cersei's feminist because she believes women should get what they want through sex? As Daenerys puts it, "The Copper King offers me a single ship on the condition that I lie with him for a night. Does he think I will whore myself for a boat?" (2.6). Truly strong women have sex because they wish to, not because they think offering men their bodies will give them power. Certainly, Robert and even Jaime grow to despise Cersei. When Cersei literally tries sleeping with men to ensure their loyalty, beginning with her cousin Lancel in the second season, she loses at her game.

When Cersei suggests that she would make a better advisor than either of her brothers, Tywin dismisses her. "I don't distrust you because you're a woman. I don't distrust you because you're not as smart as you think you are. You've allowed that boy [Joffrey] to ride roughshod over you and everyone else in this city" (3.4). "From what I saw of Joffrey, you are as unfit a mother as you are a ruler," her uncle says famously (IV.162). Cersei's love for her children is so overwhelming, it spirals into paranoia and bad judgment: Cersei pulls Joffrey off the wall and half the goldcloaks desert. She nearly kills Tommen to spare him from the enemy army. She battles to prevent Myrcella from being sent away to safety because she can't bear to lose her. As such, even more than Catelyn, her motherhood becomes human frailty and irrationality, traditional "feminine weaknesses." "She carries a lot of anger, and a lot of fear and paranoia. Her one piece of sanity is her children," Lena Headey (Cersei) adds (qtd. in Cogman, *Inside HBO's* Game 70).

Martin takes pride in his spectrum of female characters, from strong to sweet, saying:

I wanted to present my female characters in great diversity, even in a society as sexist and patriarchal as the Seven Kingdoms of Westeros. Women would find different roles and different personalities, so women with different talents would find ways to work with it in a society according to who they are.

Indeed, a *Salon* article notes:

Game of Thrones persuasively demonstrates why some of us are always yammering on about the need for increased representation of women (and minorities) on television: Through the relatively simple process of upping the numbers, the burden on any individual woman magically lightens. No single character in *Game of Thrones* has to be the show's final word on womanhood, and that's a freeing prospect. I can find Melisandre a dinner-theateresque take on the sorceress archetype; you can find Daenerys an appalling victim of untreated Stockholm syndrome. But it's OK. With the women of *Game of Thrones*, you don't have to put all your dragon eggs in one basket [Rastogi].

Certainly, medieval women had few options, and Martin's women take full advantage of their world as warriors, healers, mothers, and more. They thrive, even while relegated to second-class citizens. "Whether it's Queen Cersei or (her brother) Tyrion's consort, the former prostitute Shae, who come from completely different backgrounds and social strata, both had to learn how to cope with a world where they don't have most of the advantages in terms of gaining power," says David Benioff (Keveney). To some viewers, the women's struggle against their position mirrors their role in our world. Too many, however, ask men to take advantage of their sexual abilities, even those with career choices outside the brothels. The problem is that these women are generally "wrong" and "lose." None are playing the game of thrones with any degree of success.

Widows and Mothers: The Chatelaines and Queen Consorts

Catelyn rides into battle beside her son, Lysa commands the Eyrie, Selyse guards her husband's holdings, Cersei rules as queen regent. In fact, these women are some of the most historically accurate in Westeros, as widows often ruled and even took up arms on behalf of a young son.

In European history, the chatelaine or lady of the castle had to do far more than embroider: She managed acres of land, crops and animals, along with hundreds of dependents. She settled everything from legal arguments to actual battles. We know a great deal about the life of the lady of the manor from the letters of Margaret Paston, lady of a set of rich estates, who wrote frequently to her husband in London describing her day-to-day activities between 1441 and 1447. In her letters she mentions making marriages, supervising the preparation of huge amounts of food and other household goods (much like managing a small hotel and restaurant), making medicines, keeping tenants' houses in repair, and arbitrating complaints in the local court (Haskell 459–71). In 1642 and 1643, Lady Brilliana Harley defended Brampton Castle against seven hundred soldiers in her husband's absence, even while ill and pregnant.

Christine de Pizan, a widow and professional writer, wrote several guides for women, and included the following advice in her *Treasure of the City of Ladies* (1404): "Because that knights, squires and gentlemen go upon journeys and follow the wars, it beseemeth wives to be wise in all they do, for that most often they dwell at home without their husbands who are at court or in divers lands" (5).

In *Livres des trios vertus*, Christine de Pizan fully recognizes upper class women's contribution within the economic sphere, describing the knowledge of law, accounts, agriculture, and textile production needed by the lady of the manor. Further, she must know war, defense and strategy: "The lady who lives on her estates must be wise and must have the courage of a man. She should not oppress her tenants and workers but should be just and consistent…. She must know the laws of warfare so that she can command her men and defend her lands if they are attacked" (qtd. in Bornstein, 105–07).

CATELYN

I wanted to make a strong mother character. The portrayal of women in epic fantasy has been problematical for a long time. These books are largely written by men, but women also read them in great, great numbers…. Nobody wants to hear about King Arthur's mother and what she thought or what she was doing, so they get her off the stage and I wanted it too. And that's Catelyn ["A Very Long Interview"].

Thus Martin describes his desire to create Catelyn, the fighting mother of the saga.

Catelyn is the archetypal mother. As such, she's often seen in blue like the Virgin Mary (in later seasons, Daenerys, mother to her people, also wears blue). Most of Catelyn's personality can be defined in terms of others: She begins the story feeling unwelcome at Winterfell, surrounded by her northern husband and his northern gods. "All these years, and I still feel like an outsider when I come here," she notes in the godswood ("Winter Is Coming," 1.1).

In the first few episodes, her part in the story is as Bran's mother and Ned's wife, fighting to protect them both. Unfortunately, this reduces her to a stock character—the wife who ignores all political realities to beg her husband to stay with her. She begs, she cries, and tells him, "You do have a choice!" In the books, by contrast, Catelyn realizes they can't say no to the king. She tells Ned he must accept to create opportunities for the Starks. Family, Duty, Honor indeed. Upon hearing of John Arryn's murder, she still urges him to go, in order to save the realm and find justice for Ned's dear friend. As such, she's more practical and even conflicted about the choice, rather than being cast as the clichéd mother and wife.

As Fairley explains, women in the story have a difficult path: "They're second-class citizens. They're intelligent. What makes them more dangerous than men is that they take a longer time to work their revenge because they have to scheme it. You don't expect it to come from them. You do not expect ruthlessness from women at all" (Keveney).

Catelyn's also Jon's wicked stepmother. Michelle Fairley (Catelyn) explains, "For Cat, he's a daily reminder of Ned's infidelity, of his betrayal. I think she channels all the rage and hatred she felt toward Ned and inflicts it all on Jon" (qtd. in Cogman, *Inside HBO's* Game 30). Since more of the story is told from Jon's perspective than hers, our sympathies go to him, the mistreated child whom Catelyn abuses when he goes to bid his dying brother goodbye.

In a moment not seen in the books, Catelyn confesses her dark secret to Talisa much later:

Catelyn Stark: When my husband brought that baby home from the war, I couldn't bear to look at him, didn't want to see those brown stranger's eyes staring at me. So I prayed to the gods, "Take him away, make him die." He got the pox and I knew I was the worst woman who ever lived. A murderer. I'd condemned this poor, innocent child to a horrible death all because I was jealous of his mother, a woman he didn't even know! So I prayed to all Seven Gods, "Let the boy live. Let him live and I'll love him. I'll be a mother to him. I'll beg my husband to give him a true name, to call him Stark and be done with it, to make him one of us."

Talisa Maegyr: And he lived?

Catelyn Stark: And he lived. And I couldn't keep my promise. And everything that's happened since then, all this horror that's come to my family … it's all because I couldn't love a motherless child ["Dark Wings, Dark Words," 3.2].

In the books, Catelyn appears guiltless over her treatment of Jon. It's her husband who's insulted her by raising a bastard beside her children, and she wants Jon to know he'll never be their equal. Here, however, Catelyn is seen failing a test of love for a motherless child. She's selfish about her husband and children, and in her mind, she's cursed and loses them all because of it. In fact, her capture of Tyrion literally begins the Stark-Lannister conflict; fussing over prophecy and curses as the cause hardly seems necessary. While it's human to feel guilt, her cruelty toward Jon makes her lose sympathy.

After the attempt on Bran's life (which Catelyn thwarts with her bare hands, biting and finally slitting the man's throat in an image of the mother protecting her helpless child with her very body), Catelyn certainly has powerful moments, though many of them prove ultimately ineffectual. Using her father's connections she cleverly captures Tyrion, and she tells her mad sister Lysa, "This man is my prisoner. I will not have him harmed" (1.5). However, Tyrion is innocent, and Catelyn ignores evidence and gags him, when as he puts it, he's "starting to make sense" (1.5). In this, she's Littlefinger's dupe.

After her disastrous trip to her sister's and the war it begins, Catelyn becomes an able advisor to her son Robb, traveling with him on campaign rather than returning to Bran and Theon at Winterfell. She's present in his councils, equal to all the lords and councilors. Robb soon accepts her capability and sends her to negotiate with Renly and the Freys. When Ned is beheaded, she springs into action. Though Robb urges his mother to stay in safety, she refuses him, determined to join her son and brother in battling for the North.

Catelyn Stark: If you lose, your father dies, your sisters die, we die.

Robb Stark: Well, that makes it simple then.

Catelyn Stark: I suppose it does ["The Pointy End," 1.8].

With all their lives in jeopardy, she refuses to wait at home. She forms a mission of rescuing her daughters as well as advising her oldest son. "She has children to guide and look after, so she cannot be seen to break down and indulge in her own grief," Fairley says. "She has to be strong for her family. But at the end of Season 1, when she says, 'We will have revenge,' she means it" (Keveney). D.B. Weiss adds, "Michelle has a rare ability to play all the facets of this character: the warmth and love, but also the determination, the steel, the rage" (qtd. in Cogman, *Inside HBO's Game* 51).

Despite her strength, Catelyn undermines Robb's authority with her emotional behavior. She refuses to be sent home and the terms she negotiates for him (giving up his sovereignty to King Renly and wedding a Frey respectively) involve offering more than he's willing to give up. Finally, she betrays him and frees the kingslayer. Her presence is presented as a liability as much as an aid. Rhiannon of Feministfiction.com notes:

> In the books, Robb is a boy-king, out of his depth and somewhat reliant on his mother for help, while Catelyn is shrewd, intelligent and vehemently anti-vengeance. In its attempt to make Robb into more of a stereotypical "sexy young king," the show has stolen a lot of Cat's agency, allowing Robb to voice her ideas (such as sending an envoy to Renly Baratheon), leaving her out of strategy meetings, and transforming her desire to help Robb into a desire to return home and be with her youngest sons ["Are 'Most Women Stupid?'"].

In medieval times, women with a son too young or incapacitated to fight would sometimes lead the troops themselves in full armor. Catelyn may be only adjunct to her capable son; she nonetheless embodies the role of chatelaine as defender of the realm. Martin adds: "With Catelyn there is something reset for the Eleanor of Aquitaine, the figure of the woman who accepted her role and functions with a narrow society and, nonetheless, achieves considerable influence and power and authority despite accepting the risks and limitations of this society" ("A Very Long Interview").

Eleanor of Aquitaine rode all the way to Jerusalem in the Second Crusade and insisted on leading her own troops even into battle. Eleanor called herself "lady of the golden boot" and led a host of armored women. The Byzantine historian Nicetas Choniates describes her as another Penthesileia, queen of the Amazons, and writes of female crusaders "riding horseback in the manner of men, not on coverlets sidesaddle, but unashamedly astride, bearing lances and weapons as men do" (qtd in Newark 108). Many ladies rode to the Crusades, including the queens Margaret of Provence and Eleanor of Castile.

After the birth of her last child, Queen Eleanor of Aquitaine, age forty-four, returned to politics. She took her teenage son, the future Richard the Lionheart, to Aquitaine and had him crowned there as her heir. Catelyn likewise accompanies Robb as his link to the Riverlands of her birth, where her brother and great-uncle pledge fealty to him. Though Catelyn insists Robb rules, she remains an important advisor in his campaign, forging alliances and negotiating on Robb's behalf. At last, Eleanor led her sons in rebellion against their father, King Henry II. Catelyn strikes out as well, kidnapping Tyrion and then freeing the Kingslayer, both out of desperation to help her family. Both women were powerful leaders in a world where they could only act on behalf of husbands and sons. As such, their love and protectiveness for their families became a weapon used to strike their oppressors. Catelyn describes herself as "a widow, a traitor, a grieving mother" (III.39), all like Eleanor. As Eleanor's letter to the pope reads:

> Pitiful and pitied by no one, why have I come to the ignominy of this detestable old age, who was ruler of two kingdoms, mother of two kings? My guts are torn from me, my family is carried off and removed from me. The young king [crown prince Henry, †1183] and the count of Britanny [prince Geoffrey, †1186] sleep in dust, and their most unhappy mother is compelled to be irremediably tormented by the memory of the dead. Two sons remain to my solace, who today survive to punish me, miserable and condemned. King Richard is held in chains. His brother, John, depletes his kingdom with iron [sword] and lays it waste with fire. In all things the Lord has turned cruel to me and attacked me with the harshness of his hand ["Third Letter"].

Upon King Henry's death in 1189, Richard the Lionheart took the throne and released his mother from prison, issuing the unprecedented decree that she might have "the power of doing whatever she wished in the kingdom" as a co-regent to himself (Ralph of Diceto, qtd. in Castor 195).

Her great betrayal of Robb and the army comes when she frees Jaime Lannister to trade for her daughter—an unwise political move of uncertain outcome. As it turns out, those in King's Landing don't have Arya and don't intend to free Sansa. By accepting the offer, she allows Littlefinger and the Lannisters to dupe her again. As Robb notes, "Jaime Lannister has played you for a fool. You have weakened our position;

you brought discord into our camp; and you did all behind my back. Make sure she's guarded day and night!" (2.8). When the Lannisters and Littlefinger are plotting, it's mentioned that Robb is too politically clever to make such a bad exchange as this, but Catelyn, a softhearted woman and mother, may agree. Her motherhood plays into their hands. Rhiannon adds, "As he shouts and she frowns and cries, the audience is pushed into agreeing with Robb's point of view. Catelyn acted irrationally. She was being an irrational, impractical, non-strategic mother, and she betrayed her son by weakening his position.... Catelyn's strength and wisdom are reduced to a cliché of a meddling mother who loves her children too much to see reason" ("Are 'Most Women Stupid?'").

In the books, she's more logical, discussing with Robb that there's no proof that Arya's in King's Landing. Her betrayal comes *after* Bran and Rickon's reported deaths, and as such, it's an explosion of grief leading to the irrational decision. With two children suddenly dead, Catelyn's desperate to reclaim her last ones. Further, Robb is struck with the same grief and acts just as unwisely, suddenly wedding Jeyne Westerling, whose family are bannermen to the Lannisters. When he confronts his mother, he points out that they both succumbed to grief and must forgive each other for similar emotional outbursts. Book Robb adds, "You freed him without my knowledge or consent ... but what you did, I know you did for love" (III.192).

By contrast, television Robb is infuriated by his mother's more calculated act, saying, "You betrayed me.... You knew I would not allow it, and you did it anyway."

Catelyn defends herself with the heartfelt but illogical plea, "I have five children, and only one of them is free" (2.8). Unsurprisingly, Robb isn't moved. While book Robb freed his mother on his return, this one put her in chains in "a chamber that serves as a cell" and she doesn't say a word (3.1). In the book, the Young Wolf also makes an emotion-born mistake, but television Catelyn is seen as being as emotionally fragile and easy to manipulate as the Lannisters think—the irrational mother.

Catelyn's final, defiant act, surrounded by Lord Frey's soldiers, is to threaten his wife (his grandson in the books) with a knife and attempt to trade her life for Robb's. "Lord Walder! Lord Walder, enough! Let it end! Please. He is my son, my first son. Let him go and I swear we will forget this. I swear it, by the old gods and new, we will take no vengeance."

Catelyn pleads and bargains, but as always, her clever ideas and desperate words fail. When she sees her pleas are useless, she switches to threats, uttering, "On my honor as a Tully; on my honor as a Stark, let him go or I will cut your wife's throat!" However, Walder dismisses Catelyn with the flippant comment that he can "find another" ("The Rains of Castamere," 3.9).

Roose stabs Robb in the heart, adding, "The Lannisters send their regards." Catelyn slits Lady Frey's throat in retaliation, then stands in shock as Walder Frey slits her own. In an interview, actress Michelle Fairley describes what it was like to play Catelyn in the Red Wedding scene:

> The woman is just grief-stricken, but she doesn't lose control. She knows she's dead, but in her mind she wants to be dead and wants to get revenge as well. Because of the way it's filmed, as well, you felt incredibly static which is powerful—the fact she stays rooted to her spot. Her grief has to be expressed in some shape and form and it's vocally and through the face.... There's nothing left for her, she's dead already, she wants it. She can't go on. She wants retribution for her son's death. It's brave and it's gutsy—"I don't give a flying f–k what happens to me; I've lost all my children and my husband so what else do I have to live for?" [Hibberd, "*Game of Thrones*' Michelle Fairley"].

David Benioff said, "The look of Michelle's face just before and that howl of rage and grief—she had to do the howl 20 times, just such a terrific performance. They were both phenomenal. We had been waiting for that scene for so long and then having it turn out better than imagined—because of these actors—was just very emotional!" (De Graeve). Of course, by committing the act, Catelyn the nurturing mother becomes the Terrible Mother, slayer of the innocent. Hordes of fans were outraged at the death, or shocked and tearful. Martin describes similar feelings on the killing of two beloved characters: "The Red Wedding was the hardest thing I ever wrote. I wrote that last in that book in *Storm of Swords*. When I actually reached that, it occurs about two-thirds of the way through the book; I skipped over it.... It was tough, it was emotionally wrenching" (Harte). The audience had a similar reaction.

Lysa

Lysa Arryn only appears in three episodes, all in season one (though she's mentioned occasionally, and contracted to return in season four as Littlefinger courts her). Nonetheless, she makes a strong impression. As the head of one of the Seven Kingdoms, and one with an intact army, she shouldn't be discounted.

In the books, she's described as overweight from many pregnancies and miscarriages. Robin (Robert in the books) is her only child. Like Joffrey, he's savage and cruel, likely as a result of hyper-mothering and spoiling. Both mothers bring their sons up as little lords, convinced that all they do is allowable, so their children become tyrants. As Pearson notes, the Caregiver archetype must teach a child as well as comfort and protect it or the child will learn nothing (114). Lysa teaches her son total dependence, so that is the child she produces. When the books begin, Young Robert is six. He has epileptic seizures but his mother's coddling and breastfeeding leave him immature and helpless. Catelyn despairingly thinks that three-year-old Rickon is more independent. As shown in the later books, Lysa is insanely overprotective, sending away children who don't let her son win at games and encouraging him to sleep with her each night, even when he wets the bed.

Every character involved in Robin's life, including Jon Arryn, King Robert, Stannis, Tywin, and Catelyn, suggests fostering him out during book one and before, indicating they're all quietly horrified by Lysa and Robin's unhealthy relationship. Lysa reacts with threats and sometimes actual violence, even to her sister's offer. As psychiatrist Dr. Strecker notes:

> A mom is a woman whose maternal behavior is motivated by the seeking of emotional recompense for the buffets which life has dealt her own ego. In her relationship with her children, every deed and almost every breath are designed unconsciously but exclusively to absorb her children emotionally and to bind them to her securely. In order to achieve this purpose, she must stamp a pattern of immature behavior on her children [qtd. in Friedan 279].

Lysa has never been loved. She was infatuated with Littlefinger as a child, but he wanted Catelyn, and only accepted her as a substitute. John Arryn wed her for duty and was a cold, emotionless man. Her children died. Thus her single son is everything to her and she must be everything to him.

Lysa's home is a reflection of herself: The Godswood is dead, and icy white stone predominates. It's an empty place, "as high as honor" but vacant of love and loyalty. The place is feminized but also cast as murderous and cold with its infamous sky cells and moon door. The men treat the Eyrie with indifference and disdain, much as they treat the lady and her son. When Tyrion notes, "They say the Eyrie is impregnable," Bronn retorts, "Give me twenty good men and some climbing spikes and I'll pregnate the bitch" (1.5).

Lysa is irrational, paranoid, jealous, and easily manipulated, the worst qualities of hyperfeminized behavior. Tyrion manipulates Lysa into granting him an audience and a trial by combat, which the dishonorable Bronn wins. After the war begins, Lysa refuses to send any troops to help Catelyn and Robb's campaign, insisting that every soldier must stay in the Vale to protect her and her son. When Littlefinger courts her, he reveals to Sansa that it's her lands and status he wants, not her. "It is a rare thing for a boy born heir to stones and sheep pellets to wed the daughter of Hoster Tully and the widow of Jon Arryn" (III.929). Nonetheless, Lysa is easily won over by his sweet words. The patriarchy as authority (Littlefinger) or physical force (Bronn) beats her every time she matches wits with them. Meanwhile, she displays little or no familial affection towards her sister and her children.

Both Lysa and Cersei take literally Cersei's rule to "love only your children": Neither woman loves her husband, bestowed on both of them in arranged marriages. And both are violent and cruel toward their siblings, Catelyn and Tyrion. Because of their characters and selfishness, they turn their sons into monsters.

QUEEN SELYSE

Stannis's wife is not really a matriarch of her world, only the counterpart to her husband. She enters the show in "Kissed by Fire" (3.5). While Ygritte boasts of her sexual conquests and Daenerys rides proudly through Essos, Selyse is imprisoned in a gloomy tower, as is her young daughter. She's truly disturbing, as Stannis cringes from her jars of stored fetuses. Bryan Cogman, the writer of "Kissed by Fire," notes, "She's admittedly a bit different from the book, but what we did retain is fanaticism, her fierce devotion to Melisandre.... So we asked the question: What would bring someone to abandon their gods and seek answers elsewhere? Perhaps the stillborn deaths of three sons? And that's how that scene was born" ("Inside Season 3").

Selyse notes that Stannis need not visit their daughter (whom she calls a distraction) though she's prayed for Stannis to visit *her*. In the medieval world, queens were known to do anything to advance their daughters, as on *The Tudors* and in history, Queen Catherine demands King Henry VIII acknowledge Princess Mary as his heir. In contrast here, Selyse says, "[Melisandre] gave you a son. I gave you nothing" (3.5). Her daughter Shireen, sweet and intelligent, though disfigured by a childhood disease, is nothing to her. Cogman adds: "She's essentially the Shireen from the books. The main difference is Selyse's attitude towards her is a bit different. She has a more overt hatred and resentment of her—she wanted to give Stannis sons, not a deformed daughter" (Cogman, "Inside Season 3"). With this, another female-female relationship is abandoned, leaving almost none still existent.

In the books, Shireen is Stannis's acknowledged heir, despite her gender, youth, and greyscale scars. It shouldn't be discounted that she has Baratheon and Targaryen blood, like King Robert, who once seized the throne by those claims. Though she acts like Myrcella, the sweet marriage pawn, rather than fierce Arya, she may yet have a part to play. On the show, her teaching Stannis to read changes the course of history, though her help is quiet and passive. However, she does not free her friend through cleverness or guile, only gives him storybooks. He is the one to read the king's letters and decide what Stannis must do. This is a weak arc for her only appearance to date; by reading the letters herself or giving more aid to Davos, she could have had a plot, rather than a short cameo.

In the books, Selyse and her daughter are not confined to a lonely tower. Both stand beside Stannis at state functions, and Shireen plays around the castle with the fool, Patchface. (Patchface has been known to utter accurate prophecies, so it's interesting that on the show Shireen sings Patchface's song. She may inherit his part in the story.) Selyse brings many knights to Stannis's cause through her status as a Florent. Still, her most important act so far is that she originally invited Melisandre to Dragonstone and introduced her to Stannis. Selyse is the catalyst for Stannis to follow the Lord of Light. In the books, those who believe in R'hllor are named Queen's Men after Selyse.

Benioff calls her a "true believer," noting, "As a mother I think she thinks of herself as a bit of a failure. As a wife ... she's married to someone she admires but there's no love there ... other than that, she really hasn't had any power until she becomes an adherent to this religion" (Benioff, "A Real Sense of Purpose"). In fact, she's beyond an adherent. She welcomes Melisandre's taking the queen's traditional place as main advisor and lover to the king. Selyse is so devoted to Melisandre and the Lord of Light that she accepts Melisandre's affair with her husband and even "wept with joy" (3.5). Her status as a fanatic may eventually hurt the king's cause, as there's little evidence that R'hllor is the answer to save Westeros or that Stannis is truly his chosen one.

Selyse more than takes cues from her husband—she only exists to drive his story and possibly Jon Snow's. Cogman relates that Stannis in season three is lost without Melisandre and "he's essentially an addict going through withdrawal and as part of that withdrawal and the guilt associated with his actions in season 2, he decides to check in with his family" (Cogman, "Inside Season 3").

> It was very important that Stannis be a married man, breaking a vow, so we made a point of showing he had a wife. We came up with the idea of her being shut away in a tower, frankly, at first, as an excuse to keep her off-screen…. It was decided that we needed to create a specific emotional arc for him this season—again, using clues from the book [Cogman, "Inside Season 3"].

She is her husband's representative and she plays the role with haughty pride. Like Daenerys in her first few episodes, all Selyse's power derives from her husband and she acts as his counterpart. On the show, she builds him up, calling him "the one god's champion and the finest man I've ever known" (3.5). In book five, he's her only source of power, despite Melisandre's nearness. She constantly uses the threat that her husband "will hear of this," emphasizing her lack of any real authority, despite her entourage of fifty knights.

Up North, she demonstrates a lack of understanding, bludgeoning her way through wildling culture rather than learning about them. She stubbornly insists the wildlings act like her own people, as she appoints an acceptable "King of the Wildlings," dresses him as a southern lord, and betroths his daughters to her knights. Jon notes that the man is descended from a dead wildling leader's younger brother—a bloodline as unimportant to the wildlings as being descended from his horse (V.900). In her stubbornness, Queen Selyse ignores all of Jon Snow's advice. She also decides to marry off Val, known to the people of Westeros as "the wildling princess" and known among her own people as no one particularly important. She promises to find the insolent Val "a husband who can teach you courtesy" (V.708). When Val tells her that free folk do not kneel, she replies coldly, "Then they must be knelt."

Val at times plays the part of the maiden Selyse expects, but the stubborn queen remains unaware that Val's act is meaningless as Val promises, "I will be a proper wildling princess for your queen" yet does whatever she wishes (V.705). Selyse's willful ignorance remains a source of contention in the north, though she has little effect on events. After Selyse's introduction of Melisandre to Westeros, she has a negligible part in the plot in five books and even less in three seasons.

CERSEI

There's a quote widely attributed to Gloria Steinem, a leader of the women's liberation movement in the '60s and '70s: "Men should think twice before making widowhood women's only path to power." Indeed, Cersei is the classic femme fatale: She secretly poisons her husband (all right, with strongwine and his own idiocy but the result is the same) and chases power for herself and her offspring even if she has to tear the kingdom apart to do it.

In a male-dominated world, Cersei seizes power, but only to indulge her own selfishness.

> In *A Game of Thrones,* Cersei commits a series of dark deeds. In a sadistic act of petty revenge, she has Sansa's direwolf, Lady, killed. She murders her husband, setting in motion many of the horrors that ensue. She has Ned Stark imprisoned and branded as a traitor. She sets her sociopathic son, Joffrey—who is a result of her affair with her brother, Jaime—on the throne, hoping to rule Westeros through him. All the while, she's manipulating everyone she can to achieve her own ends [Spector 181].

This makes her a bad person, but not specifically an anti-feminist one. Her anti-feminism comes from *how* she gains power. Resorting to stereotypical feminine scheming and poisoning is bad. Worse is offering her body to men she doesn't like as a way of compelling them to help her (this has mixed results). It's unfortunate that she's almost the only one giving speeches about women's rights and why women should have the right to rule, as her selfishness and cruelty mar her agenda.

Likewise, Cersei stands up to Tyrion and Tywin but she keeps losing. In one famous moment, Cersei's sure she's outwitted Tyrion and captured the woman he loves, but she's guessed wrong and found, not Shae, but a different prostitute. When her daughter is shipped away or the women of her castle are under threat, she does nothing but drink, complain, or make idle threats. Tywin and his army confiscate her regency at the end of season two, and he doesn't bother to listen to her then or in the following season. He allies with the Tyrells, encourages Margaery, and plans unwanted marriages for both his children. In the King's Landing power struggles, Cersei never gains the upper hand. "She lacks the ability to see how her personal and ethical shortcomings hamstring her quest for power and respect. She's wicked and pathetic at the same time" (Spector 171).

> *Tywin Lannister:* You'll marry Ser Loras.
> *Cersei Lannister:* I will not.
> *Tywin Lannister:* The boy is heir to Highgarden. Tyrion will secure the North, you will secure the Reach.
> *Cersei Lannister:* No, I won't do it.
> *Tywin Lannister:* Yes, you will. You're still fertile. You need to marry again and breed.
> *Cersei Lannister:* I am Queen Regent, not some broodmare!
> *Tywin Lannister: You're my daughter!* You will do as I command and you will marry Loras Tyrell and put an end to the disgusting rumors about you once and for all ["Kissed by Fire," 3.5].

Lena Headey (Cersei) notes: "It's a similar story to this [entertainment] industry, where you're sort of a second class citizen. I think [Cersei] feels that, but she would never admit it to herself" (Armstrong). Nonetheless, she grows in power. Her costumes reflect this, evolving from bird embroidery to lions and finally a sort of armored corset.

She's a bit different on the show than in the books. The books show her indulging in dozens of murders, while in the show she's shocked and helpless in the face of Joffrey's brutality. The producers chose Headey to play her because they liked her unique portrayal—"funny" and "vulnerable" with a "discomfort" of "not being at home in her own skin" (Mitchell). One critic notes:

> Making Cersei's motivations clear on the page didn't click with me in the way it did immediately from Lena Headey's nuanced, arched-eyebrowed interpretation. Beginning in Season 1, the writers added multiple scenes that filled Cersei out, especially an exchange between her and Robert (Mark

Addy) during which she told him that she had loved him when they first married; it was sad and lovely. Headey's high-water mark was the "Blackwater" episode toward the end of Season 2 during which she delivered one sinister monologue after another and ended up almost mercy-killing her beloved (and genuinely sweet) son Tommen when she thought they had lost the war [Arthur].

Some of Cersei's rage is quite justified. She wed the heroic king and was to be queen of Westeros and a force of power in the land. However, her new husband loved dead Lyanna Stark more than his living wife, the greatest, most sought-after beauty of the kingdom. She takes her secret revenge by having children with her brother instead of her husband, denying Robert progeny and placing full Lannisters on the throne. Like Guinevere, her adultery brings down the kingdom.

Cersei's falseness and its consequences are a symptom of patriarchal culture. Ned's bastard son and Robert's many infidelities are dismissed as typical lordly behavior, but hers is a national crime. "When woman becomes man's property, he wants a virgin, and he demands total fidelity at the risk of severe penalty … conjugal infidelity on the part of a woman is considered a crime of high treason" (de Beauvoir 91). Otherwise, the male head of a household may be deceived into raising another man's offspring, which in fact occurs in this story.

> In Westeros, as with many male-dominated societies, a man's power lies not just in himself but also in the line of sons he leaves behind. Cersei usurps the line of succession, substituting another man's child for Robert's own, an act that is both treason and the ultimate emasculation. The only sons who will sit on the Iron Throne after Robert dies are those of the queen's Lannister bloodline alone. That they are children by her twin implies a mirroring of herself in their creation, a startling statement of control and self-defined identity [Spector 181–182].

Cersei bemoans being trapped in a woman's body, ruling through men and not being heir to Casterly Rock. Headey explains that Cersei is so angry "because she wasn't born a man," and her inner monologue in the books reflects as much (Keveney). *Oh for a sword and the skill to wield it. She had a warrior's heart, but the gods in their blind malice had given her the feeble body of a woman"* (V.719). As a child, she sometimes wore Jaime's clothes, and was surprised how differently she was treated (IV 345). "If Lord Tywin could see me now, he would know he had his heir, an heir worthy of the Rock," she thinks (IV.758).

However, though she has these thoughts, she never seeks training in arms as Arya or Meera Reed does. Instead, she spends her time seething over men's advantages. Brienne and Arya, lords' daughters, choose differently, ignoring their duty as highborn ladies rather than being bound by them. Rather than acting to improve her lot, Cersei condemns such women as unfeminine and considers Brienne "a huge, ugly, shambling thing" (V.726). She longs to be a man, yet she despises women who have chosen that path.

She's obsessed with her father's respect, which will always go to Jaime, rather than herself, though she considers herself nearly identical to her brother. Her attempts always fail. She faces her father and demands:

> Did it ever occur to you that I am the one that deserves your confidence and your trust? Not your sons. Not Jaime or Tyrion, but me. Years and years of lectures on family and legacy, the same lecture really, just with tiny, tedious variations. Did it ever occur to you that your daughter might be the only one listening to them, living by them, that she might have the most to contribute to your legacy that you love so much more than your actual children? ["And Now His Watch Is Ended," 3.4].

Cersei appears to buy into the patriarchy as much as she despises it. Tyrion notes she "lusts for power with every waking breath" (I.368). She considers her best friend Taena "more man" than her husband—thus more fit for political office, though she regrets she could never appoint a woman. She even tries reenacting King Robert's brutality, casting herself as the powerful Robert.

> "You hurt me," she complained…. "It was not me my lady," he said in a sulky sullen tone, like a child caught stealing apple cakes from the kitchen. "It was the wine. I drank too much wine."… Sooner or later there would always come a night where he would drink too much and want to claim his rights [IV. 686].
> The Myrish woman gave a gasp of pain. "You're hurting me."
> "It just the wine. I had a flagon with my supper, and another with the widow Stokeworth. I had to drink to keep her calm." She twisted Taena's nipple too, pulling until the other woman gasped. "I am the queen. I mean to claim my rights" [IV.692].

She wants the feeling of being dominant, with herself as the seducer at last.

Without an absent husband and lover who must be concealed, Cersei's focus turns toward her children. As Tyrion points out, her one redeeming feature is loving them (that and her cheekbones). She tells Sansa to love no one but her children, for in that a mother has no choice. She's desperate to protect her children: "She would kill half the lords in Westeros and all the common people, if that was what it took" (IV.774). As the producers note, "Cersei is someone who does the most horrible possible things ... the only thing she cares about is her children. She'll do anything to protect her kids, including sacrificing someone else's kids" (Mitchell). She indeed loves them with all her heart, even as she acknowledges that Joffrey is a monster. Little is seen of the younger children's personalities: Myrcella and Tommen are sweet, docile, and obedient, both brought up to support their older brother. Joffrey is not seen persecuting them much, though he does insist Tommen should act like a prince and not cry at his sister's departure.

Nonetheless, Cersei's indulgent mothering is shown as turning Joffrey into a monster. "Cersei's mistake is that she really can't face the truth about Joff," Headey comments (qtd. in Cogman, *Inside HBO's Game* 70). "Cersei is in a powerful seat, but it's slipping away very dangerously from her. She doesn't face a lot of her truths. She's put her power in Joffrey, and Joffrey is misusing it greatly" (Keveney). In their first scene alone together on the show, she tells him that as king he can do what he likes, including cheating on his wife with a string of mistresses. "Anyone who isn't us is our enemy," she notes (1.3). Robert, though brutal, has acted the absent father and Cersei appears to be Joffrey's influence. Joffrey quotes her advice often, though generally flouting it to hit Sansa or execute Ned.

In season three, she attempts to advise her son, but she grows increasingly jealous and paranoid about Margaery's influence. "Margaery Tyrell dotes on filthy urchins for a reason. She dresses like a harlot for a reason. She married a traitor and known degenerate like Renly Baratheon for a reason," Cersei insists. Though she plays the political game herself, she fears and hates the others who do. Joffrey, who's grown up disrespectful and sexist despite Cersei's smothering influence, only comments that Margaery "married Renly Baratheon because she was told to. That's what intelligent women do: what they're told" (3.2).

While Tyrion builds a strong case that Myrcella will be safe and beloved in Dorne, his rational arguments make little impression on Cersei, who's only concerned with losing her child, not that child's ultimate

Cersei has several strong historical parallels that provide insight into her character: The War of the Five Kings is in many ways a retelling of the English Wars of the Roses (1455–85), with the rival Houses of Lancaster and York recast as Lannister and Stark. "Many first names, only altered slightly, are shared between series: Jon, Robert, Edmund, Edward/Eddard, Richard/Rickard, Geoffrey/Joffrey, Thomas/Tommen, Walter/Walder, James/Jaime, Jane/Jeyne, Margret/Margaery, Marcella/Myrcella, Caitlyn/Catelyn, and Lisa/Lysa" (Frankel, *Winning the* Game of Thrones 82).

The historical Henry VI of House Lancaster was a mild, obedient fellow, with a personality much like Tommen's when well and Robin's Arryn when ill; he alternated between childish complacency and debilitating fits. His wife, Margaret of Anjou, the Cersei character, determinedly clung to power, ruling through her husband and son as she and Richard Plantagenet, Duke of York, fell into political opposition.

The heir to the throne after Margaret's family, Richard declared Margaret's young son illegitimate and marched on London. The Lancasters arrested him and forced him to swear allegiance to Henry VI, much as Ned Stark must to Joffrey. Nonetheless, a compromise was reached: Richard became "Protector of the Realm," regent, and heir for the incapacitated king, cutting the king's son from the succession.

At this, Margaret went to war. Northern Yorkists battled Lancaster supporters in the south. The Lancastrians had a victory when they ambushed the Duke of York and even stuck his head on a pike on the gates of the city (echoing Ned Stark's fate), but York's heir Edward won the war at last. After he took the throne, Edward quietly had Henry VI executed in the Tower of London. Henry's son died in the famous Battle of Tewksbury, and Margaret went into exile, her cause lost. Her forcefulness and rage seem a strong model for Cersei, like her efforts to rule through her young and incapacitated royal family.

The new king was crowned King Edward IV and, much like Robb Stark, made an imprudent marriage out of infatuation rather than wedding for political connections. He was fat and eager for pleasure, whether prostitutes, wine, food, or other overindulgence. Robert Baratheon is based on him, as Martin acknowledges ("Correspondence with Fans," August 15, 2001). Edward died suddenly, possibly from poison, and his youngest brother snatched the regency. The future Richard III arranged

welfare. Cersei's fury at the marriage appears in her chilling speech to her brother: "One day I pray you love someone. I pray you love her so much, when you close your eyes you see her face. I want that for you. I want you to know what it's like to love someone, to truly love someone, before I take her from you." In this and other matters, Cersei is the quintessential irrational woman. On the show she's seen winning a squabble with Littlefinger by threatening him with beheading, something he's unlikely to forget. By the fourth book and third season, jealousy and paranoia motivate Cersei's every action. She loathes Margaery for her influence over Joffrey and sees the Tyrells as rivals, not allies. Margaery comments, "We're going to be sisters soon; we should be friends,"; in response, Cersei tells her the story of the Castameres, who were the second wealthiest family, like the Tyrells, before her family destroyed them. She then adds, "If you ever call me 'sister' again, I'll have you strangled in your sleep" ("Second Sons," 3.8).

Archetypically, Cersei is Hera, the raging stepmother of the pantheon. While a stately queen, she's constantly cuckolded and must maintain her dignity while surrounded by her husband's bastards. When Robert has an affair near Casterly Rock, Cersei reputably kills two of the bastards and has their mother sold into slavery (I.381). As the older queen, Cersei fears being displaced. She is Jung's "Terrible Mother as witch or mother-in-law, furious at being supplanted and relegated to cronehood" (Frankel, *Girl to Goddess* 131). Margaery, the fair young queen, first in Joffrey's heart and beloved by the people, is her greatest threat, as she thinks. Margaery becomes the Capitol's new fashion trendsetter (leaving Cersei quipping about her lack of fabric) and she usurps Cersei's influence over Joffrey but also over Sansa and the court. By book four, Cersei is fuming each time Margaery is called "the queen." This reflects her character, as "Cersei's personality is marked by paranoia, instability, impatience, and imprudence" (Silverman 68).

"An Aphrodite woman may be distrusted by other women, especially by Hera women" (Bolen 251). The Aphrodite woman, an adored goddess of desirability like Margaery, is often shocked by this reaction, as she isn't possessive or jealous herself. She has a circle of best friends and attendants, as Margaery's book counterpart possesses, and gets along well with other girls interested in love and marriage, like Sansa. By contrast, jealous, spiteful Cersei continues to make digs about Margaery's growing popularity. Natalie Dormer (Margaery) notes: "The dialogue is going to get increasingly cattier and cattier—this is all the foreplay for the fight between Cersei and Margaery, and those who know their *Ice and Fire* know that it's going to get incredibly serious. This is the preamble" (Vineyard). As she and Margaery fight over a man, as if the kingdom is secondary to who is most important to Joffrey, they look comical and frivolous.

Cersei had few childhood girlfriends, considering them "vapid, weepy creatures" (IV.683). Her friend Melara Hetherspoon "fell" down a well and drowned but also "screamed and shouted" (IV.685), demonstrating that Cersei pushed her as punishment for her wanting to marry Jaime. On the show, it's mentioned that she beat a nine-year-old until she lost an eye (3.1). Tyrion notes, "Cersei is as gentle as King Maegor, as selfless as Aegon the Unworthy, as wise as Mad Aerys. She never forgets a slight, real or imagined. She takes caution for cowardice and dissent for defiance. And she is greedy. Greedy for power, for honor, for love" (V.281).

In the fourth book, one source of Cersei's paranoia is revealed: As a child, Cersei received a prophecy from Maggy the Frog (a mispronunciation of Maegi). Much of the prophecy has already come true: Cersei married not Prince Rhaegar but King Robert. She has three children and he has sixteen (but no children together). And last comes her downfall. Maggy warns in true *Macbeth* fashion, "Queen you shall be ... until there comes another, younger and more beautiful, to cast you down and take all that you hold dear" (IV.771).

This younger, fairer queen might be Sansa, Margaery, or Daenerys. Cersei's hyperawareness of the prophecy is clear as she controls Sansa, bringing her up as a strictly controlled protégé. She unleashes all her fury on Margaery, who is powerful enough to be a true rival. "All she holds dear" suggests her three children and her crown, which derives from those children. The Maegi notes, "Gold shall be their crowns and gold their shrouds," suggesting all three will rule, and then predecease Cersei. Certainly, Sansa, Margaery, or Daenerys might kill Cersei's children or allow them to come to harm. According to the laws of Westeros, Joffrey, then Tommen, then Myrcella (through a consort or son) will inherit the iron throne. However, Myrcella has been sent to Dorne, whose laws of succession place her before her younger brother. A

Myrcella-Tommen civil war provoked by Dorne is a possibility. In fact, by the fifth book, harm comes to Myrcella through the beautiful young princess Arianne of Dorne and her political maneuvering—perhaps a taste of things to come. Margaery and Cersei's squabbles escalate, but in the first five books, Cersei has not yet lost everything—more tragedy is to come.

All this said, *Feminist TV* makes a fair point in its defense of Cersei:

> I would never proclaim that Cersei Lannister is a "good person"; she is cruel, conniving, and callous. She often acts impulsively based on her passions, and is occasionally blinded by the love she bears for her children and her twin brother Jaime.... However, I would very much say that Cersei is operating in the same value system as the vast majority of characters in this world.... But here's the thing; most of these "corrupt value system" characters are men, and are therefore seen as "bad-asses," "heroes," or "rebels." Meanwhile, Cersei gets labeled "bitch," "terrible and whiny," and "stupid whore" (all quotes taken from various Tumblr conversations). Want to know why? Hint: misogyny! Female characters are traditionally singled out and held to vastly different standards than male characters are, mostly because society at large teaches us that double standards are a-ok (spoiler alert—not true). So while Tywin, Tyrion, and Jaime Lannister get to be cool rebel dudes, Cersei is viewed with an amount of contempt and hatred that's actually rather shocking ["In Defense of Cersei Lannister"].

She goes on to point out that Cersei's incestuous affair with her brother is just as much Jaime's fault, though the Internet fans' blame seems to fall on her. Cersei is often called "mean," "whiny," and a "bitch." However, since Cersei is playing the cruel political game alongside Joffrey, Tywin and others, and voicing similar complaints about powerlessness as Tyrion, Robb, and Jon in a similar way, she should not be condemned gender-specifically. Critics who condemn her as whiny may be protesting that she's speaking too much, in a culture where women are supposed to decorate the screen rather than speak.

> All that said, it really doesn't matter if you like Cersei Lannister or not. She doesn't need to be your favorite character. But the way people talk about the female characters they don't like is intrinsically tied to how they think about women in the real world. You can dislike Cersei's character without participating in the sexist policing of female bodies and voices. Also using gendered slurs, even when talking about fictional women, matters. It matters because it propagates a way of thinking and describing women that is deeply and historically sexist. So love Cersei or hate her. Just don't call her a bitch ["In Defense of Cersei Lannister"].

Cersei has several strong historical parallels that provide insight into her character: The War of the Five Kings is in many ways a retelling of the English Wars of the Roses (1455–85), with the rival Houses of Lancaster and York recast as Lannister and Stark. "Many first names, only altered slightly, are shared between series: Jon, Robert, Edmund, Edward/Eddard, Richard/Rickard, Geoffrey/Joffrey, Thomas/Tommen, Walter/Walder, James/Jaime, Jane/Jeyne, Margret/Margaery, Marcella/Myrcella, Caitlyn/Catelyn, and Lisa/Lysa" (Frankel, *Winning the* Game of Thrones 82).

The historical Henry VI of House Lancaster was a mild, obedient fellow, with a personality much like Tommen's when well and Robin's Arryn when ill; he alternated between childish complacency and debilitating fits. His wife, Margaret of Anjou, the Cersei character, determinedly clung to power, ruling through her husband and son as she and Richard Plantagenet, Duke of York, fell into political opposition.

The heir to the throne after Margaret's family, Richard declared Margaret's young son illegitimate and marched on London. The Lancasters arrested him and forced him to swear allegiance to Henry VI, much as Ned Stark must to Joffrey. Nonetheless, a compromise was reached: Richard became "Protector of the Realm," regent, and heir for the incapacitated king, cutting the king's son from the succession.

At this, Margaret went to war. Northern Yorkists battled Lancaster supporters in the south. The Lancastrians had a victory when they ambushed the Duke of York and even stuck his head on a pike on the gates of the city (echoing Ned Stark's fate), but York's heir Edward won the war at last. After he took the throne, Edward quietly had Henry VI executed in the Tower of London. Henry's son died in the famous Battle of Tewksbury, and Margaret went into exile, her cause lost. Her forcefulness and rage seem a strong model for Cersei, like her efforts to rule through her young and incapacitated royal family.

The new king was crowned King Edward IV and, much like Robb Stark, made an imprudent marriage out of infatuation rather than wedding for political connections. He was fat and eager for pleasure, whether prostitutes, wine, food, or other overindulgence. Robert Baratheon is based on him, as Martin acknowledges ("Correspondence with Fans," August 15, 2001). Edward died suddenly, possibly from poison, and his youngest brother snatched the regency. The future Richard III arranged the death of their third brother and declared Edward's sons illegitimate, before finally killing them in the Tower. In many ways, his plot echoes that of vilified Stannis.

At the war's end, the last Lancaster, the future Henry VII, sailed to defeat Richard in battle. Henry wed Edward IV's daughter Elizabeth, and united the red and white roses of their house sigils to create the Tudor Rose. While the last scions of Lannister and Stark, Sansa and Tyrion, might unite to bring peace to Westeros, the prince coming from over the sea to end the civil war is most likely to be Daenerys.

Queen Isabelle of France, wife of Edward II of England, most likely had her husband murdered (much as Circe does) and campaigned to become regent for her young son. All the while, she kept her known lover beside her at court. She was famous for accusing her two sisters-in-law of adultery. After announcing that Margerite de Bourgogne and her cousin Blanche de Bourgogne were dallying with knights in the old guard tower, the *Tour de Nesle*, Isabelle arranged for them to be put on trial. The two knights accused of being their lovers were executed, while the women had their heads shaved and were displayed to the crowd and humiliated in the streets, and then imprisoned. Queen Isabelle, however, lost much popular support for starting the *Tour de Nesle* affair. Much of this has parallels in Circe's plot of the fourth and fifth books.

Catherine de Medici, queen of King Henry II of France from 1547 until 1559, was neglected and despised in favor of the king's mistress, Diane de Poitiers. When the king died, Catherine became regent and political mastermind on behalf of fifteen-year-old Francois II, her son. Francois II wed Mary, Queen of Scots, and her uncles proved as difficult for Catherine to live with as Cersei finds her Tyrell in-laws. When Francois died young, she ruled for her second son, and then her third, as Nostradamus prophesized would happen. Similar fates are likely to befall three Lannister children and Cersei, who is prophesized to outlive them all thanks to a childhood meeting with a Maegi who told her, "Gold shall be their crowns and gold their shrouds" (IV.540–41). Catherine was known for being a ruthless schemer and occasionally poisoner. Her subjects considered her ruthless, and sometimes politically inept, but all was intended to keep her three children on the throne.

Of course, Martin notes that his characters are only loosely historical:

You can do one-for-one conversions of the real-world to fantasy, but if you're going to do one-for-one, you might as well just write straight historical fiction.... It makes more sense to take certain interesting elements of Henry VIII and certain interesting elements of Edward IV, and maybe something from here and something from there, and put them together and use your imagination to create your own character—someone who is uniquely himself and not exactly like someone from history [Roberts].

Maidens: The Innocent, the Orphan, and the Femme Fatale

A popular archetype is the fairy tale princess or ingénue, from the French for virtuous and candid. Carol Pearson in her archetypes study suggests "the Innocent" for this category. Innocents "assume they will be cared for by the universe and other people, because they are so special and so good" (78). Such a princess is Sansa. Her archetype of course is the fairy tale princess, a child-woman, unassertive and youthful. She's unthreatening and passive, wanting to accommodate others and in turn expecting to be rescued.

"Sansa is naive and quite vulnerable at the start," Sophie Turner (Sansa) observes. "She's a complete romantic and lives in a fantasy world. She just wants to be the girl that her father and her mother expect her to be. She just wants to make her family proud, and her good intentions can be manipulated, mainly by Joffrey. I think she's very immature for her age and she needs a wake-up call" (Nguyen).

Of course, she gets that call soon enough. As soon as the second episode, she takes the prince's side against her sister, and her wolf Lady is unjustly executed as a result. When Bran has a vision of his family, he saw his father "pleading with the king, his face etched with grief. He saw Sansa crying herself to sleep at night, and he saw Arya watching in silence and holding her secrets hard in her heart. There were shadows all around them" (I.136). Sansa's first choices—begging to wed Joffrey and then taking his side before the king—set her family on their path to tragedy. "She makes a lot of mistakes that lead to some really bad consequences," Turner tells TVGuide.com. "I think the fans of the books and of the television show are angry at her. People who haven't dug deep enough into the character can't really see the good intentions in Sansa's decisions" (Nguyen). She's a peacemaker, but in a world of treachery and violence, being a peacemaker will only leave her a victim.

Sansa, though she publicly takes Joffrey's side, is also punished, with her demure Lady killed only for being born a wolf. This punishment reflects the abuses Sansa suffers in court. For the Starks, the wolves represent power, inner strength, and magic, their link with warg abilities and deeper perception. While Arya must send away her source of magical strength and appear to conform, compliant Sansa loses her wolf permanently. This symbolizes Sansa's losing her wild power and inner magic, which to date she has not regained.

When this happens, Sansa is cut off from the deep insight that makes Grey Wind growl at the Freys and Ghost protect Jon from the White Walker. When a fan asked Martin if all the Stark children are skin changers with their wolves, he replied, "To a greater or lesser degree, yes, but the amount of control varies widely," adding also, "Bran and Summer are somewhat of a special case" ("Correspondence with Fans," February 12, 2001). Sansa has likely lost that power, while Jon and Bran, who stay close to their wolves, slowly develop the ability. Alone in King's Landing, Sansa trusts the wrong people and is used by them over and over. Her magical perception has been lost.

Irrational optimism is one of the Innocent's worst qualities, as she will delude herself that she's not in terrible peril. As late as moments before Ned's death, Sansa still believes in Joffrey. Though courtly and gallant, Joffrey shows his true face to her as early as the second episode when, humiliated, he yells at her savagely. He is the one to have Arya's playmate killed, who lies to the court to protect his own reputation. Through the season, his behavior worsens, though he does have polite moments. "I fear I have behaved monstrously in the past few weeks.... Will you forgive me for my rudeness?... I'll never be cruel to you again," he tells Sansa and she's eager to believe ("A Golden Crown," 1.6).

The Innocent's best girlfriend is often a girl with a stronger personality like Margaery or a similar Innocent like Sansa's best friend Jeyne. The princess is compliant and passive, acted upon instead of acting. "She represents the young girl who does not know 'who she is' and is as yet unaware of her desires or strengths" (Bolen 199). She's determined to please others, certain that if she's appealing enough, the world will be kind to her.

The character most seen looking at herself in mirrors is Sansa. This suggests that she's considering herself as an object. Will her new gown please the men in her life? Does she look pretty enough? Archetype scholar Wind Hughes describes the Maiden, saying, "She may be the dutiful daughter, her self-worth linked to pleasing others in order to receive their approval. She has not developed a strong sense of self." Daenerys is such a figure in the first episode but she grows, far outpacing Sansa. Likewise, Arya begins trying to please Septa Mordane and follow the Starks' rules, but she soon breaks out with Needle, the gift from outsider Jon Snow.

"Sansa completely disapproves of everything that Arya does," says Turner. "She finds her sister a complete nuisance. Sansa is so different from Arya she can't relate to her" (Nguyen). In her first appearance, Sansa can be defined as all Arya is not, and Arya fits the same definition. Sansa conforms, is polite and ladylike, wants conventional marriage with the handsome prince. She's her mother's girl. Arya codes herself masculine as she competes with Bran at archery and Jon gives her first sword. "Sansa can have her sewing needles. I have a Needle of my own," she remarks (1.1). When Ned discusses her future with her, Arya once against defines herself as Sansa's opposite. Siblings in real life tend to polarize, half-consciously dividing attributes like "I'm the bright one and she's the pretty one" (Downing 111). As Jungian analyst Christine Downing puts it, "She is both what I would most aspire to be but feel I never can be *and* what I am most proud *not* to be but fearful of becoming" (111).

At breakfast together in the book, Sansa wears a delicate white silk gown, which Arya stains with the juice of a blood orange, reflecting the upcoming carnage. Arya, by contrast, wears "ratty leathers and rough-spun" (I.447). Arya sees her older sister as the perfect one who is all her parents expect of a daughter, as she is not. Sansa can sing and dance, sew and write poetry, play the high harp and the bells. "Worse, she was beautiful," Arya thinks. "Sansa was two years older; maybe by the time Arya had been born, there had been nothing left" (I.70). However, trapped, helpless Sansa finds herself envying her sister's strength and independence. Though she doesn't become another Arya, she learns guile and self-defense as she struggles through the world of politics. "She was very vulnerable and naive, and now she's independent and has to survive in this world. That's a lot of pressure for a 13-year-old girl,"

Turner says. Moving forward, "one of the main challenges is the mental and physical torture she's going to get from the Lannisters and all the people around her" (Keveney).

Carol Pearson contrasts two types of young heroes, the Innocent and the Orphan. While the Innocent believes people are essentially kind, the Orphan operates from a more traumatized and cynical place. While the abandoned Innocent tries harder to be perfect and lovable, the abandoned Orphan learns that people are essentially alone. "At some point, Orphans give up on failed authorities and take control of their own lives, and when they do, they become Rebels" (Pearson 85). The Orphan as Rebel works for justice, especially with other wounded outcasts. These are the contrasting paths of Arya and Sansa, sisters who see their betrayal quite differently. While Sansa tries to charm the Lannisters, then finally withdraws into herself, Arya leaves the system, determined to fight from the outside.

Margaery, a third maiden archetype, is the femme fatale or "bad girl"—the one who appears sweet and innocent but is more manipulative, even murderous to win her desires. Traditionally, she uses femininity and sensuality to achieve her goals. A certain amount of feigned helplessness is traditional, and thus Margaery asks Joffrey for hunting lessons and appeals to Joffrey's eagerness for approval as well as violence. Margaery doesn't appear to kill, but her enemies have a habit of mysteriously dying around her ... only time will tell how much she has controlled those events. The only reason she's likable is that she's not manipulating good people, but the disturbing Lannisters, from cruel Cersei to sadistic Joffrey. However, as she walks the fine line to ingratiate herself to Joffrey, she's enabling his eagerness for violence.

True to form, Margaery is cast against good girl Sansa, as she replaces Sansa as Joffrey's fiancée. She's pretending to be the Innocent Sansa actually is. (By contrast, Sansa as "the imp's wife" is expected to be plotting alongside him.) Margaery is also a foil for Cersei. Cersei was raised by her father to be only a marriage pawn, furious at the patriarchal system but abandoned to be raped and abused by King Robert. Her attempts to play the game of thrones often fail as Joffrey, Tywin, and Tyrion ignore her wishes. By contrast, Margaery was raised by Lady Olenna to play the game and win. She knows how to win over both city-folk and court, while Cersei brutally alienates both.

Margaery's a consummate liar, twisting her relationship with Renly and her feelings about homosexuality to please Joffrey. She appears to fool him into thinking she's a sweet innocent who can be easily controlled, all the while controlling him. While her father "swears she's still maiden," her dialogue with Sansa on the show and her seeking moon tea in the books make this appear unlikely. She's at least morally dubious, though she appears to be a better person than Cersei at least. Cersei has killed and maimed others by this point; there's no evidence Margaery has directly done so or even given the orders. In the books, her motivations are less clear, as she's perceived more at a distance by Cersei and Sansa. Her actress, Natalie Dormer, comments:

> I'm watching her unfold every time I get the script myself, which takes the pressure off. David and Dan were the first to admit that they weren't sure at first what to do with Margaery. They genuinely weren't sure, and we've been working it out as we've gone along. Hopefully I've given them something to anchor her to, but I am curious about how dirty her hands will get. It could be played either way, couldn't it? [Vineyard].

She's more effective than the Lannisters, and has the makings of a sympathetic figure as she's kind to Sansa and Joffrey, the abandoned children so different from each other. Dormer adds: "I really loved Margaery getting close to Sansa. Sophie [Turner] and I have had so much fun together. I love that big sister dynamic—Sophie and I are pretty much agreed that if the circumstances were different, Sansa and Margaery would actually be good friends" (Wieselman).

Certainly, Margaery is the anti–Sansa or possibly the future Sansa, one who's a player not a pawn, one who can spar with Queen Cersei and make choices for herself. All her moves seem carefully orchestrated down to the last word, and this makes her resemble the oh-so-careful Littlefinger or Varys, a schemer cleverly playing the game.

MARGAERY

Yes, Margaery is pretty great in the books too. But the show has made her formidable sooner, abetted by her wily portrayer, Natalie Dormer. Because *A Song of Ice and Fire* relies on specific point-of-view characters as third-person narrators—the story jumps among them and them only—and Margaery is not one of them, it takes readers a while to see how strong and smart she is, and how wary she is of the Lannisters [Arthur].

Her marriage to King Renly appears to be the act of a dutiful marriage pawn; book Margaery is only fourteen, about the age of Daenerys. There is no seduction scene in which she strips and offers to share Renly with her brother, no proud moment when she decides to be *the* queen. She is merely Renly's pretty and sweet adjunct. Likewise, in King's Landing, she isn't seen manipulating Joffrey or spending time alone with him, only being adored by the cheering populace. Together with her many girlish cousins and friends, she's the prize offered by her family in the political game, as they barter her in marriage after marriage (she is even proposed as a replacement queen for King Robert if he sets Cersei aside). Lord Tyrell is the one negotiating for concessions, not his daughter or his mother. Without much seen of Margaery's personality, it remains possible she's ambitious, but it's more likely she's just following her family's dictates.

Television Margaery echoes in viewers' minds with Anne Boleyn, the political schemer played by Natalie Dormer on *The Tudors*. Martin comments, "My Margaery is younger than Loras, not older than Loras. So she's really just like a sixteen-year-old kid. And Natalie is brilliant, but she's clearly not a sixteen-year-old kid. She's very smart. She's almost what my Margaery will become in ten years" (Anders). She's older and gets more dialogue. As she dresses provocatively and travels alone to the worst slums of the city, she shows herself a different kind of player. Kate Arthur notes, "In the premiere of this third season, we got a glimpse at Margaery's larger strategy with her fiancé, Joffrey, and it is ripped from the Princess Diana playbook: She jumped out of her carriage and won over the orphans of King's Landing while Joffrey cowered."

Both versions of Margaery are the Aphrodite archetype or Hetaera, the lover desired by all who is sent to improve the life of her chosen king. She's sexy and worldly, advising Sansa to seize pleasure where she finds it, noting, "Most women don't know what they like until they tried it and sadly so many of us get to try so little before we're old and gray," along with the provocative "We're very complicated, you know; pleasing us takes practice" (3.7). When Margaery gives Sansa advice on experienced men, she demonstrates that she has more than a little experience herself. The Aphrodite woman travels from one relationship to the next, embracing life and sensuality, as often-widowed Margaery does. She acts as an inspiratrice for the man in her life, guiding him to wisdom and spirituality. When alone with her men, she presents herself as the perfect complement or Anima woman: She's loyal and self-effacing with Renly, willing to invite her brother into their relationship. With Joffrey she's sensual but not pushy, showing a demure excitement of his savagery. She's the archetypal lover and bride—the perfect woman for a variety of men.

One common match for the Aphrodite figure is Ares, the handsome, immature, raging god of war.

> He is an emotional, passionate, blustering man, who has supermacho affectations. Lacking a real father as a role model and disciplinarian, and used to getting his way with his mother, he is impatient and has a low tolerance for frustration. He likes to be in charge, yet he may lose his head when pressured, which doesn't make him a good leader [Bolen 249].

This archetype is perfectly realized by vile Joffrey. The gods of love and war make a problematic relationship. His jealousy can turn to violent outbursts and she can find her affection for him is transient. While they may have a tempestuous romance, it is generally doomed.

Though their relationship is based on Joffrey's covering his true viciousness beneath a courtly veneer, Margaery handles him expertly. In one episode, she subtly seduces him not by touching him (a clear mistake as a pair of prostitutes once proved), but instead by touching his crossbow and fantasizing about how it must feel to hunt and kill. "The angle at which he holds his crossbow when firing will be immediately recognizable to anyone who sat through one of those 'subliminal sexual imagery in advertising' movies in school," Christopher Orr of *The Atlantic* notes ("*Game of Thrones*: A Feminist Episode"). As she (ahem) holds the tool of Joffrey's power, she's exerting control over him. Though he fights Cersei's attempt to boss him around earlier in the episode, he beams at Margaery's subtler approach. Dormer notes:

> You have to appreciate how badly that could have gone for her, too! Because Joffrey turned dark on a knife's edge the way he did with Sansa, and Margaery very quickly has to play a game of three-dimensional chess in her head to outmaneuver him and learn what makes him tick. That was the first scene I shot of the third series, Jack [Gleeson]'s and my first scene together. We didn't know each other as actors; we were trying to figure out the dynamic of how these two would interact, figure out each other's rhythms. But you have to marvel at Margaery—she passed the test, as it were. He's a very, very dangerous and tricky human being, and who knows what will happen in the

future? Will she be so adept at outmaneuvering or fall foul of it the way Sansa did? [Vineyard].

She adds that Margaery is a true inspiratrice, acting as the perfect mate rather than voicing her own opinions: "She is playing a role. She is trying to create a persona for herself that she thinks Joffrey will like and will trust and will listen to" (Vineyard). Later, she listens attentively to Joffrey's savage retelling of Targaryen history but coaxes him outside to meet the cheering crowd. Whereas Cersei wheedles and Sansa begs (and both go ignored), Margaery seems capable of tricking him subtly and getting away with it. As such, she may actually be a good match for him. However, Joffrey has not yet hit her or publicly humiliated her as he has with Sansa.

In season three, Joffrey is still in the courtly stage. One assumes he feels a bit cowed by Lord Tywin and Margaery's many Tyrell relatives. Still, with all the terrible acts Joffrey has committed, viewers are waiting for his next attempt, and wondering when he'll reveal himself to his future bride. Margaery knows from Sansa, or possibly before, that Joffrey is a monster, and her character is too smart to become Joffrey's victim. Dormer adds:

> She has not seen the dastardly, dark, sadistic side of Joffrey and it will be very interesting when it happens—I think it's only a matter of time [*laughs*]. When she comes directly against it, how she will handle it? We had a taste of that where she managed to flip the conversation on its head and gained control of it in a way Sansa would have never been able to, but as we all know, Joffrey can go to a physically malicious place. If he gets that extreme, it's going to be very interesting to see how Margaery will handle that. She'd definitely be changed by it, that's for sure [Wieselman].

SANSA

"The culture we live in also conditions girls to equate femininity with passive, dependent behavior. They are encouraged to act like Cinderellas waiting for a prince to come, Sleeping Beauties waiting to be awakened" (Bolen 200). Sansa's character reveals the flaws in that kind of upbringing as she's hopelessly naïve, trusting in beauty and rank over character.

In the first few episodes, Sansa is charmed by the handsome prince who chooses her over all the other ladies of Westeros. In the second episode, Sansa's flawed judgment becomes clear: Ser Ilyn and the Hound are monstrous to her because of their scarred faces. By contrast, she lies to defend Joffrey, for she is "his lady, his princess." This choice of course results in the death of her wolf, Lady, and with her, Sansa's romanticized belief that handsome princes are perfect within. In the book, Sansa begins "crying herself to sleep at night," clearly mourning her lost illusions as well as her wolf (I.136).

Sansa's wolf represents her inner magic and fierceness, sacrificed so early in the story. "If Lady was here, I would not be afraid," Sansa thinks much later (III.799). Thus, Cersei and Joffrey literally kill Sansa's spirit, foreshadowing both killing her father and inflicting the slow emotional death that follows. Her siblings are human masks over the wolf magic and wildness developing within until Bran can shed his human form and enter the wolf. Sansa, by contrast, is only mask. As she imitates the queen's hairstyle in season one and Margaery's in season three, she floats from imitation to imitation, while the strong core has faded away. The Innocent is "the 'nameless maiden'; she represents the young girl who does not know 'who she is' and is as yet unaware of her desires or strengths" (Bolen 199). As such, she's on a quest for identity.

The first season sees Sansa in attractive low necklines, then increasingly mirroring Cersei in hairstyle and dress through her father's execution. After, she wears more drab, high-necked gowns. "She's wearing something closer to her mother's look. She's come full circle," costume designer Michelle Clapton notes (qtd. in Cogman, *Inside HBO's* Game 44). Even her wedding dress is surprisingly understated and demure (whereas in the books it's her first truly adult gown with plunging neckline). The heavy gold fabric is elegant, but her neckline is high, with a rigid heavy structure to the dress, suggesting her high position and the structured society that traps her. Her arms by contrast, are vulnerably bare.

In season two, she hates Joffrey but learns to manipulate him, even as she rejects Cersei as a role model. Sophie Turner, her actress, says, "She was very vulnerable and naive, and now she's independent and has to survive in this world. That's a lot of pressure for a 13-year-old girl." Moving forward, "one of the main challenges is the mental and physical torture she's going to get from the Lannisters and all the people around her" (Keveney).

In the book, the knight saved by Sansa at season two's beginning pledges his loyalty. They meet in the Godswood, and he vows to be her knight and defend her in a pattern of courtly love. In fact, he promises he'll smuggle her from the castle and take her home. Thus, Sansa refuses more problematic protectors, as she trusts Ser Dontos. (A parallel can be seen with young Daenerys, who trusts the witch Mirri Maz Duur because she saved her life and expects gratitude. Both of these innocents will have an awakening.)

On the show, her attitude is more puzzling. She doesn't want to be queen, shown by her delight when her engagement crumbles. She isn't gathering information or working for the Starks—she's merely enduring. Clearly, she's suffering from massive trauma, frightened that even a hint of treason will see her executed. That's the most logical reason she refuses Sandor Clegane and Littlefinger's offers to see her home in season two and Tyrion's offers to end her engagements. She drifts through the Red Keep, compliant and cool as a statue, passively enduring Joffrey's plots. "I am loyal to King Joffrey, my one true love," Sansa tells Tyrion, full of dignity after Joffrey has had her beaten. Though she cringes and pleads before Joffrey, her words here are colored with sarcasm and cool dignity. "Lady Stark, you may survive us yet," Tyrion observes (2.4). Like him, she knows when to hold her words back and when to release them, when to set aside dignity and when to shield herself in it.

Her lack of resistance encourages Joffrey to keep mistreating her; she's not improving her situation with her actions. Of course, she's growing smarter and she manages to endure three seasons in King's Landing while other characters like Ros, Janos Slynt, and Sandor Clegane rise in power and then ingloriously tumble.

In season three, she's grown from Joffrey's plaything to a desirable marriage pawn; the Tyrells, the Lannisters, and Petyr Baelish all want her. Of course, she's only sought for her claim to the North and the heir she can produce. Sansa is polite to all these offers, suggesting she's learned her true status: She will never be allowed to choose for herself, only be traded and fought over. She and Margaery smile and chat like sisters—Sansa admires and is envious of the confident, powerful older girl who is protected in a way lost Sansa may never be again. As she grows close to Margaery in season three, Sansa imitates her, especially in hairstyle.

Sansa's girlish crush on Ser Loras makes her seem hopelessly naive as she gushes about the red rose that actually means nothing to him. Every character on the show and most in the books seems to know Loras would make a bad husband for her ... except Sansa herself. Loras "is very good at hitting men with sticks" as Olenna mentions, but there hasn't been any evidence that Loras is a wonderful human being or anything more than a handsome face with skill at jousting. Nonetheless, Sansa is smitten. "Sansa truly thinks the Tyrells are the answer to all her problems. Just when she thought all chivalry and heroism was dead— here's this amazing family come to get her out of there. And not by sneaking around and escaping! Through a proper marriage in the sight of the gods," writer Bryan Cogman explains ("Inside Season 3"). It seems she still values looks over substance.

However, Tywin blocks the Tyrell alliance and weds her to Tyrion against both their wills before she can escape.

> *Tyrion Lannister:* Joffrey has made this poor girl's life miserable since the day he took her father's head. Now she's finally free of him and you give her to me? That's *cruel* even for you.
>
> *Tywin Lannister:* Do you intend on mistreating her? The girl's happiness is not my concern, nor should it be yours.... You wanted to be rewarded for your valor in battle. Sansa Stark is a finer reward than you could ever dare hope for. And it is past time you were wed ["Kissed by Fire," 3.5].

On their unconsummated wedding night and after, Sansa is cold toward Tyrion. In the books, he offers to refuse the match, leaving her to wed the more handsome Lancel Lannister. However, Sansa decides that the entire family is her enemy; which one she weds hardly matters. She enters her marriage with a resigned suffering that bothers Tyrion and also some viewers. In the books she exercises a single moment of defiance and silently refuses to kneel and aid Tyrion during the wedding. He finally must stand on the fool's back, as laughingstock to the court, to place his cloak around her. By kneeling on the show, Sansa is being the compliant good girl instead. Rhiannon of *Feminist Fiction* demands:

> Why does she have to be *nice*? Why should she not be defiant and bold, fighting back in whatever small way she can.... She has *one* moment of defiance, one moment where she gets to stand up for herself, in an almost insignificant way, and say, "I do not consent to this. I will not be part of this." She cannot stop the wedding, but she can refuse to make it easier for anybody. She can be dignified and detached and refuse to participate. And

that strength and non-consent was taken away from her. To make her nicer. To make her kinder to Tyrion, and to smooth things over so that we see them *both* as victims, in this together, with Tyrion's kindness there to save her ["Sansa Stark Does Not Kneel"].

Though he chooses not to exercise his power as husband over her, Sansa has lost her childhood dreams of wedding a handsome, gallant protector. Her husband, the hideous imp, has made her a Lannister forever, whose children will give the North to her enemies. It's not surprising she retreats from the well-meaning Tyrion. She doesn't care that Tyrion is a wounded outcast like herself; he is a Lannister, and that's enough. He promises not to hurt her, but Joffrey and Cersei once promised that as well. Is it any wonder she doesn't believe?

A look at history reveals much about her character. With her constant insistence on "courtesy as a lady's armor," Sansa demonstrates her love for medieval "courtesy books"—primers on proper behavior written mainly between the twelfth and fifteenth centuries (Bornstein 13). While many were written by men, one famous set was penned by the early feminist Christine de Pizan. She writes:

> It seems to me that it is the duty of every princess and high-born lady, excelling in honour and status above all others, to excel in goodness, wisdom, manners, temperament and conduct, so that she can serve as an example on which other ladies and all other women can model their behaviour. Thus it is fitting that she should be devoted to God and have a calm, gentle and tranquil manner, restrained in her amusements and never intemperate [141].

In this tradition, Sansa comforts the ladies of the court and leads them in prayer during Stannis's siege. De Pizan advises ladies with husbands who "conduct themselves abominably" to "bear all this and to dissemble" for responding harshly will gain her nothing (*Cyte of Ladyes*, qtd. in Bornstein 69). When Joffrey humiliates her and beats her in public, Sansa bears it all, but sneaks around the Godswood (in the books) or with Littlefinger (on the show), contriving an escape.

In medieval Europe, the queen's traditional power was that of the Intercession "to soften his heart toward his subjects and improve his rule," as she would publicly plead with the king to show mercy for a petitioner (Parsons 147). This was a prearranged staging, a way for the king to show mercy as a gift to his queen rather than acknowledging weakness or arbitrarily changing his mind.

"As the possibility for the direct exercise of power became more remote, writers began to stress the queen's duty to use the less direct, but no less potent, means of persuasion and intercession" (Huneycutt 131). As queens became more consort than co-ruler in the early twelfth century and onward, the intercession was their singular power, a reason for supplicants to approach the queen and for her to influence policy non-threateningly. "The queen's idealization as a virtuous maternal figure complementing the king as ruler and lawgiver" continued, as the books of the time revered her for humbling herself for others, comparing her to Biblical Esther pleading for grace (Parsons 147).

In "The Pointy End" (1.8), Sansa kneels before the court and sweetly begs Joffrey for her father's life. This is her great talent—courtesy and courtly behavior. As she asks that her prince save Ned "for love of me," Joffrey is provided with an excuse to preserve peace. Of course, being Joffrey, he prefers a vicious strike at Sansa and his court rather than political expediency. He suddenly orders Ned's death on the steps of the holy Great Sept, even as Sansa and Cersei are convinced he'll offer mercy. Sansa faints: She has discovered the prince's true cruelty far too late. Thus he rejects Sansa's role as the beloved he should honor and treats her with increasing contempt through the second season.

Sansa in turn grows craftier, saving the drunken Ser Dontos by praising Joffrey's wisdom. She urges Joffrey to be brave and ride in the vanguard as her brother would do during the Battle of Blackwater. Under her claims that Joffrey is her one true love, a certain guile develops, until she evolves from innocent to survivor.

GILLY

Gilly is a similar Innocent, with a terribly problematic story arc. Craster, living in almost the only safe stronghold beyond the Wall, weds his daughters, granddaughters, and so on, while sacrificing the baby boys to the Others in the forest. His daughters are completely isolated and have no chance for escape. Jon Snow confronts his commander about it, and Mormont responds with a speech about how disturbing allies are better than none. Jon is forced to accept it. The women are taught to agree to this life, until Gilly comments that her father and husband wedding her daughter wouldn't be that bad. Benioff notes:

Hannah [Murray] brings a wonderfully damaged quality to Gilly—the character is a bit like one of those girls who is kidnapped and abused for years, and brainwashed by her captor into thinking he's a prophet and a righteous man. Hannah understands that intuitively; her Gilly is also lovable and fetching and sympathetic [Lacob, *"Game of Thrones' Creative Gurus"*].

When some of the Night's Watch rebel and kill Craster and Commander Mormont, Sam and Gilly escape to save her newborn. In the books, the older women, including Gilly's mother, bring supplies and horses to Sam and tell him the Others will soon arrive and kill them all. Upstairs, Sam can hear the men raping Craster's younger wives. The older women seem resolved to their fate. Everyone in the house, women and rapists, small children and livestock, vanish into the snow and are not heard from again. Gilly and Sam make no attempt to save them. Any love Gilly has for her mother, stepmothers and sisters goes unmentioned as Gilly calmly leaves them to die, only Gilly is beloved of Sam, so only Gilly can be saved. This deliberate sacrifice on everyone's parts, even in the unforgiving North, suggests the entire household are abominations who would do better to be wiped out than survive. Thus a disturbing current of "blaming the victim" is present.

As the pair travel, Sam takes a more manly role than ever seen, as protector to his beloved and her child. Gilly, by contrast, has no defense against the White Walkers. She is a mother, but seems to fit well in Sansa's category as the Innocent, the young woman who makes herself sweet and charming as she begs for a protector. Thus she pleads to marry Sam, since she believes she must trade her body for protection.

Gilly is technically a wildling, but she lacks the self-confident attitude seen in Ygritte and Val. This appears to be the product of her education—women in Craster's house are taught to serve him all their lives rather than seeking adventure and the strongest man to claim as theirs. Gilly seems like the ultimate weak woman, but she shows strength in keeping her baby son alive through the terrible trek to the Wall, beset by monsters. As she puts it, "I'm Craster's wife, and Craster's daughter, and a *mother*" (V.105). She defines herself in relation to others, but makes it clear she'll kill to protect her child. On the Wall, she finally becomes a foster mother as well. When Jon presents her with a terrible choice, she must decide the welfare of both children, not just her own.

The Prostitutes

Prostitution has always been an ambivalent area to address. In "Prostitution: A Difficult Issue for Feminists," Priscilla Alexander explains:

> As feminists, we abhor the exploitation of women's sexuality by profiteers, and some of us feel, instinctively, that prostitution supports an objectification of women's sexuality and of women, that is somehow related to the pervasive violence against us. In addition, we are defined, by ourselves and others, by our place in the age-old whore/madonna dichotomy. However, there is a growing realization among many feminists that the laws against prostitution, and the stigma imposed on sex work, keep all women from determining their own sexuality [342].

Forbidding prostitution rather than regulating it for the women's protection creates many problems, both physical and social. At the same time, women selling their bodies so they can survive is rarely empowering. Around 50 percent of adult prostitutes and 75 percent of juvenile prostitutes are reported to have experienced sexual abuse as children, and become prostitutes because they want to reclaim their bodies or because they see them as commodities (Alexander 344). Costumes and personas are worn for the benefit of the man's fantasy, not the woman's. As she fulfills his vision, she makes herself the object of his fantasies, and thus she becomes objectified.

The media offer a stereotypical and unrealistic view of prostitution, from the "whore with the heart of gold" and "sex goddess" to the degraded prisoner. In the seventies, characters on *Police Woman* and *Charlie's Angels* went undercover as prostitutes, but most actual prostitutes were shown as stereotypes.

> These early prostitution storylines would set the standard for how prostitution would be dealt with on TV for decades. The profession was used as a plot device for crime dramas, but rarely as the central premise for a program. The prostitutes were rarely given complex characterizations, often acting as one-dimensional examples of "fallen women." It would be many more years before complex prostitutes would be shown on television [Cummings, "From *Gunsmoke* to *Game of Thrones*"].

On numerous episodes of *CSI, House, The Shield,* and similar programs, the prostitute is either dead or in danger of becoming so.

There are a few exceptions of sympathetic, well-rounded prostitutes, such as Inara on *Firefly* who defies expectations as much as Shae. Inara, a sophisticated courtesan, is in fact higher-ranked that the ship's captain. Nonetheless, prostitutes archetypically are considered the negative aspect of the lover: they are not joyously embracing their own sexuality, but allowing it to be exploited for the use of another. Using it to advance in life is another example of the negative lover, as she is trading her bodily autonomy rather than claiming it.

Prostitution is rightly called the world's oldest profession, as it goes back through the beginning of recorded history.

> Prostitution has existed in every society for which there are written records. For a long period in history, women had only three options for economic survival: getting married, becoming a nun (earlier, a priestess), or becoming a prostitute. The invention of the spinning wheel, around the 13th century, enabled a woman working alone to produce enough thread to support herself, for the first time, as a spinster [Alexander 343].

For most women, prostitution was a means of survival, no more. The men in power regarded them as a necessary evil. Saint Thomas wrote, "prostitutes are to a city what a cesspool is to a palace: get rid of the cesspool and the palace will become an unsavory and loathsome place" (qtd. in de Beauvoir 113). However, a few particular women managed to gain the influence of wives or even queens as they played with politics.

> The king's mistress, such as Madame de Pompadour or Diane de Poitiers, was often more influential than the politically chosen queen. Her spiritual sisters, the courtesans of Venice and other parts of 17th- and 18th-century Europe, wielded significant political power. Often poets, performers, and artists, the courtesans were expected to be skilled courtiers (the original meaning of courtesan), educated entertainers, delightful conversationalists, and perfect companions. Across the world, Japanese geishas (literally artists) learned music, dance, the tea ceremony, literature, and poetry. The similarly roled hetaerae of Greece were scholars and leading public figures, such as Plato's students Lashena of Mantua and Axiothea. The hetaerae were the only women who took part in the Symposia [Frankel, *Girl to Goddess* 223–24].

Veronica Franco was more than the most famous courtesan of Venice: Though self-educated, she published three books of poetry and argued down the Inquisition in open court. She bested the male poets of Venice and awed the visiting dauphin of France. "Had Veronica married the biggest swell in Venice, she would have been shackled, gagged, and lobotomized. Despite the occupational hazards of her job (which were considerable), she was able to slip the feminine traces and reinvent herself as a suprema" (Prioleau 124).

Charles VII, newly appointed by Joan of Arc, met his match in the witty Agnes Sorel. As his official mistress and chief counselor, she dazzled the court with exotic eastern silks and perfumes. In time, however, Charles' eldest son Louis the "universal spider" plotted against her and saw her banished, an intriguing reflection of Martin's series (Prioleau 238). Diane de Poitiers rode and hunted beside her king and advised him on statecraft as well. She was an older widow, and King Henri of France was smitten with her. Under Diane's tutelage, he read Machiavelli and grew shrewd and insightful. He made her a duchess, gave her the crown jewels, and sent her a quarter of the national revenues. She was "renaissance prince and courtesan, abbess and baud, lady charity and hardball powerfrau" (Prioleau 93).

As Tyrion's "lady," Shae is the closest parallel before season four, when Prince Oberyn Martell and his paramour Ellaria Sand arrive. While a courtesan of sorts, she acts as her prince's lady in public as well as private, scandalizing the court yet demanding the rank to which her lover has elevated her. In book three, Tyrion reflects on the mess it will cause that Cersei won't want a courtesan seated at the high table, but Oberyn will be offended if his chosen lady isn't honored. Even without Prince Oberyn, Ellaria is valued and protected in the court of Dorne, together with her bastard daughters.

However, *Game of Thrones* has few high-class courtesans among the many show characters and even more book characters; the only women who try such an arrangement lose in spectacular fashion. For instance, Tywin as a young man hurls his father's mistress out of the house to be paraded through town, weeping and begging "as she hobbled barefoot and naked through the streets to exile" (V.853). Shae and Ros may try climbing to power through prostitution, but their real status is clear: Both can be threatened, tortured, or even killed by the men in power, and they are helpless to prevent it. When they try to affect politics, their influence is terribly limited. "The prostitute does not have the rights of a person; she is the sum of all types of feminine slavery at once," de Beauvoir cautions, and this becomes their role more than the dazzling mistresses of kings and emperors (600).

Though Tyrion loves Shae and even rescues Ros from his vengeful sister, Littlefinger and Tywin both regard prostitutes as subhuman, women who can be exploited in any way possible. "In prostitution, masculine desire can be satisfied on any body as it is specific and not individual. Wives or courtesans do not succeed in exploiting man unless they wield a singular power over him" (de Beauvoir 600). That power goes unseen in Westeros.

SHAE

Shae is a misogynistic caricature in the novels. As Tyrion's beloved concubine, she is astoundingly stupid, greedy, and whiny. There are a number of female characters in Martin's books that are just non-people. They have no agency, inner lives, personalities, or charm; Shae represents the nadir of those.... On *Game of Thrones*, however, the writers have transformed Shae. She is intelligent, multidimensional, and loyal (or appears to be, anyway). She seems to have true affection for Tyrion—at the end of Season 2, she begged him to leave King's Landing with her—which in the books she fakes. (Badly.) It's not only Tyrion she's good to; she tries to help Sansa as well, becoming her confidante. As played by Sibel Kekilli, she is shrewd and worthy of Tyrion's love [Arthur].

In the world of archetypes, Aphrodite women attract Hephaestus men, among others. Hephaestus was shunned for being ugly and crippled, though he had many talents. He was introverted and controlled but with a temper capable of volcanic explosions. Their relationship echoes Shae and Tyrion's. Abandoned by both parents, a Hephaestus man has problematic relationships with others. "He may have a love/hate relationship with women, whom he resents for being both terribly important to him and untrustworthy. And he may feel very little closeness with men, whom he often feels estranged from and inferior to" (Bolen 247).

Tyrion assumes that no woman will ever want him because of his appearance. Every action when he contracts Shae is defensive, as he insists Bronn warn her in advance of what he looks like to avoid "a look that Tyrion Lannister did not ever care to see again" (I.679). His requests that she share his tent and laugh at his jokes affirms a lack of real relationships in his life, if he must manufacture this one. Tyrion suspects she's faking pleasure, but lets it go, since "*that* much truth he did not crave" (I.680).

Shae is introduced saying she can speak for herself in contrast with tongue-tied Podrick. Her smile is "shy, insolent, and wicked," like her personality (I.679). "Feelings of anger, inferiority, and fear of loss are likely to be triggered in him by an Aphrodite woman's attractiveness or her attraction to others," Bolen warns (248). Indeed, book Tyrion alternates between terror for Shae's safety, jealousy as she favors a lowborn singer, and growing affection for her. He's flattered beyond anything he's known when she calls him her giant and her lion, coding him as manly in a way he rarely hears.

While Tyrion treats his early relationship with Shae as a business arrangement, laying out his requirements that she pour his wine, rub his legs, and sleep with no one but him, he also cares for her as a person. As he rides into battle after their first night together, he gallantly orders Pod to escort her home if he should die. Sibel Kekilli, who plays Shae, explains, "In the very beginning, it was more like a working relationship. Like, 'I give you this,' so I get something for that. After a while, there emerged some feelings, and I'd call it love" (Parker). Varys tells her, "You've been a good influence on our mutual friend, you know. He used to drink from sundown to sun-up, visit three brothels a night, gamble away his father's money. Now it's just the drinking" (3.10).

In the books, Tyrion's seen asking her to the Capitol seconds after his father forbids him to bring her; Shae is a pawn in their battle. However, he soon becomes genuinely fond of her, so he hides her thoroughly. While Tyrion ostensibly has control of the relationship, Shae manipulates him for entertainment and delights in King's Landing, even as he pleads for her to be cautious. She's foolish and greedy, planning to keep her "gold collar with the black diamonds" even while working as a lady's maid (II.715). She craves books, jewels, and gowns, while on the show she simply wants an end to boredom. Tyrion satisfies all these cravings and visits her often, even at risk to her life. When Cersei captures the wrong prostitute and tortures her, Tyrion admits to himself that he would have done anything to protect Shae; only Cersei's ineptitude has freed him from this. With their love being played as sincere on the show, it's uncertain how the relationship will end. Martin comments:

> A lot of beautiful young women read for Shae.... But there's another dimension to Shae as well. She's not as practiced and hardened at this as a more seasoned pro. There's still a girl next door quality to her, a sense of vulnerability, playfulness, and, yes, innocence.... All of our Shaes were hot as hell.

But only a handful of them captured that other quality, maybe three out of twenty, and Sibel was the standout.... Watching those auditions, any red-blooded male would want to take every one of our Shae candidates to bed. But Sibel made you fall in love with her as well ["You Guys Are Scary Good, the Sequel"].

Shae is the woman as Aphrodite figure but also the woman as mystery. Her early drinking game establishes that. In fact, both drinking game and Free Cities origin are new to the show; she's more ordinary in the books. While many fans note with amusement that she breaks all the stereotypes, Shae is being exoticized as "mystery woman" and unknowable object for the story's men, rather than human being. Only a few tantalizing hints of her past exist as she makes comments like "I stopped being a child when I was nine. My mother made sure of that" (3.10). Sibel Kekilli reveals some of her character's third season thought process:

She's in love with Tyrion, but she was always scared about [loving someone or hoping for a better life]. And [with Tyrion], there was a small, short moment where she started to hope to have a new life maybe, to be loved. I'm sure that Tyrion has real feelings for her, but, of course, power is more important to him, and now she understands.

I think it was in the seventh episode where she says to Tyrion, "In the end, I will be the whore again." I think that's the point where she thinks, "Okay, I shouldn't trust anyone, just myself. I shouldn't love anyone, you can just trust yourself," that there's no place for her because she's not high-born. She understands now. She was right to be afraid [Ghahremani].

Shae's role as Sansa's defender is created just for the show, giving her a reason to appear more. In this area, she seems selfless, putting herself at risk simply because Sansa is an innocent. "Men only want one thing from a pretty girl ... love is not the thing he wants," she says of Littlefinger (2.2). When Sansa and Tyrion wed, Shae's position becomes increasingly conflicted. Shae rejects Tyrion's calling her his "lady," insisting on the label "whore" for herself. She likewise complains of being forced to care for her lover's wife and "brush her hair and clip her nails and empty her chamber pot," though she adds, "I love that girl. I would kill for her. Do you think that makes it easier for me?" (3.10). In fact, she still longs to protect Sansa, even from Tyrion's advances. She smiles quietly when she discovers their marriage remains unconsummated.

Her exchanges with Ros are predictable as they contrast their experiences as women of the world. Her conversation with Varys at season three's end is more interesting: Varys urges her to leave the city, explaining, "Tyrion Lannister is one of the few people alive who could make this country a better place. He has the mind for it, he has the will, he has the right last name. And you—you are a complication" (3.10). It has not been absolutely revealed whether Varys is trying to bring peace as he assures Ned Stark, or (as suggested in the fifth book) he wants to trick Starks and Lannisters into wiping each other out so his chosen heir can take the throne. As such, his advice to Shae may not be sincere.

ROS AND HER FRIENDS

The role does call for actress Esmé Bianco [Ros] to be naked a lot. Yet despite being the embodiment—literally—of the Game of Thrones-has-too-many-needlessly-naked-women argument, Ros has evolved into a shaded, badass character. She wept for the murdered baby in Season 2 (one of Robert's bastards, all assassinated); she warns Shae to protect Sansa from Littlefinger in season three. Since she's not in the books, you never know what's coming for her or from her. Team Ros! [Arthur].

In the first episode, Benioff and Weiss introduced their first original *Game of Thrones* character, Ros the prostitute. With Ros set thus apart from all the book characters, viewers were uncertain what her fate would be. While invented as a "plot device" with a single appearance, Ros became a recurring character with a plot arc (Lacob, "Esmé Bianco"). The many prostitutes under her command occasionally are repeat characters with names but none have plot arcs, save a bit for the mother of Robert's bastard daughter. They exist only to sensationalize the show.

Ros spends time with several characters in the North, and then decides to seek her fortunes in King's Landing, where she works for Littlefinger and then Varys. She becomes a connection between many characters: Tyrion, Theon, Jon Snow, Joffrey, Pycelle, Littlefinger, Varys, Shae. "There's definitely something to be said for the fact that she's a common thread between all of these people, which I don't think any of them realize," Bianco said. "People are unguarded around her, which will prove to be interesting" (Lacob, "Esmé Bianco"). As the recipient of secrets, she becomes the sexposition character—the one to whom people tell things in order to inform the television audience.

In discussions of Ros's role, a few particular scenes stand out: In season one, Ros and another female prostitute "practice" on each other while Littlefinger indulges in a monologue. For critics of the sexposition, this scene is everything wrong with the show: It's a scene of Littlefinger's lasciviously directing the prostitutes how to perform rather than offering dialogue important to the plot. His lack of interest in the women in front of him shows his obsession with Catelyn, but that also serves to emphasize their role as subservient to him.

> "There was no way that the scene with Littlefinger in the brothel wasn't going to ruffle a couple of feathers," Bianco said. "The books are not an easy read. They are brutal and have their fair share of sex in them. It would be naïve to think that HBO would take a story in that genre and just do the safe … version of it. That scene is beautifully shot and shows quite clearly the kind of world that the characters are living in" [Lacob, "Esmé Bianco"].

"Beautifully shot" and "accurate to their world" are not arguments that would satisfy critics of the scene, for it's not plot or character—just sex. Nonetheless, one aspect of character growth does stem from this: In the first episode of season two, a better-dressed Ros directs the acting lessons for a prostitute and echoes Littlefinger's closing line with "Go wash yourselves. Put some clothes on. Both of you are working tonight" (2.1). She's become his second-in-command but also turned from posable doll to director of the brothel scenes. At the same time, Ros shows a lack of camaraderie as she too reduces and dismisses the women. She uses the scene to show her superiority.

Ros grows and changes, as she's promoted from the sex worker to Littlefinger's deputy. As Ros tells Shae, "We've done rather well … given where we started. It's not easy for girls like us to dig our way out" (3.1). Afterwards, Ros meets with Varys and decides to work for him instead of the untrustworthy Littlefinger. Ros knows how to read. ("Rare for a woman in your profession," Varys notes. "Former profession," Ros replies.) She cleverly interprets Littlefinger's schemes from his ledgers.

Nonetheless, she succumbs to physical and emotional torture, showing that she remains a pawn in the men's schemes. In an often-criticized scene, Joffrey forces Ros to beat, burn, and torture Daisy with a stag's head scepter. Ros and Daisy literally have no choice but to obey his terrible whims. Class, gender, and their profession make them helpless against the young king, who isn't punished for his brutality in any way.

At the same time, Joffrey's fear of women is subtly shown. When the pair offer themselves to him, Joffrey is terrified by the adult women prepared to have sex with him for the first time. He immediately insists they touch each other, not him, and then makes Ros hurt Daisy as he controls the women, rather than offering them control. Joffrey appears drawn to sheltered Sansa because of her unworldliness; men uncomfortable with grownup women often seek out such an Innocent as lover. Thus "a man feels he can be perceived as a powerful, dominant man and not have his authority or ideas challenged. He also feels that he can be innocent, inexperienced, or incompetent and not be criticized" (Bolen 210). With Sansa and the prostitutes, Joffrey maintains a careful line and makes other people strike them, never himself. Thus his fear of those he abuses is shown. However, any point made about women trying to survive in a man's world is undermined behind the titillation factor. This scene, like Littlefinger's earlier "performance," is about nudity and power as the men force the women to demean themselves and the naked women comply.

The third scene in this vein is Ros's abrupt death. Littlefinger, once again the man in charge, is preaching to Varys as different characters are shown, tying them together thematically:

> You're so right. For instance, when I thwarted your plan to give Sansa Stark to the Tyrells ... if, I'm going to be honest, I did feel an unmistakable sense of ... enjoyment there. But your confidante [Ros], the one who fed you information about my plans, the one you swore to protect, you didn't bring her any enjoyment. And she didn't bring me any enjoyment. She was a bad investment on my part. Luckily, I have a friend who wanted to try something new. Something daring. And he was so grateful to me for providing this fresh experience ["The Climb," 3.6].

The shot pans from Joffrey, smirking with his bow, to Ros, naked, bloody, and lifeless, hung by her wrists. Her body is on display, centered, completely mastered and helpless in death. An arrow protrudes from between her breasts and one from between her thighs. Joffrey has escalated from his previous scene; he wants to control the sexual woman, and he chooses to use physical violence, substituting weapons for actual sex. While he doesn't touch her, he is the direct instrument of her death.

Playing the game and trying to rise above her circumstances gets Ros killed, in a lesson about social class Shae has yet to learn. More significantly, Ros is another character who exists to push forward others' stories. She displays emotion but has no personal life or relationships with other characters—only the physical.

The Crones

Westeros is ruled by men, but the Crone is one of their goddesses … the power of the ancient woman still echoes through their world. "The Crone was the most powerful of the Goddess's three personae" in ancient times (Walker 29). While this was true in many cultures, often only the trappings linger in patriarchal religions as the diminished Hecate, underworld crone, or Sophia, Biblical spirit of wisdom. "The patriarchy feared the feminine in connection with her role in birthing and dying even more than in her association with sex. The wise crone transformed into the ugly hag, the death-snatcher. The elderly woman, in the prime of her wisdom, was likewise cast out by patriarchal cultures as useless and grotesque" (George 222). Male power could not abide the midwife or wisewoman, whose knowledge of healing and the natural world competed with their own. Thus she was dismissed from ancient religions, and centuries later, the witch-hunts began.

Most archetype scholars note that the Crone connects with the Great Beyond, rather than children or lovers.

> The ancient wisewoman crone was the Dark Goddess's earthly representative to society. She was venerated as elder sought out for advice, as seer called upon for prophecy, and as healer asked to tend the ill. The crone acted to bridge the transition from the dark to the new moon; she was the funerary priestess who helped the old to die and the midwife who assisted the new to be born [George 222].

As such, she understands lore that the younger generation does not. She is the keeper of the ancient tales, like Old Nan, who knows the stories that have faded out of print in Castle Black's archives. From the earliest scenes of the first episode, Old Nan has been the voice of the past, offering viewers' only knowledge of the Otherworld. Likewise, the old woman is released from some of society's rules. Like Lady Olenna, she can say the things no one else would, as someone outside the conventional hierarchy but still deserving of respect.

In most stories, the Crone is a teacher rather than a questor in her own right. In fact, Old Nan, Septa Mordane, and Lady Olenna are all guardians for the next generation. They take the role of grandmothers—figures of love and support who provide a different kind of affection than mothers do. Actress Natalie Dormer (Margaery) comments: "The Starks were a very close family, and the Tyrells are too. There's real affection and loyalty there, and having the adding [sic] dynamic of Diana Rigg was so wonderful. It was incredible that the authority of this family, and Margaery's mentor, is a matriarch" (Wieselman). Even for powerful Olenna, Margaery is the prospective queen, not her grandmother. Nonetheless, it's clear who holds the power.

OLENNA

Arriving in season three as Joffrey's "future grandmother-in-law from hell," matriarch Olenna Tyrell makes a powerful statement about female power. "She's one of our favorite characters," says Weiss. "In a world where there are few powerful women, she is definitely one, scathing, witty and powerful, with a bawdy sense of humor" (Hill).

When the role was first envisioned, intimidating actress Dame Diana Rigg showed up for the part—as the producers joked, "You don't audition her, she auditions you." Upon arrival, she called the producers "naughty boys" and said the show has "an awful lot of bonking ... I like it." She also fixed their grammar in the script pages (Mitchell). On camera, she's just as imposing yet gleeful a figure. For season three, the producers hoped Emilia Clarke and Diana Rigg in particular would get Emmys (Mitchell).

Lady Olenna of course is the terrible old woman who says what no one else dares. Upon her introduction to Sansa as well as the viewers, she mocks her husband, her son, her former son-in-law, and her grandson. She prides herself on being plain-spoken, knowing she's important enough that no one will challenge her.

Olenna Tyrell: Loras is young, and very good at knocking men off horses with a stick. That does not make him wise. As to your fathead father…
Margaery Tyrell: Grandmother! What will Sansa think of us?
Olenna Tyrell: She might think we have some wits about us, one of us at any rate ["Dark Wings, Dark Words," 3.2].

While she directly ridicules authority figures like Varys and Tyrion, and stands up for her goals, she also uses pacifying genderspeak as Daenerys does. She comforts a terrified Sansa by telling her they're just a group of women chatting. "We mothers do what we can to keep our sons from the grave," she notes modestly a few episodes later (3.4). Nonetheless, she scoffs at the men in power and notes that having the world belong to them is "a ridiculous arrangement in my mind" (3.4).

She's politically astute, noting, "The people are hungry for more than just food. They crave distractions. And if we don't provide them, they'll create their own. And their distractions are likely to end with us being torn to pieces" (3.5). She appears to know what ruling requires, as dowager of one of the most prosperous of the Seven Kingdoms. When she mocks Renly ("Gallant, yes, and charming, and very clean. He knew how to dress and smile and somehow this gave him the notion he was fit to be king" [3.2]), she places faith in true leadership and morality, not the showiness other leaders prefer.

Olenna also cares for family. She isn't necessarily eager to see her grandchildren in positions of power, but she's willing to play the game to keep them there and she's concerned about Joffrey marrying her granddaughter. Sansa reveals that her soon-to-be son-in-law is a "monster," and Olenna replies with only mild disappointment: "Hmm. That's a pity" (3.2). However, viewers are certain that isn't the end of the story.

With all this, she's a wonderful force to be reckoned with, on the show at any rate. In the books, the constant presence of her son, Margaery's father, steals her political force. Olenna only appears in two scenes, meeting Sansa to ask her about Joffrey, then attending Joffrey and Margaery's wedding; she's only seen from Sansa's or Tyrion's point of view after all. On the show by contrast, she's the one negotiating cleverly with the men of King's Landing. Olenna sets herself as their equal in all dealings and shows herself as a powerful figure. Since her son, lord of Highgarden, takes this role in the books, her presence on the show is a wonderful addition to the patriarchal web of intrigue in King's Landing. Her expanded role may be intended to counter the antifeminist accusations from critics or to emphasize an interesting new kind of character (Lord Tyrell in the books is much like a greedier Tywin Lannister). Either way, her many scenes add an excellent new feminist perspective.

Though Olenna comments on gender roles, she is not seen succumbing to Cersei's emotion, irrationality, or other feminine-coded behaviors. This may be due to her age or her role as seasoned matriarch of her House. Her character is decisive, clear-headed, and as powerful as Tywin, Varys, or Tyrion, as she matches wits with all of them. As Walker notes in her book on the Crone archetype, the Crone's "intellectual gifts were not based solely on what is now called 'feminine intuition,' emotion, or unconscious responses. She was equally credited with analytical intelligence of the sort that has become stereotyped as 'masculine'" [65].

Despite her delightful vigor, Olenna "loses" in her season three negotiations: Her beloved grandson Ser Loras will wed undesirable Cersei or join the Kingsguard and have no heirs at all. Sansa is wed to the Lannisters before Loras can become Lord of Winterfell. Margaery is to marry Joffrey the monster and Olenna will even pay for half the wedding. Her teasing about the family relations that will result after the many planned weddings shows her criticism of the arrangements, carefully buried in humorous flippancy:

> *Lady Olenna Tyrell* [to Loras]: So, their son will be your nephew after you're wed to Cersei, of course. And you will be the king's stepfather and brother-in-law. [To Margaery:] When you marry the king, Joffrey's mother will become his sister-in-law. And your son will be Loras' … nephew? Grandson? I'm not sure. But your brother will become your father-in-law, that much is beyond dispute ["Second Sons," 3.8].

Admittedly, she isn't done playing politics against the Lannisters, but like Cersei in seasons two and three, she keeps losing when she plays the game. As such, she must take her place among other feminized females in the series.

THE DOSH KHALEEN

The Dothraki are the most patriarchal of the cultures seen: The men are so hyper-masculine that only their warrior-status counts and they have no warrior women. However, the former khaleesis are their rulers. In the books, Daenerys meets the crones of the *dosh khaleen*. They are the permanent guardians of the only Dothraki city, where Daenerys eats the horse heart and Khal Drogo kills her brother. In the expanded scene shown in the book, the crones escort her to the lake marching as proudly as khals in front of the warriors. "Even the mightiest of *khals* bowed to the wisdom and authority of the *dosh khaleen*" (I.492). All were once khaleesis until they lost their khals and retired to the stronghold of the crones. They are the ones to prophesize her child will be the Stallion that Mounts the World. Though Daenerys originally accepts the idea of being one of them, she soon rejects this retirement, even with the power the crones hold, in favor of becoming a conqueror.

Prophecies and visions suggest these crones will have a further role in the story. In her vision in the House of the Undying, Daenerys sees crones from the Dothraki city "knelt shivering before her, their grey heads bowed" (I.411). As the ending of book five indicates, Daenerys may return to the Dothraki and rule them at last. She will enter the city of the *dosh khaleen* and take her place as their initiate, learning their wisdom before becoming queen.

OLD NAN

Old Nan, the wise grandmother and matriarch, is seen caring for a crippled Bran and telling him stories. In the books, her fate is unknown after Winterfell burns. On the show, the actress died after season one and the show seems to have made that part of its canon. She's a stereotype, the wisewoman telling tales as exposition. Nonetheless, her role may be important.

Old Nan's stories describe giants and the children of the forest, fabled creatures soon revealed to still exist North of the Wall. Further, she tells of the Time of Heroes, with an endless winter covering the land and the First Men's successful battle against it. Old Nan explains to Bran in the first episode:

> Thousands of years ago there came a night that lasted a generation. Kings froze to death in their castles, same as the shepherds in their huts, and women smothered their babies rather than see them starve, and wept and felt their tears *freeze* on their cheeks. So is this the sort of story that you like? In that darkness, the white walkers came for the first time. They swept through cities and kingdoms, riding their dead horses, hunting with their packs of pale spiders big as hounds.

Obviously, this time has come again. The White Walkers, vanished for a thousand years, are now returning, and Old Nan's stories may be the key to the world's salvation.

In the book, after this speech, Old Nan entertains Bran with a story of the White Walkers, who hated "iron and fire and the touch of the sun," clearly a hint that Jon would find useful up north (I.240). Continuing the tale above, the last hero of the First Men set out with his horse, his dog, and twelve hero-companions to find the children of the forest, whose ancient magics could save mankind. As Bran and his wolf travel north with Hodor, Osha, Rickon, Meera, and Jojen, his story becomes a mirror of the one in Old Nan's tale.

> When Bran and Rickon leave Maester Luwin in the Godswood at season two's end, six of them set out—exactly half of twelve, just as half of Bran is left to be a hero.... If one adds the people, from guides to fellow travelers, the children find on the way North, the number reaches exactly twelve companions, at least for a night here and there. As Bran and his wolf travel steadily north, his story echoes the Last Hero's. He's even a descendent of the First Men, as all Northmen are. On his hero-quest, it's clear that Bran will descend into the darkest place all alone, as the Last Hero once did. There, he will confront the Other beyond the curtain, the one he has seen in his dreams [Frankel, *Winter Is Coming*, Kindle Locations 96–102].

With the blood of the First Men and the warg and greenseer powers, he appears destined to end the permanent winter and bring spring to the world. Without Old Nan's ancient wisdom, this would not be possible.

OTHER MATRIARCHS

The books have several other no-nonsense elderly women, including Jaime Lannister's aunt Lady Genna Frey. She makes "ribald jests," mocks her husband, and sends him from the room when it pleases her. "Men are greedy," she notes disparagingly, commenting that her son will do well if he learns from her, not his father (IV.712). Though she protests that the game of thrones is "not for girls," she gives Jaime insightful advice and shows far more cleverness about the politics of the Riverlands than her stubborn and ignorant husband (IV.716). In her single appearance, she comes across as charming, clever, and likable.

Septa Mordane has little effect on the plot: She's Sansa's chaperone, and the motherly voice that tells Sansa she's doing well at her studies, or chastises Arya for being rambunctious. Joffrey beheads her and mounts her head beside Ned Stark's. Thus Joffrey demonstrates his contempt for the priesthood as well as the entire Stark family. Meanwhile, Sansa is truly isolated with her best friend Jeyne and her chaperone stolen from her as well as her father and Winterfell guards. At the same time, Septa Mordane remains an influence on Sansa, as the bereft girl reminds herself of the Septa's teachings: that courtesy is a lady's armor, that she will find something beautiful in any husband (though, as Sansa decides, Tyrion is the exception). With the Septa's teachings at being passive yet enduring, Sansa may survive her adventures.

In Meereen, the high priestess known as the Green Grace, Galazza Galare, advises Daenerys. Though she's nearly eighty, she's quite alert to the political situation of her day. Daenerys respects her as a force of peace in the warring city. She takes her advice on how to quell the rebellious mobs, and Barristan sends her to treat with their enemies. Though more of a stereotype than a character, the Green Grace stands out as one of Daenerys's few older female advisors.

In Westerosi history, Aegon the Conqueror defeated six of the Seven Kingdoms but failed with Dorne. His sister Rhaenys flew there, but always found near-empty castles, with the warriors reportedly "away." She finally journeyed to the Capitol of Sunspear and confronted Mariya Martell, Princess of Dorne. She was 80, fat, blind, and almost bald. Her rival ruler, Argilac the Arrogant, had nicknamed her the "Yellow Toad of Dorne." When Rhaenys demanded a surrender, Mariya replied, "This is Dorne. You are not wanted here, return at your peril." When Rhaenys threatened to return with "Fire and Blood," Mariya replied with her own house words: "Unbowed, Unbent, Unbroken." As the many kings of Westeros and the beautiful lady of the Eyrie were conquered, this one stubborn matriarch resisted, leading her people through passive resistance and cunning guerrilla attacks rather than strength of arms. Dorne remained independent until they made a peaceful marriage alliance with the Targaryens ("Chicon 7 Reading"). This story is coming in 2014 in *The World of Ice and Fire: The Official History of Westeros and the World of* A Game of Thrones.

In all these cases the clever crone defends her people through negotiation and wordplay, rather than strength of arms. She succeeds and protects her grandchildren and subjects alike. Though these characters are rare in Westeros, they are all depicted as forces of positive strength, female yet not hyper-feminized, clever at outwitting the patriarchy with deeper wisdom.

The Seers

Mirri Maz Duur, Melisandre, and Quaithe are the wisewomen of the saga. All are presented as complete mysteries—none reveal their complete histories or motivations, and all offer cryptic prophecies with room for misinterpretation. The medial woman's job is to interpret the mysterious messages of the universe and communicate them to the world. As such, she's rarely a viewpoint or main character. She advises men (Jon, Stannis) and women (Daenerys) alike, but that is her main and often only role.

The seer archetype emphasizes a woman's role as mystery figure, unknown and unknowable by men. "Of these myths, none is more anchored in masculine hearts than the feminine 'mystery'" (de Beauvoir 268). Unfortunately, this myth emphasizes the woman's place as an object in men's stories: Viewing the woman as inexplicable justifies everything—if the man cannot understand her, it is not his fault—she is "mysterious" after all. If her desires make no sense to him, well, again, she is not meant to be understood.

Melisandre takes this a step further, combining feminine birth magic with stripping naked—and shaved—and inviting men and audience members to gaze on her. The taboo breaks and all the secrets of magic and the private birthing chamber are brought to light. She is the woman with mystery origins, motivations, and powers, but also a sex object. Between that and her callous and sometimes murderous agenda, she rates no one's empathy.

While the medial woman crafts her identity, she can even be a mystery to herself, as the psychic uttering words in a trance then forgetting her message, or as the ego who sacrifices rationality to hear the inner voices. Jung notes that religious devotion is common in medial women. "As a rule, they cannot exploit their 'art' for egoistic purposes, and this proves that their faculty is not subject to the will of the ego [but to] the dominance of the unconscious" (qtd. in Molton and Sikes 274). As the voice of the unconscious, they embody the words of the universe.

Historical seers include Hildegard of Bingen, an abbess of twelfth century Germany. In her cloistered life of meditation and prayer, she often saw glimpses of other places and times. She insisted a scribe write down all her visions, preserved through today. Corresponding with important religious figures, she directly influenced policy in Rome. By the time she was fifty, crowds from across Germany and Gaul surrounded her, with both sexes beseeching her for her wisdom.

Born in 1342, Julian of Norwich was the first known female writer in English. She had many visions, which she recorded in the book *Sixteen Revelations of Divine Love*. She was nearly unique in her imagery of God's femininity, writing, "As truly as God is our Father, so truly is God our Mother." Angela of Foligno, a similar religious figure, dwelt in a thirteenth century Italian convent. She had ecstatic visions, which she confided to her confessor. Her *Book of Divine Consolation* lasts through today, and she was sainted in 1693.

Benedetta Carlini, an abbess of Pescia, predicted that a plague would strike in 1631. She spoke with angels in trances and her hands bled in the phenomenon called stigmata. After she allegedly died and returned with messages from the next world, church officials came to investigate her claims. When they discovered she was having a torrid affair with a nun, they determined she was possessed and locked her in a convent cell for thirty-five years.

All this said, Martin's seers have a greater connection to fantasy tropes than to history. In fiction, this trope appears as Circe in the *Odyssey*, Madame Dorothea from *The Mortal Instruments*, Drusilla on *Buffy the Vampire Slayer*, and Tia Dalma in *Pirates of the Caribbean*. (All in fact are villainesses generally disguised as harmless women, only to spring on their victims when least expected.)

The medial woman has three major shadow forms in which she turns her creative powers toward destruction. "One is chicanery, one is the possibility of a serious delusional pathology, and one is evil intent" (Molton and Sikes 255). The seer is often disconnected with society: The blind seer, the flaky and distracted prophetess, the Cassandra figure who is never believed are all popular tropes. Above all, heroes may disregard or misunderstand their cryptic warnings, casting seers as figures of little helpfulness. The three witches set Macbeth on his path to destruction: While their prophecies are accurate, they're too obscure for Macbeth to understand in time. The Fates often act this way in Greek myth, inciting tragedies for Oedipus and other heroes because of their self-fulfilling predictions.

Charlatans and lying mediums are a common trope, but a more

popular one is the evil seer. She is the murderous Medea or Morgan le Fay more often than she is the helpful and stable Galadriel. Most often she embodies female rage rather than acting as an inspiratrice and counselor. Mirri is the former, Quaithe is the latter. Melisandre displays qualities of both, and her true role as bringer of light or darkness has not yet been revealed.

MIRRI MAZ DUUR

> My mother was godswife before me, and taught me all the songs and spells most pleasing to the Great Shepherd, and how to make the sacred smokes and ointments from leaf and root and berry. When I was younger and more fair, I went in caravan to Asshai by the Shadow, to learn from their mages. Ships from many lands come to Asshai, so I lingered long to study the healing ways of distant peoples. A moonsinger of the Jogos Nhai gifted me with her birthing songs, a woman of your own riding people taught me the magics of grass and corn and horse, and a maester from the Sunset Lands opened a body for me and showed me all the secrets that hide beneath the skin [I.672].

Mirri's description of herself as a healer who knows the secrets of the birthing bed and has trained in all kinds of magic is comforting, and Daenerys takes her expertise in trust. The concept that a maegi "was a woman who lay with demons and practiced the blackest of sorceries, a vile thing, evil and soulless" (I.671) seems to come from the Dothraki misogyny. Mirri is not clearly an evil figure, and her appearance prepares fans for Melisandre's even more ambiguous arrival in the next season.

Mirri Maz Duur, like many other Lazareen women, is raped by the Dothraki and rescued by Daenerys. However, this scene demonstrates Daenerys's naiveté. She assumes that rescuing the prisoners will leave them grateful, and she's stunned when Mirri Maz Duur still treats Drogo as her enemy.

On the show, she deliberately poisons Khal Drogo; in the book it is more ambiguous. Drogo tears off the poultice and ignores her instructions—Mirri insists that her cure would have worked if he had kept using it. Regardless, Drogo becomes fatally ill, and Mirri offers Daenerys a desperate chance. As she says, "There is a spell.... But it is hard, lady, and dark. Some would say that death is cleaner. I learned the way in Asshai, and paid dear for the lesson. My teacher was a bloodmage from the Shadowlands" (I.710). The woman is careful in her phrasing, only promising explicitly that she can keep Khal Drogo alive, and adding, "Only death can pay for life." Daenerys asks if her death is meant, and when she learns it isn't, she asks no more questions.

In the books, Mirri tells her, "My song will wake powers old and dark. The dead will dance here this night. No living man must look on them," as she seals herself in Drogo's tent (I.712). However, Ser Jorah breaks the taboo and carries Daenerys into the tent of death to save Drogo—Dany's in labor and most of the Dothraki have abandoned them. Mirri, the only midwife remaining, is a disturbing medial woman of death as well as life, reminding Daenerys how closely the two are linked. Indeed, Daenerys comes closer to death than she does before or after that night. In the tent, Daenerys's baby dies and Jorah too is marked with death and later appears haggard and ill. Daenerys realizes his actions have killed her baby.

At the same time, Mirri of book and show freely admits that the baby's death was the price for Drogo, suggesting Daenerys was fated to enter the tent once she made the terrible bargain. Mirri's careful word choice that she can restore his life is certainly malevolent, as is her offer to save Drogo from his inevitable death. As she bribes desperate, unschooled Daenerys with forbidden knowledge, her counsel is cruel rather than wise and supportive.

Her final prophecy of when Drogo will return is just as painful for the heroine: "When the sun rises in the west and sets in the east," said Mirri Maz Duur. "When the seas go dry and mountains blow in the wind like leaves. When your womb quickens again, and you bear a living child. Then he will return, and not before" (I.635). While these conditions, like Drogo's literal return, seem unlikely, they all appear to take place at the end of the fifth book, depending how metaphorically the text is read. Daenerys does not bear a child then, but her body, infertile since her miscarriage, appears to recover.

Mirri's prophecy offers a challenge to Daenerys as do her offers of aid. In fact, Mirri is the terrible catalyst to Daenerys' growth, forcing her to grow into widow and queen and then birth the dragons.

> The cruel mentor's job is to force the innocent heroine to face the harsh realities and ugliness of her own mortality.... Snow White's stepmother makes her eat the apple, the thirteenth fairy pricks Sleeping Beauty with a spindle. And the Maegi strikes her terrible bargain: a life for Drogo's. She

teaches Daenerys the value of life and of making bargains without considering: When Daenerys protests that she would not have willingly sacrificed her child, the Maegi can only say that Daenerys secretly knew the true cost. The mentor's job is to make the heroine accept these grim realities, rather than ignoring them. A girl can live in innocence, but to be a mother, one must know the pain and ugliness of real life [Frankel, *Winning the Game of Thrones* 117–18].

Mirri carries the ancient lesson that death must be honored as well as birth—cutting out what is no longer needed is a path to new growth. The hero's journey is the cycle of dying then returning to life with new wisdom and enlightenment. "Until we really acknowledge that we are going to die, we will not feel the pull to be who we really are" (Pearson 249). After losing her husband and son, Dany has gained the strength to execute the Maegi in the fire and walk in herself, allowing her dragons to be born.

MELISANDRE

Melisandre is everything wrong with the story from a feminist perspective. She is a wise woman of unknown agenda who can see the future in the flames. She's strong, but she gains her (apparent) power as a seductress, like Cersei, Ros, and Shae. And like Cersei, Ros, and Shae, she wheedles power from the men, ignoring the concept that it may be taken away.

In many ways Melisandre is the classic femme fatale. In her scene with Gendry, she seduces him only to use and discard him. While she appears devoted to Stannis, the day may come when she discards him as well, and viewers won't be at all surprised. In a memorable season three scene, Stannis tries to seduce her and create another shadow baby, but Melisandre gives him a cutting, pitying look and tells him, "Your fires burn low, my king." Her dark red robes are distinctive, like the red lipstick, red shoes, and other trappings famously worn by all types of "fallen women." Even Thoros of Myr, the red priest, doesn't dress that way. The producers also chose the actress who plays her carefully:

Benioff: Melisandre is a tricky role, and very few actresses have all the attributes required. Drop-dead gorgeous? Check. Charismatic and fiercely intelligent? Check. Able to convey a sinister, menacing presence without going over-the-top villainess? Check. In Carice's hands, Mel is like Lady Macbeth and the three witches rolled into one.

Weiss: When you put it that way ... yeah, it is a tricky role to cast. If we hadn't gotten Carice, we might've just had to put Lena [Headey] in a red wig [Lacob, "*Game of Thrones*' Creative Gurus"].

The femme fatale attempts to exceed the boundaries of what society considers acceptable in order to gain power over her body and her future. (Indeed, Melisandre, a former starved and abused slave, makes it her mission to seduce, direct, and dominate the patriarchal Stannis, the very embodiment of the hidebound establishment.) The femme fatale is usually defeated—and indeed, it's unlikely Melisandre will win in the game of thrones; she appears unlikable and misguided as Cersei. However, while Cersei and her agenda are remarkably transparent, all Melisandre desires remains concealed.

Though Melisandre displays her body to Davos and Gendry as well as Stannis, she is metaphorically masked. Her abilities, her true agenda, and most of all what she's seen in her prophetic fires all remain hidden from the men and from viewers. They're even hidden from her fellow priests. Martin notes, "Melisandre has gone to Stannis entirely on her own, and has her own agenda" ("Interview in Barcelona"). She appears to be a true believer, whether or not she feels Stannis is the chosen one or is using him for some other purpose. Nonetheless, she's not above cheap illusions: His magic sword of light is a fake created by Melisandre to capitalize on the ancient Lightbringer legend.

Of course, Melisandre cultivates her mysteriousness to gain worship and respect. De Beauvoir notes that this is common: "Like all oppressed people, woman deliberately dissimulates her objective image; slave, servant, indigent, all those who depend upon a master's whims have learned to present him with an immutable smile or an enigmatic impassivity; they carefully hide their real sentiments and behavior" (de Beauvoir 271). Some of Melisandre's powers come from the illusion powders described in the fifth book, while others appear to be more mystical. She calls herself "a knight ... of sorts. A champion of light and life" (2.4). She's also caught in a larger mystery—is she correct about the Lord of Light who must battle the evil Other, or is she misguided about her world's upcoming apocalypse? As she thinks, the world's survival depends on the choices she makes.

"Make no mistake, good sers and valiant brothers, the war we've come to fight is no petty squabble over lands and honors. Ours is a war for life itself, and should we fail the world dies with us."

...All of them seemed surprised to hear Maester Aemon murmur, "It is the war for the dawn you speak of, my lady. But where is the prince that was promised?"

"He stands before you," Melisandre declared, "though you do not have the eyes to see it. Stannis Baratheon is Azor Ahai come again, the warrior of fire" [III.884].

By contrast, Thoros of Myr, Melisandre's male counterpart as a red priest, reveals his entire history and motivation in conversation. He has dwelled in Westeros for decades, gone drinking with King Robert, participated in tourneys, been regarded as something of a joke. He buys his flaming swords in King's Landing from Gendry's master. On the show's third season and in the books, he reveals aloud his moment of revelation that magic has returned and that his Lord of Light is real. By contrast, it's unclear how long Melisandre has had magic.

Thoros of Myr (traveling with the Brotherhood without Banners in season three) is a red priest of R'hllor. He came to Westeros to convert Aerys Targaryen, after learning of his obsession with fire. Later, as he fought in the Riverlands, true powers awakened in him. Since Melisandre the Red Priestess is first seen in *A Clash of Kings*, a stranger to all in Westeros, her powers may be just as new, brought with the birth of dragons and the return of magic to the land. Like the Maesters, who try and fail to light dragonglass candles, the Maegi may have practiced the rituals with little or no power behind them, until recently [Frankel, *Winter Is Coming*, Kindle Locations 228–34].

The other mentors, the maesters, gain their knowledge from books and study. There is little mysterious about their powers. In fact, they cling to a magic-free world, where the rationality of a modern audience takes priority, insisting, "The world the Citadel is building has no place in it for sorcery or prophecy or glass candles, much less for dragons" (IV.683). Their tools of surgery, arithmetic, and literacy make sense to a modern audience.

Giving birth to a shadow creature appears to be a female-only power, as it requires a womb. However, the feminine birth power is subverted: Melisandre creates a force of evil that enables Stannis to kill his closest relative and frames the good women Brienne and Catelyn for the death. As such, the most primal female power is depicted as twisted, vile, and obscene. According to *The New York Post*, Melisandre the red priestess has "some mysterious witchy power in the amulet she wears around her neck. She's also got it in other places, as we saw in one graphic scene where she gives birth to a murderous shadowy wraith" as teaching viewers the following helpful message: "Have a shadow demon in your loins and no one will mess with you. Less specifically: Develop a special skill that only you can offer, it will make you invaluable—whether getting ahead at your office job, or seizing the Iron Throne" (Stewart).

Offer your boss sex and an illegitimate monster-child to get ahead in the office? Kill men with disturbing sex magic to gain power? While this may be meant humorously, the effect is disturbing. This isn't the powerful feminine, but the monstrous feminine with a demonized, vile body, not a respected one. Associating with her "drains Stannis of his fires," emphasizing that she is a destroyer of all she touches.

Every act is done to aid Stannis (at least ostensibly). The Medial Woman often acts as the Anima for a single man, tutoring him in feminine paths. By doing so, she may draw him and herself into chaotic turmoil: "With men, she may sense and animate psychic contents which should be made conscious but which do not belong to his ego and cannot be easily assimilated without preparation" (Molton and Sikes 276). For instance, she enriches Stannis's life by drawing the duty-bound, colorless man into a sensual affair foreign to his nature, leaving him guilt-struck. "In such cases, her influence is destructive and bewitching" (Molton and Sikes 276).

Some would say she's incredibly powerful, as Stannis's second-in-command. But she gains that power as she does her magic—by taking off her clothes. She seduces Stannis, a man who preferred loyalty to his wife before Melisandre removed her red robe. However, he does not love her or submit to her; he uses her as she uses him. When he leaves her behind so she cannot share his glory and credit for the Battle of Blackwater, she is helpless. "Where is your god?" Stannis asks, strangling Melisandre in his rage.

"Inside you," she chokes (2.10). Now there's a bad relationship.

She speaks alluringly to every other man she meets in an attempt to gain power over them. "You want me. You want to see what's beneath this robe ... and you will," she tells Davos, a happily married man (2.4). In a single Melisandre viewpoint chapter in five books, she considers her pageboy and thinks, "He fears me, he wants me, and he worships me" (V.409). This complex tangle is Melisandre's goal. If men do not fear her and want her, she does not control them.

In a terribly gratuitous scene that seems wholly unnecessary, Melisandre seduces Gendry in order to tie him up and drain blood out of his private parts with leeches while Stannis and Davos watch. She does all this to extract a few drops of blood, which she certainly could have had simply by requesting them. (In the book, with Robert's bastard Edric Storm, it's implied that he consented to the leeches.) Stannis feels ambivalent about the necessity of this.

> *Stannis Baratheon:* Why bathe him and dress him in fine clothes? If it needs to be done, then do it. Don't torture the boy.
> *Melisandre:* Have you ever slaughtered a lamb?
> *Stannis Baratheon:* No.
> *Melisandre:* If the lamb sees the knife, she panics. Her panic seeps into the meat, darkens it, fouls the flavor.
> *Stannis Baratheon:* And you've slaughtered many lambs.
> *Melisandre:* And none have seen the blade ["Second Sons," 3.8].

Interesting justification, but holding Gendry down in a creepy sex scene and leaching him where he doesn't want it is torture and fear, not the stealthiness Melisandre brags about above. It's one more indication that her incarnation of the show likes to dominate and control men sexually. Thoros of Myr has raised Beric from the dead multiple times, and though he shares Melisandre's faith, he hasn't been seen stripping or seducing people to do it. As such, Melisandre becomes a parody of religious and political power rather than its embodiment.

QUAITHE

Book fans were pleased by Quaithe of the Shadow, who appeared briefly in season two. So briefly in fact that show fans possibly didn't notice her. Played by Laura Pradelska, she appears in "The Ghost of Harrenhal" (2.5) just long enough to give Ser Jorah some cryptic advice: "I am no-one, but she is the Mother of Dragons. She needs true protectors, now more than ever. They shall come day and night to see the wonder born into the world again. And when they see they shall lust ... for dragons are fire made flesh ... and fire is power." Two episodes later, she gives Jorah a more concrete warning: that Daenerys is in danger from the man who stole her dragons. Apparently she will return in season four to offer Daenerys additional aid, echoing her book prophecies or offering new ones for the show's new directions.

Quaithe wears a red lacquered wooden mask all in hexagons like Melisandre's ruby necklace (since they both were trained in the Shadow Lands beyond Asshai). The mask, worn in book and show, makes her the ultimate mystery figure; even the reason for the mask has not been revealed. The concealing mask has prompted some fans to speculate that she actually is the ghost of Mirri Maz Duur or Melisandre traveling in visions (the timing of book two makes these highly unlikely). It's also possible she was burned by dragonfire or has some identifying characteristic.

Mostly the mask accentuates her mystery. She is the unknown, unknowable medial woman, bridging the gap between Dany and the universe itself. "We touch her realm when we wonder about our dreams, and we come close to her when we note strange coincidences in our everyday lives" (Molton and Sikes 225). Her mask makes her a puzzle but also comments on femaleness as the ultimate puzzle for the patriarchies Daenerys must conquer. Masquerade "constitutes an acknowledgment that it is femininity itself which is constructed as a mask—as the decorative layer which conceals a non-identity" (Doane 6). Daenerys must master the power of the feminine if she hopes to claim her inner strength and rule.

In the books, Quaithe has a larger role. She is a representative of Qarth who visits Dany alongside Xaro Xhoan Daxos and Pyat Pree. Oddly, she's been staying in Qarth since before Dany's dragons were born, and speaks the tongue of Westeros. It's unclear who she truly is or what she wants. Later, she urges Dany to leave the city, and touches Dany's wrist, which tingles. When the khaleesi asks for clarification, Quaithe offers the following prophecy:

> "To go north, you must go south. To reach the west, you must go east. To go forward, you must go back, and to touch the light, you must pass beneath the shadow."
>
> Asshai, Daenerys thought. She would have me go to Asshai. "Will the Asshai'i give me an army?" she demanded. "Will there be gold for me in Asshai? Will there be ships? What is there in Asshai that I will not find in Qarth?"
>
> "Truth," said the woman in the mask. And bowing, she faded back into the crowd [II.426].

The masked woman is the feminine power of the mysterious shadow in Asshai, which Daenerys must master before she journeys to Westeros.

Possible treasures waiting in Asshai include the dragons Bran has seen flying there in his visions or a lost Targaryen sword that will be the fabled Lightbringer needed to fight the White Walkers.

> Apparently, to reach Westeros in the northwest, Daenerys must journey to Asshai in the southeast to find magic, dragonlore, or perhaps Lightbringer. It is a land of magic and lost knowledge, called "beside the shadow," indicating it has a knowledge of darkness but is not a source of darkness itself. Another possibility is that one of the Maegi from Asshai, like Quaithe, will teach her what she needs. The "light" may be Lightbringer or enlightenment or goodness, and the shadow suggests the land near Asshai, or perhaps the shadow of danger and death. Melisandre births shadows and uses them to kill, but she comments that they need light to be cast—they represent magical strength, but not pure darkness [Frankel, *Winter Is Coming*, Kindle Locations 240–58].

Quaithe does not protect Daenerys in the House of the Undying or offer any advice that isn't truly cryptic. Daenerys thinks of Quaithe often, attempting to decipher her words. Though she seems benevolent, her motives are even more obscure than Melisandre's, as are her warnings. Nonetheless, like Mirri Maz Duur, she's Daenerys's mentor—the wise female who teaches Daenerys how to grow into adult and queen. In book five, Quaithe appears again, as a vision only for Dany. She says: "The glass candles are burning. Soon comes the pale mare, and after her the others. Kraken and dark flame, lion and griffin, the sun's son and the mummer's dragon. Trust none of them. Remember the Undying. Beware the perfumed seneschal" (V.152–53).

The events of book five enact all of this, as men of all these house sigils sail toward Daenerys. The glass candles signal a return of magic in the Maesters' citadel, and their plot to rid the world of power they cannot understand, including dragons. They may prove Daenerys's great enemy.

The House of the Undying prophecy reminds Daenerys she must abandon her power and return to a simpler time. In a final cryptic moment at book five's end, Daenerys is wandering in the desert, possibly going back to go forward as Quaithe suggested. She dreams of Quaithe's instructions, and then sees her once more, with a mask made of starlight. She says: "Remember who you are, Daenerys.... The dragons know. Do you?"

She is the last child of the Targaryens, whose ancestors once conquered Westeros. Her mentor's challenge that she learn to know herself is the heart of each hero's quest, with a mentor who represents the hero's future. Whether or not Daenerys will become another Quaithe, she must master the arts of magic and prophecy within her, along with the mysterious, unknowable power that is woman.

Tricksters: The Sand Snakes

Tricksters, like women, are marginalized figures, so the women of folklore often use a trickster's talents to get ahead. Such a woman is the outsider, wrecking the status quo and turning the government on its head. "She seeks to expose and protest oppression and create social and political justice for both genders," explains Marilyn Jurich in *Scheherazade's Sisters: Trickster Heroines and Their Stories in World Literature* (230). Tricksters are sexual, occasionally coarse characters, always traveling and ignoring traditional morality and convention. Thus the deceit is a tool of rebellion against traditional society. The female trickster "embraces such contrarieties and the oppositions are more certain, more apparent for her, being a woman. Her very nature is considered contrary by the traditional male ordered society" (Jurich 33).

The ladies of Dorne, introduced in the fourth book, cover a number of archetypes, all of them tricksters of a sort. Princess Arianne, heir to her elderly father's throne, is caught between roles of Daenerys and Sansa, as she wonders why no marriage has been arranged for her, yet itches to strike at their enemies and lead her kingdom to war. Arianne willingly seduces men to make them her allies, as Cersei does. Her "clumsy conspiracy" as she attempts to seize power goes terribly wrong, and Arianne thinks, "I was a foolish willful girl, playing at the game of thrones like a drunkard rolling dice" (Martin, "Arianne"). Unfortunately for gender roles in the series, another young woman plays at the game of thrones and loses, only to have her father inform her she must follow his orders, as he knows a better way.

Actress Indira Varma (who played Niobe on *Rome*) has been cast for season four as Ellaria Sand, paramour of Prince Oberyn Martell "The Red Viper" (played by Pedro Pascal). Arianne's uncle remains devoted to revenge, though Ellaria does not have a significant plot arc to date.

When she arrives at King's Landing, she will be involved with the political sniping and backbiting accompanying Margaery and Cersei's scenes. She may even reveal the deadly side that's required to be the Red Viper's lover.

Oberyn's many bastard daughters, the dazzlingly deadly Sand Snakes, are all variously talented and vicious. (While it's not guaranteed all will appear on the streamlined show, they set out on clandestine tasks in book five, suggesting their importance in books six and seven.) The Sand Snakes represent the spectrum of options for strong women in Martin's world and in medieval times: Clever Sarella was once a pirate captain, while Tyene embarks for the High Sept and a religious road to power. The daughter of a Septa, she maintains a sweet, pious exterior over a core of viciousness. Meanwhile, Sarella is known to be "playing a game" in Oldtown. Fans are certain she is disguised as the maester-in-training Alleras (Sarella spelled backwards), who is slim-shouldered and calls himself "no lord's *son*" (IV.10). With dark Summer Islander skin from her mother and the look of her father, she's working on a complex scheme, in a citadel that allows only men to train.

Fourteen-year-old Elia, called "Lady Lance," is known for her skill in jousting.

> "I am almost a woman grown, ser," she responded haughtily. "I'll let you spank me, though ... but first you'll need to tilt with me, and knock me off my horse."
>
> "We are on a ship, and without horses," Joss replied.
>
> "And ladies do not joust," insisted Ser Garibald Shells, a far more serious and proper young man than his companion.
>
> "I do. I'm Lady Lance."
>
> Arianne had heard enough. "You may be a lance, but you are no lady. Go below and stay there till we reach land" [Martin, "Arianne"].

More swarthy and sturdy than beautiful, Obara leads her country's army on behalf of her crippled uncle. She's trained as a warrior, battling with spear and whip. Obara "always rode stallions and had been heard to boast that she could master any horse in Dorne ... and any man as well" (IV.43). Though Nymeria and Tyene adorn the court with their beauty, they are mistresses of poison, no less deadly for their demure qualities. Elegant Nymeria "was sure to have a dozen blades concealed about her person" (V.501) and even a brush of Tyene's fingers can mean death, though she dresses as "the most chaste of maids" in concealing white lace (V.502). The Red Viper, their father, tells his girls they should wed or have affairs if they wish but if they find themselves stuck with "a fool or a brute, don't look to me to rid you of him. I gave you the tools to do that for yourself" (IV.850). His daughters are each commanding and wonderfully self-sufficient.

"As nurturer and protector, the traditional roles allotted to her, woman seeks to benefit those for whom she cares and tries to improve her community," even if trickery is involved (Jurich 225). In their first appearance in the books, each Sand Snake approaches the prince, using all her persuasion, charm and guile to convince him to pursue her plan for justice—each different and each devastating.

Obara urges her uncle to let her lead troops into battle. Nymeria suggests political maneuverings, as her mother was a noblewoman from Old Volantis. Tyene volunteers as an assassin. As the fifth book concludes, Nymeria is sent to court, Obara to battle, Tyene to the Great Sept, where they will meddle in the political upheaval. Arianne discovers the secrets behind the Dornish agenda and heads off to fulfill her father's great mission.

As a jouster, an heiress seeking the best marriage, a courtesan, a warrior, a politician, a student disguised as a boy, and a religious devotee, the ladies of Dorne cover many of the roles available to medieval women who wanted to impact their world. While their appearances have been limited, their characters shine even in brief cameos. These ladies are tricksters, fond of disguises and role-playing as they entice their enemies into complacency. "Highly creative, Tricksters are able to create lifestyles that fit them and allow for the full expression of all the things they love to do, even if those things seem unusual to many" (Pearson 65). The Trickster archetype comes late to Westeros, only beginning to impact the story in the fourth and fifth books, and only for a few chapters. One hopes it will have a stronger presence in the last two volumes as long-concealed plots come to fruition.

Great Goddess: The Heart Trees

In the spectrum of archetypes, the Great Goddess's absence echoes through the epic. R'hllor and his counterpart the Other are male as is the Drowned God. The Seven represent a division of roles with only the flimsy Mother among them.

Trees themselves are feminine symbols, like the great Tree of Life appearing in many legends. Thus the ancient godswoods take the place of the Great Goddess, nature incarnate. They are most notable for their dwindling belief in the North and absence in the South. In the Eyrie, where Lysa rules irrationally and keeps her son dependent, the godswood of feminine strength has died. At the Red Keep there is only "an acre of elm, alder and black cottonwood trees" with a great oak, limbs overgrown with smokeberry vines, in place of a heart tree (I.255). Though Ned and his daughters pray there "as if it had been a weirwood," the old gods do not protect them. By the first book's end, Ned is executed on the steps of the Great Sept of Baelor, the strongest worshipper of the Old Gods sacrificed to the New.

The Heart Trees of the druidic Old Gods are even color-coded as feminine. Their red leaves and white branches echo the ice and fire dichotomy and hearken back to older legends:

> The three original sacred colors were white, red, and black, signifying the goddess as maiden, mother, and crone: purity, maternity, and wisdom. Upheld by Indian and Greek legend, these colors were later adopted by the Christians as symbols of faith: virginity, martyrdom, and death.... White, red, and black are goddess colors: young moon, full moon, and new moon [Frankel, *From Girl to Goddess* 192].

White was the color of purity, or snow, bone, and sterility; red was the color of blood, birth, menstruation, and life; black was the color of the earth, fertility, wisdom, and the hidden womb. The colors appear in women's legends around the world, from the tale of Deirdre in *The Tain* to the rote phrase still lingering at the beginning of *Snow White*.

The godswood of Winterfell is a "dark primal place" with forest "untouched for a thousand years" (I.22). The ancient trees grow strong, even when the castle is destroyed. Near Riverrun, Catelyn's childhood godswood is "bright and airy" with birds and flowers (I.22). The Heart Trees are long gone, and only pretty redwoods remain. It's the contrast between the ancient strength of the ruling Mother Goddess and the diminutive femininity encouraged under the patriarchy. In the presence of such primal female power at Winterfell, Catelyn feels uncomfortable. Osha, by contrast, routinely swims in the dark lake there and does honor to the ancient powers. When she kills a dying Maester Luwin under the Heart Tree, and leads Bran and Rickon to safety, she is like the godswood's ancient champion, the mother-protector rising in power over the patriarchy.

Like the female monster, the female divinity frightens because all people had a time when they were tiny and dependent on an all-powerful mother. While she can be all-providing, like an earth goddess, she can also be all-devouring and consume the child like Snow White's evil step-mother. This terrifying, powerful figure who doesn't need a divine spouse is mostly left out of Martin's world.

The Old Religion offers no holy texts or priestly intermediaries—it is a quiet religion where men and women can commune with the quiet-ness of the earth, as Ned and Sansa do. "The singers of the forest had no books. No ink, no parchment, no written language... When they died, they went into the wood, into leaf and limb and root, and the trees remem-bered" (V.452). Lore seems to pass through Old Nan and those like her, storytellers who remember the old legends, as the wildlings do. Old Nan reports: "The children of the forest were the first people, small as children, dark and beautiful.... They worshipped the old gods and their wisemen, the greenseers, carved the faces that keep watch in the weirwoods" (I.736–37). While the children, like Ygritte, Brynden Rivers, and other followers of the old ways, use weirwood bows, these feminized tiny figures of nature have largely faded away. The old religion is dying out, with the misogy-nistic High Septon or the male god R'hllor taking its place.

Weirwood stumps are scattered through Westeros, emphasizing the loss of the feminine magic like scars upon the land. With his head on one, Jaime dreams of Cersei and Brienne, the conflicting voices of female honor and treachery in his head. Inspired by them, he chooses honor and rescues Brienne from the bear pit. The weirwood table of the Kings-guard, weirwood rafters at Harrenhal, and weirwood throne of the Eyrie signify opulence, but also a lost feminine spirituality in these places where compassion has died and honor is a brittle semblance. Only at the Black Gate of the Nightfort does the ancient power remain.

Brienne has her own weirwood encounter. "Most old castles had a godswood. By the look of it, the Whispers had little else.... Mounds of poisonous red ivy grew over the heap of broken stones" (IV.416). There among the trees, Brienne battles rapists who call her "mad with moon blood," a typical male insult for females (IV.420). She fights beside the sea and a dark cave, also feminine symbols of the primal, uncivilized world. Though the South has few remaining, Brienne sees a slender young weirwood tree "with a trunk as white as a cloistered maid" that echoes herself, just beginning to grow a feminine side in the midst of a masculine world (IV.416). At last, she corners the jester Shagwell (a sexual name in itself) who attempts to yield. As he condemns women for not finding his abuses as funny as the men do, he is another voice of the patriarchy.

> "You are no better than the rest of them. You have robbed and raped and murdered."
> "Oh, I have, I have, I shan't deny it ... but I'm amusing, with all my japes and capers. I make men laugh."
> "And women weep."
> "Is that my fault? Women have no sense of humor."
> Brienne lowered Oathkeeper. "Dig a grave. There, beneath the weirwood." She pointed with her blade [IV.421].

She slays him beneath the tree, and strikes a blow for female power.

Monstrous Woman: Stoneheart

Another archetype unseen (or barely seen) is the female monster—Medusa, Echidna. Lamia, Grendel's mother. The wights and Others are almost entirely male, as the horror comes from the fact that they used to be Black Brothers. Unnatural humans such as Pyat Pree and the Frankenstein-like Ser Robert Strong are male, as is Beric Dondarrion, a very human character who nonetheless has a bit of Frankenstein about him. The single giant character is male. Only the children of the forest are female as well as male, and they are tiny, appealing, non-threatening, and benevolent—inherently feminine characteristics.

The female monster, left out of the tale, is a powerful and primal force of terror:

> The maternal figure as monster has various guises ... dominant amongst which is the figure of "the archaic mother." This figure, "the generative mother," the "mother as the origin of all life," is monstrous ... from her perceived self-sufficiency. As parthenogenic mother, she offers "a notion of the feminine which does not depend for its definition on a concept of the mas-

culine." In the patriarchal world of the horror film, this "horrifying image" has two manifestations. One is the image of the "gestating, all devouring womb," the other is the threat of obliteration, of reincorporation, which she poses [Thornham 231].

The only female monster is Lady Stoneheart, who appears at the end of book three. (Many fans anticipate her appearance in the fourth season.) Though formerly human, she is on a mission of vengeance, and ignores all please for mercy or attempts at reason; she is stonehearted in function as well as name. The lady who was once highborn, conformist, lovely, well-spoken, and proper has become her own shadow, a monster that lurks in the wild and subverts the patriarchy as a fearsome outlaw. She embodies the female as monster:

> Released by her monstrousness from the constraints of culture (or perhaps made a monster by her disavowal of them), she completes a dialectic of womanhood. As a woman, she is the most familiar, but as a monster, the unknown; this combination makes her uncanny.... She is unspeakable, and therefore cannot speak. She is the awful, and for this reason powerful; the Terrible Female [Ruberg 3].

Women with agency are often depicted as monsters or villainesses (many Disney witches take this role, contrasted against the innocent princesses). In fact, monsters often represent the shadow of the hero—all he or she refuses to become. Gollum is disturbing because Frodo feels Gollum's greed and treachery rising inside himself when he wears the ring. Similarly, Brienne, protector of morality and the innocent, sees Lady Stoneheart as vengeance personified—justice without mercy, the possible dark side Brienne may become if she continues to serve others' missions rather than fighting for herself. Lady Stoneheart's limited appearances (two brief ones in thousands of pages) leave her a minor figure. The lady herself appears to be more monster than hero—Martin has said she will not be a point-of-view character, and her possible growth appears unlikely.

Female monsters produce shock, not because they are unusual (which they are) but because of their unwomanly conduct. With their immorality and amorality, they challenge human conventions. In her essay on the female monster in video games, Bonnie Ruberg explains:

> Here in front of the player is a woman, a symbol of comfort and submissiveness. Yet she bears claws, fangs, rotting flesh. Suddenly, that femininity

which culture has taught him should be beautiful comes before him as unrelentingly, unapologetically ugly. That femininity which he believed should serve him attempts, without sympathy or remorse, to devour his very body. That femininity which society has told him to protect, he must kill—not peacefully, respectfully, but in the most violent of manners, one befitting the slaughter of an animal. Now, that which was the most tamed is most wild; that which was once most humane is most foreign. It is precisely this unwillingness to yield to expectations that makes the female monster so terrifying [3].

This is often a reaction against culture: There's a trope in world folklore in which women die powerless, betrayed by men, and then rise as monsters. They are Japanese *yuurei*, German *lorelai*, Russian *rusalka*, the Mexican *Llorona* or Venezuelan *Sayona*. Lady Stoneheart, only operating for her children in life, has risen as a powerful figure seeking selfish revenge. Though a monster, dead, disfigured, and apparently amoral, she has become an outlet of female power.

Monsters are a physical representation of the outcast, in stories from *The Hunchback of Notre Dame* to *Frankenstein*. "The defining characteristic of monsters is that they somehow exist outside of society, whereas heroes walk that line" (Blair 119). As many have noted, *Game of Thrones* is a saga of outcasts: Tyrion, Jon, Bran, Theon, Jorah, Barristan, Yara, Arya, Brienne. The heroes are the Night's Watch or Brotherhood Without Banners, bravely defending the common people as the lords and knights rape and kill the smallfolk for material gain. It would not come as a terrible shock to find the White Walkers (or rather, the mysterious force behind them) are misunderstood, as necessary to the balance of the world as fire and ice, summer and winter, rather than Tolkien's force of pure evil. Jon Snow has already bonded with the enemy wildlings, and Daenerys is uniting Dothraki, exiles, slaves, and slave-owners into a new kingdom of freedmen.

In all this, the female monster is largely nonexistent. Female outcasts survive by imitating men (Arya, Yara, Brienne) or serving them (Shae, Gilly). None truly subverts or attack all the tenets of civilization. By contrast, female monsters are the ultimate outcast—women with power who are demonized for having it.

The series' other monster of female rage is Nymeria, Arya's wolf. She represents Arya's fury and savagery, which Arya must chase away in order to conform to the Lannisters' rules and live in King's Landing.

In the second book, Arya hears about an enormous female wolf who has risen to packleader and has no fear of men. In time, Nymeria leads hundreds of man-eating wolves and fills the forests with her fury. In Arya's dreams, she thinks, "Some of her little grey cousins were afraid of men, even dead men; but to her meat was meat and men were prey. She was the night wolf" (V.593). As a killer of knight and peasants alike, howling in the forest, Nymeria becomes the bane of society.

Though the wolf hasn't yet impacted the plot, she remains at the edge of Arya's consciousness, like a sixth sense. Arya reflects to herself that she may be "no one," but the names she repeats to herself are "the night wolf's prayer. Someday she will find them, smell their fear, taste their blood" (V.593). Nymeria is her seething magic, rage, and power, distant from her but still thriving. When Arya returns to Westeros, Nymeria may do more to aid her.

The Hero Queen: Daenerys

Illyrio Moptis, who sets up Daenerys's wedding to Drogo, later notes: "There is no peace in Westeros, no justice, no faith ... and soon enough, no food. When men are starving and sick of fear, they look for a savior" (V.30). This savior will be Daenerys. In Westeros, whoever has the dragons will receive the people's allegiance, and she has the first in centuries.

Melisandre prophesizes the return of a great warrior with a flame-lit sword as "the cold breath of darkness falls heavy on the world": "When the red star bleeds and the darkness gathers, Azor Ahai shall be born again amidst smoke and salt to wake dragons out of stone" (II:110). He will be the one to save Westeros from the White Walkers and the eternal winter. While there are hints that Stannis, Jon, and a few other characters fit, Daenerys is the strongest correlation. She was born on Dragonstone, a saltwater-enclosed isle in a night of storms and mist while the world around her burned. In season one, she was reborn as the Mother of Dragons on a tear-stained funeral pyre of flame and ash. This second birth "woke dragons from stone," and on that morning, the "bleeding star," the Red Comet, appeared. She may wake more secrets on the Targaryen stronghold of Dragonstone in the future.

Further, Maester Aemon tells Sam that Daenerys is the prophesized hero in *A Feast for Crows*: A child of the forest said that "the prince that was promised would be born of their line," the line of Aerys and Rhaella, Daenerys's parents (V.300–01). Aemon notes: "No one ever looked for a girl. It was a prince that was promised, not a princess…. What fools we were, who thought ourselves so wise! The error crept in from the translation. Dragons are neither male nor female" (IV.520).

Daenerys is thus the prince who was promised, champion from over the sea, and the one female who could rule Westeros. She undergoes the full arc of the heroine's journey, while Brienne and Arya are rejecting their femininity. As such, most of the feminism on the show must be attributed to her. However, her role in the first episode is the most subjugated pawn seen on the series. Critics are divided on how much this weakens her character. Jennifer Armstrong's "*Game of Thrones*: Feminist or Not?" describes her as "first seen fully naked, fresh out of a bath, being creepily ogled and fondled by her power-hungry brother, Viserys" and adds that he weds her to "hulking warlord Khal Drogo (Jason Momoa), who consummates their union, businesslike, having barely exchanged a word with her."

Daenerys has other problematic moments on the show. There are her rapes in episodes one and two. There's the moment she shows off her body for Daario. And there's the slaves' worship of her in "Mhysa." Otherwise, she's a glowing warrior queen who revels in being a woman. Most of her moments shine. But how destructive are her weaknesses? Are there any other flaws? Caroline Spector explains in "Power and Feminism in Westeros":

> Daenerys's journey from child bride to first female ruler of a khalasar is one of the more dramatic examples in the Ice and Fire series of a woman taking power. However, hers is not a journey without problems—both for the character and for readers. The most obvious of these is the fact that she falls in love with Khal Drogo. For a modern reader, this is inevitably problematic— being a mere thirteen, she can hardly be said to have consented to her marriage, much less to the sexual acts that take place within it. However, in Westerosi society, she's considered of marriageable age once she has physically matured to a point where she can bear children. Her emotional maturity and personal desire for the union are irrelevant in a culture where the woman's role is to bear a man's children and to submit to him [183].

By today's standards the marriage is shocking but in medieval Europe where Martin's series is based, this was far less so: "Women married young, often at the onset of puberty, at 12–13, and normally before 20; the average age was between 15 and 16" (Haskell 466). In modern society, an impressionable twelve-year-old's being ordered by older men to have sex with an older man is still rape. But in medieval times, adulthood for women began at puberty. Certainly, Daenerys is young—less than thirteen in the books—and completely sheltered. On the show she's older, but still naïve. Martin explains her aging-up:

> We had some real problems because Dany is only 13 in the books, and that's based on medieval history. They didn't have this concept of adolescence or the teenage years. You were a child or you were an adult. And the onset of sexual maturity meant you were an adult. So I reflected that in the books. But then when you go to film it, you run into people going crazy about child pornography and there's actual laws about how you can't depict a 13-year-old having sex even if you have an 18-year-old acting the part—it's illegal in the United Kingdom. So we ended up with a 22-year-old portraying an 18-year-old, instead of an 18-year-old portraying a 13-year-old [Hibberd, "EW Interview: George R.R. Martin"].

Arranged marriages were expected, and marriage to strangers or near-strangers was common, especially for royalty. In context, most royal young persons of both genders had similar marriages thrust upon them. However, Edmure Tully insists, "The laws of gods and men are very clear: No man may compel another man to marry" (3.6). This is a disturbing pronouncement, as men compel women to marry in many scenes: Daenerys, Cersei (twice!), Sansa (with multiple betrothals and finally a wedding) and so forth. This emphasizes women's status as pawns and dependents in their system.

For the ceremonies, she wears vulnerable, soft clothing. The "viewing dress is essentially designed to make her look good naked, as Drogo's come by to see the goods, basically," notes costume designer Michelle Clapton (qtd. in Cogman, *Inside HBO's* Game 158). Her body is visible through it, and her brother eagerly gropes her (she's the property of two different men in the first episode). Her wedding dress is likewise nearly skin-colored, emphasizing her nakedness and vulnerability. It wraps around, inviting Drogo to unwrap it. Daenerys burns in it at season's end, shedding her life with Drogo and reincarnating as Mother of Dragons.

Dany's weddings in book and show have different vibes, contrasting her joyous shout that her husband has given her the wind (the silver horse) with Jorah's chilling comment that the horselords are so alien and sullen that they have no word for thank you. Likewise, the "no" of Dany's wedding night becomes a question from Drogo, rather than a command.

> He stopped then, and drew her down onto his lap. Dany was flushed and breathless, her heart fluttering in her chest. He cupped her face in his huge hands and she looked into his eyes. "No?" he said, and she knew it was a question.
> She took his hand and moved it down to the wetness between her thighs. "Yes," she whispered [I.108].

The show never sees this exchange, leaving tearful Dany raped by her new husband. It appears to be Emilia Clarke herself who set the tone for Dany and Drogo's abusive sex scene. As she explains:

> It was something that we discussed in great depth. As an actor, for me, it was a really important part of Dany's journey that I kind of wanted us to get right.... With the book, it just seems too sudden. It just seems that she's introduced to this guy who's the most fearsome person she's ever come across and, within one moment, that's it. It's done. What we kind of wanted to show, we wanted to track the real growth of the relationship; I don't think it would have made too much sense to instantly go into that. It wouldn't have let Dany's journey really kind of blossom. I don't know, we kind of thought it needed to take more than that to crack Drogo, you know? Because in the book it kind of happens instantly and we thought it was important to show, I don't know—a bit more reality. And I think it helped the progression of Dany and Drogo [Ryan].

With the wedding, Daenerys exchanges a brother for a husband. For most of her life, Viserys has been Daenerys's only protector and parent, the one who tells her of the Targaryens and Westeros. He represents the patriarchy as selfish and entitled, demanding his sister treat him as a king and cower before his temper. Viserys is all greed and ambition. He's like a child, wanting what was taken from him but having little idea how to rule when he regains it. Dany too is childlike. Dragons are a constant threat to her, as Viserys always warns her about waking the dragon, his temper. This is an idle threat: Viserys, not a true dragon and vulnerable to fire, only imagines his dragon-born power. Nonetheless, Daenerys cringes from her birthright.

"You dare? You give commands to me? To me? You do not command the dragon. I'm lord of the Seven Kingdoms. I don't take orders from savages or their sluts. Do you hear me?" he rants (1.3). However, as he blames the victim he created, Daenerys is finding power in her new life. It's the power afforded her by Drogo's bloodriders as Drogo's wife and mother of his unborn son. "I am a Khaleesi of the Dothraki. I am the wife of the great Kahl and I carry his son inside me. The next time you raise a hand to me will be the last time you have hands," she cries (1.4). When she claims she's not a queen but a khaleesi, she clings to the title that means a khal's obedient concubine.

Drogo takes credit for her change, noting that she's grown so fierce because his son grows inside her, "filling her with his fire" (I.670). Emilia Clarke notes, "My favorite moment is when [Khal Drogo is] riling up the *khalisar* and I'm looking at him with such love: 'That's my man. He's gonna kill for me'" (qtd. in Cogman, *Inside HBO's* Game 170). At this point, Drogo decides to win the crown of Westeros for his son—Daenerys will not be participating. Even Ser Jorah calls Daenerys "child" and "fool" while they travel the Dothraki sea.

She redefines the title Khaleesi, from meaning concubine and Khal's counterpart to meaning the queen over the men who have never served a woman, only warriors. Seducing her husband and publicly demanding he spare the slave women the Dothraki are abusing, she becomes a co-ruler as well as wife. "Before long, she was actively inciting change in the hyper-masculine Dothraki culture—particularly when she appealed to her husband to stop the systematic rape of captured women," Scott Meslow comments in "*Game of Thrones* Finale: The Powerful Women of Westeros." Her power still comes from her husband, but she chooses to use it in unprecedented ways.

The Dothraki value a nomadic life based in freedom and the open sky. Always closed in before this, Dany flourishes with her beloved Silver, the horse gifted to her by Drogo. She gradually sets aside her silks for lighter clothes and finally a Dothraki vest, acclimating closer to the plains. She considers braiding her hair like Drogo's to signal that she's inherited his strength. As she begins this new stage of her life, she's offered the dragons that were no more than myth while she lived in her brother's charge. Dragons become a gift to her on her wedding day, and then a comfort, as she cradles the eggs when she's distressed. Of course, these dragons represent the potential that could be, eggs apparently frozen in stone for thousands of years.

"It's the story of a girl growing into being a woman," Clarke says of her character. "It's a beautiful arc. I kind of fell in love with her strength, which you don't see for the first couple of episodes, but I believe she has" (Armstrong). She protects her people and fights her enemies, not with a sword, but with words and finally dragonfire. Having decided she wants the Iron Throne, she's going to get it, not by marrying but by forging alliances and taking revenge on those who betray her. D.B. Weiss notes, "To be a young actress and make the journey from frightened young woman to a fantasy Joan of Arc ... so much was riding on the ability of the actress who played Dany" (qtd. in Cogman, *Inside HBO's Game* 155). She was a near-unknown who auditioned with the funeral pyre scene and swept the producers away.

On the heroine's journey, the woman faces the wicked stepmother, wielder of death magic and slayer of children. By studying with her, learning from her, and finally confronting her, the childlike heroine learns the power of death and experience to balance her innocence and lifegiving power. This dark witch of course is Mirri Maz Duur. Dany rescues her and naively expects gratitude and loyalty in return.

She trusts the sorceress, and her husband and unborn son die. This teaches her a valuable lesson: showing kindness and believing in the goodness of others will not always be rewarded. The television show reveals that the Maegi poisoned Drogo; the book is more ambiguous. In both, the Maegi offers to bring him back with the darkest of death magics, which will cost a life to fashion. Dany naively agrees. When the price is not just Drogo's horse but a rebellion and a miscarriage, Dany unwillingly pays and then discovers what she has bought with the blood-price. Drogo lives, but no more than that. Dany tries to revive him with the power of her love, taking him beneath the stars, bathing, kissing, and coaxing, but the spark that was Drogo has vanished. Her love magic is born from emotion, but still naive and untutored, lacking real magic. She leaves Drogo behind, executing him and growing from queen-consort to queen in her own right. Across the world Cersei does the same, but fails, as Joffrey claims the throne and ignores her counsel. This is why Dany must lose her child, dismantling the male power structure that surrounds her as brother, husband, and conqueror-son to create a newer form of rule, one centered in willing cooperation and freedom. She releases her slaves and asks her khals to become her bloodriders.

Nonetheless, she is rebuffed: They follow strength and will not be led by a woman.

Dany learns well from the Maegi. With the words "Only death can pay for life" (I.803), she binds her to the funeral pyre, slaying the woman who slew Drogo and her child. Dany is harnessing the magic of her death to bring the eggs to life and enter a new reality of power and life herself. She wakes the eggs, turning them and herself from potential sources of power to living, fiery ones prepared to reclaim her royal birthright.

> The hero and heroine always descend into death only to be reborn more powerfully—as the Ironborn would say, "What is dead may never die, but rises again, harder and stronger." In fact, the Ironborn embody this journey, deliberately drowning themselves literally or symbolically to enter new stages of life. While this is a metaphor for undergoing trauma or despair and growing stronger from the challenge, fantasy tends to address this literally. Daenerys faces death in the first book when Drogo is fatally wounded: She loses her child, she enters the tent of death, she nearly dies herself, and she finally gains the wisdom and pitilessness to slay the shell that remains of Drogo. "If her treatment of the witch Mirri Maz Duur in last night's episode is any indication, Daenerys has no mercy left in her," one reviewer comments [Meslow, "*Game of Thrones* Finale"]. Indeed, she lashes the Maegi to the fire and enters it herself, vanishing into the flames all night and burning down to her core—clothing, hair, all that concealed her is burned away, and a new Daenerys rises from the ashes, no longer the marriage pawn and subservient wife of Drogo, but a leader of men and the Mother of Dragons [Frankel, *Winning the Game of Thrones* 123].

She crosses into the otherworld that night, close enough to see Drogo mount his shadow stallion and ride away. She vanishes into the fire, potentially dead, and then reappears in the morning with dragons hatched about her. Only when she enters the pyre and emerges unburnt do the remaining Dothraki kneel before her. She has become a worker of miracles, mother to the first dragons in centuries. When Dany sees her subjects kneel, she knows they're hers as they were never Drogo's—won by the power of life and fire, not that of conquering and rule. On the threshold of death, she calls herself Daenerys Stormborn of House Targaryen for the first time. She's claiming her own birthright of dragons and the Targaryen legacy, not just her role as Drogo's counterpart. "All her fear was gone, burned away" (I.755).

Having faced death, she establishes herself as queen, inheritor of

House Targaryen and its legacy. "I was a child yesterday. Today I am a woman," she utters (I.800). However, as she dresses in a Dothraki vest like Drogo's and claims her khals as bloodriders, she's becoming a second Drogo, a male-coded leader. She also channels Aegon the Conqueror, her hero-brother Rhaegar, and other patriarchs of her family. "How many had Aegon started with," she wonders (I.802).

"You watch the growth of this young girl blossoming into a strong young woman," says Emilia Clarke. "When we finish Season 1, you see her in almost a spiritual level. In Season 2, there's a little bit of a crash back down to Earth when you see her again. [But] she is developing a much more iron core. She has Targaryen blood running through her, and they're very fierce people" (Keveney).

Season two follows Daenerys and her people as they suffer through the Red Waste. This is a crucible that burns her people down to their essence, killing them and depriving them of all they have. At last, Daenerys reaches Qarth, where she must battle the patriarchy. The Qartheen dignitary Xaro Xhoan Daxos is cold and calculating, eager to marry Daenerys for her position, while Pyat Pree the Warlock is a figure of prophecy and trickery. These two types of schemers both try to outwit Daenerys, and she must battle to outmaneuver them. This she does, slaying them both and plundering Xaro's house for the means to sail onwards and build an army.

Her expediency leaves her cruel and notably sexist: Dany appears to whore out Doreah, noting casually, "Xaro is our host, but we know nothing about him. Men like to talk about other men ... when they're happy" (2.5). Doreah leaves the room. Later, Dany executes her for treason when she finds her in Xaro's bed. Her harsh lessons come with a price.

Dany undresses less as she grows in power. In the book, her journey to Qarth sees her dressed in their fashion, with a breast bared, but she doesn't do that in the show. When presented with a silky sky blue gown, she realizes it's not the look for her and adds metal filigree corset-armor that emphasizes she's no soft maiden. She only appears naked again in the bathtub scene with Daario in season three. David Benioff explains: "She's in the most vulnerable possible position—naked in the bathtub ... it's one thing to be intimidating and full of authority when you're sitting there with your three dragons.... It's another thing entirely when you're in this situation." He calls the fact that she manages to turn it around "one of the more impressive things that we've witnessed from her" (Benihoff, "Unflappable"). Certainly, Daenerys would say she owns the situation as she demands Daario swear himself to her service and he complies. But stepping naked from the tub to show off her body as a sort of bribe or reward for Daario makes her seem more prostitute than conqueror.

It's not her only disturbing tool. "Here I am, are you afraid of a little girl?" Dany shouts in the House of the Undying (2.10). Her favorite phrase in the later books is "I am only a young girl and know nothing of war, but ..." Jon Snow, roughly the same age, would never shout "I'm just a little boy, come and get me!"

Season three begins with Daenerys buying the Unsullied. She has learned trickery as she trades her dragon to the slavers of Astapor, and she's also learned queenship, staring down her counselors and outwitting them as well. Her dragons are gaining size and strength, emphasizing her growing power in the world. Clarke adds:

> Coming from Season 2 her confidence in herself and others was rock bottom. In Season 3 coming up the scene [sic], she took a plunge—didn't discuss anything—it was a risk she was taking. All the trust she put into her dragons. She's testing herself, if that doesn't work—then that's game over! And if it does work then it's—game on! She does build from that and listens to herself more, takes less advice [De Graeve].

As the male kings battle in Westeros, Daenerys and her army represent a new kind of war, one of cleverness and freedom from tyranny. Ser Jorah explains the violence of war, comparing men to beasts but acknowledging the Unsullied as different, a new type of warrior who will fight for Daenerys's ideals:

> I saw King's Landing after the Sack. Babes were butchered that day as well, and old men, and children at play. More women were raped than you can count. There is a savage beast in every man, and when you hand that man a sword or spear and send him forth to war, the beast stirs. The scent of blood is all it takes to wake him. Yet I have never heard of those Unsullied raping, nor putting a city to the sword, nor even plundering, save at the express command of those who lead them [III.328–329].

In Westeros, love and lust ignited several wars, both Cersei's for Jaime's and Rhaegar's for Lyanna. As the slave master of Astapor points out, the Westerosi men sworn to chastity soon break their vows. "Their days are a torment of temptation, any fool must see, and no doubt most succumb to their baser selves" (III.317). The Unsullied have left behind these urges to be a perfect fighting force, completely obedient to the will of Daenerys. She ends the practice of killing and torturing children to make Unsullied and thus forever transforms the Unsullied, turning them from victims into protectors as she evolves. The Unsullied worship a goddess: "the Lady of Spears, the Bride of Battle, the Mother of Hosts" (V.477) who seems to echo Daenerys herself.

Traveling in Slaver's Bay, she expresses interest in Daario Naharis, the sellsword captain who proclaims himself in love with her beauty. "I count no day as lived unless I have loved a woman, slain a foeman, and eaten a fine meal," he says upon meeting her (III.576). As such, he represents sensuality and experience. Though he's a fighter, he pledges himself to her service wholly. With long hair and well-groomed appearance, he's somewhat feminized. Daenerys considers his "almost hairless" skin like "silk and satin" (V.564). "You are beautiful," she blurts out (V.566). Thus Daenerys evolves from the captive wife "sold" to Drogo to a queen who can choose a subordinate lover, like widow-queen Cersei and her cousin Lancel. With no lordly status in Westeros or Slaver's Bay, Daario is unsuited to be her husband. But he can be her kept paramour until she weds a co-ruler. Daenerys has not yet fallen truly in love with an equal, with such a relationship most likely awaiting her near the end of her epic.

Daenerys is a warrior queen conquering the cities of Slaver's Bay from the patriarchal, slave-owning cultures that hold it. The symbol of Ghis, a harpy, denotes the degraded feminine, made grotesque and banished to the underworld for being powerful. The queen of "Mhysa," adored by the slaves, represents a new kind of ruler for them. Along with warrior-queen, Daenerys is the mother-protector of her growing community in the east. She makes it her mission to end slavery everywhere, before setting off for slave-free Westeros. However, this leaves her ruling one poverty-stricken city, full of famine and midnight murders. Martin notes, "Daenerys is still very young. She has lessons to learn. [Conquering a city and killing hundreds of slave owners] was one of them. It is not as easy to do good as it might seem, no matter how noble your intentions" ("Correspondence with Fans," August 15, 2001). He adds:

> You never actually see the nitty-gritty of ruling. I guess there is an element of fantasy readers that don't want to see that. I find that fascinating. Seeing

someone like Dany actually trying to deal with the vestments of being a queen and getting factions and guilds and [managing the] economy. They burnt all the fields [in Meereen]. They've got nothing to import any more. They're not getting any money. I find this stuff interesting. And fortunately, enough of my readers who love the books do as well [Anders].

Emilia Clarke notes that season three in Slaver's Bay has "been a phenomenal season to film, to get on the journey—you think she's peaking at episode 5 getting her army. The final episode was absolutely exhilarating" (De Graeve). However, this ending is problematic as well, especially from a racial standpoint. The brown-skinned slaves are free now that the foreign white girl proclaims them so. They raise her up to the sky and chant as if she's their new messiah, answer to all their prayers. They are instantly trusting, desperately grateful and worshipful. A comedown seems inevitable as Daenerys must struggle to feed and protect them all. There's also the knowledge that she "belongs" elsewhere and that her time in the east is temporary.

There are a few females who mix male and female archetypal roles, becoming fully female women who nonetheless want to climb the political ladder and play the game of thrones. Unfortunately, only two come to mind: Daenerys and Lady Olenna. Olenna has a minimal part in the books, and loses most of her negotiations through her season three appearances. Daenerys is flawed, multifaceted, conflicted, female and powerful—a wonderful character. However, as the critic who wrote the essay "I Hate Strong Female Characters" puts it, "We need get away from the idea that sexism in fiction can be tackled by reliance on depiction of a single personality type, that you just need to write one female character per story right and you've done enough" (McDougall).

Most female characters embody a single archetype. Brienne never has a love interest in five books, as she is the chaste warrior woman. In the same five books, Sansa learns rudimentary manipulation but remains a good girl and marriage pawn, fought over by different factions. Her sister is a tough warrior girl in every scene. Cersei and Catelyn always put their children first. Margaery is careful to preserve her alluring image, as is Melisandre. Daenerys by contrast cycles through many archetypes. She is the child bride and helpless princess, then warrior woman and conqueror queen. Sometimes she dresses in sky blue silk with gold filigree armor, sometimes she wears Dothraki leathers. She is a sensual lover in the first and fifth books (and tries a lesbian relationship on rare occasions). She's a loving wife as she struggles for a night to return Drogo to life. She is a mother to her dragons and to the people under her protection. And she's a medium when she has visions of future and past in the House of the Undying and in her dreams. As such, she's a fully rounded character, rather than a stereotype on curvaceous legs.

Whatever her pitfalls, Daenerys the conqueror has lent her image to *Game of Thrones,* so much so that she is the main character for many readers. Daenerys represents powerful feminism in the ancient world—the former pawn who would be queen and more. Emilia Clarke comments:

> One of the most glorious experiences as an actor is to play Dany, [I] would never have dreamed to ever play such a strong woman. Reading the scripts and following her journey is a phenomenal experience. And as a young girl—it sort of empowers me as a woman. So getting to play that is incredible. So the possibility that I've helped other women feel empowered is just the most wonderful feeling I could possibly imagine. I'm incredibly grateful really! [De Graeve].

Of course, Daenerys as conquering queen has her own reflections in history, suggesting her fight for Westeros will concern her gender as much as her abilities. Two generations after the Norman Conquest. King Henry I had all his nobles swear fealty to his daughter Mathilda. However, the widowed and childless "Empress Mathilda" had been sent off as a child bride to King Heinrich V of Germany and was a German-speaking stranger to her birth country and its customs. A few generations past, the son of the king had not inherited, but rather, the Saxon nobles voted for the most able male leader. With this recent history in place, and Mathilda far from the seat of power, her male cousin, Stephen, seized the treasury and persuaded the bishop of Winchester to crown him. Civil war broke out.

> When Matilda the empress had received homage from those who had come to her, she left Bristol and rode through the country and waged war very hard against King Stephen her nephew and his son. The empress rode every day with the army, and she gave good advice on the most difficult matters; in the whole army there was not a baron so skilled and experienced in war as she was, and there was much talk about her throughout England. The war between her and her nephew continued until the two armies met outside

Lincoln. There they fought until the king was defeated and taken by force and imprisoned, and lost everything [Nicholson].

Mathilda captured Stephen and won the war. However, her new subjects called her "haughty" and "willful," complaining that she acted outside her gender. Mathilda was forced to name her son Henry II, and he indeed inherited her crown. "The risk these queens ran was that their power would be perceived as a perversion of 'good' womanhood, a distillation of all that was to be feared in the unstable depths of female nature" (Castor 31). This too may be the fate of Daenerys, winning the throne from a people only ruled by men.

Many generations later, Queen Elizabeth famously proclaimed she had "the heart and stomach of a king," but she also used feminine identifiers, linking herself with minor pagan goddesses Diana and Astraea (goddess of justice) (Prioleau 201). At Tilbury, she encouraged her troops "habited like an Amazonian queen" with golden arms and armor (Jones 64). She set herself as the love object of her entire court. In jewels and perfume, she danced beautifully and bantered wittily with her many courtiers. Like Daenerys, some members of Elizabeth's family were executed in her childhood, and her country was split between supporting her and her rival, "Bloody Mary." She was loved by the common people as she walked among them: At her coronation, "during the procession to Westminster Abbey, she 'wonderfully ravished' the people through press-the-flesh declarations of love" (Prioleau 202).

Before the violent reign of Elizabeth's sister Mary, England had never seen a female sovereign. Elizabeth used many tools, from dazzling to beguiling, to maintain the love and support of her courtiers. She spoke six languages and mastered history, philosophy, rhetoric, and many kinds of subterfuge. She disarmed the men's hostility toward female sovereigns with flirtation and charm. "She scintillated, teased, flattered, prevaricated" and much more (Prioleau 203).

Daenerys too must compete with male claimants back home like Stannis and Joffrey. As she slowly sets her eyes west, she begins a campaign of winning the people, seen as she frees the slaves and becomes their "mother." Like Elizabeth, she uses disarming banter and charm to win courtiers to the idea of a sovereign, but she warns newly arrived Ser Barristan that her brother was not the last dragon—*she* is.

If *Game of Thrones* is the War of the Roses retold, Daenerys parallels

Henry VII, who arrived when the Lancasters and Yorks (or Lannisters and Starks) had nearly wiped each other out. He wed the last of them (many fans believe Daenerys and Jon will end up together) and began the Tudor dynasty. After winning the throne in the Battle of Bosworth Field against Richard III (who parallels Stannis in a few ways), Henry founded the "Yeomen of the Guard," his personal bodyguard that lives on through today, and created many dynastic marriages for his children. Queen Elizabeth I was his granddaughter.

Sansa and Tyrion also could end up together, as the last Lannister-Stark survivors, and usher in an era of peace. Martin notes, "The Lancasters and Yorks fought themselves to extinction until the Tudors came in. But the Tudors were really a new dynasty; they weren't Lancasters. So ..." ("A Very Long Interview with George R.R. Martin"). It seems the Targaryens will take the throne from both, after a fight nearly "to extinction."

PART III

Gender Roles in Westeros

Women in Westeros

Women's treatment in medieval Europe is somewhat reflected in their treatment in Westeros. However, it is a fantasy kingdom that reimagines the world, and some of the gender differences are particularly significant:

Female warriors in armor are unusual, but not unheard of (the same is true in European history, in fact). Outside Westerosi culture, wildling women are fighters beside the men. Bravos appears to train male and female assassins both. The Dothraki, however, have far stricter gender roles, and no female warriors are seen.

Women engage in the crafts seen in medieval Europe: embroidery and dance for the highborn, cooking and scrubbing for the lowborn. Highborn women are literate. They are kept chaperoned, and virginity is expected. While few tradeswomen are seen, they appear to manage inns and other businesses alongside the men. Prostitution is common among women and appears unheard of for men and boys in Westeros, though such practices appear in the east. Slavery, of any race, is forbidden in Westeros.

Inheritance laws are interesting: Daughters inherit after their brothers, except in Dorne, where the oldest child of any gender inherits. However, women are not permitted to inherit the Iron Throne unless they rule through a male family member. This began with the Dance of the Dragons, in which a princess and her half-brother competed for the throne and began a civil war.

Stannis, who has only a daughter Shireen, must abide by this as well. For this reason, young Daenerys is not considered a threat to King Robert until her marriage and pregnancy. It is not clear what Daenerys will do about such a law, though practically, her arrival with dragons and an army might waive such requirements. As one of the prequel stories notes, "If a living dragon appeared again in Westeros, the lords and smallfolk alike would flock to whichever prince could lay claim to it" (Martin, "The Mystery Knight" 721). As such, Daenerys might be able to change her country's laws. "Daenerys Targaryen is remarkable and dangerous in every sense because her very existence is perilous to the current power structure" (Spector 170). She is the anti-patriarchy, and she's heading towards Westeros.

CHIVALRY

Knights in Westeros vow to protect women, though not all keep their vows. Part of the vow (the only part printed in the books) is as follows:

> ... in the name of the Warrior I charge you to be brave. In the name of the Father I charge you to be just. In the name of the Mother I charge you to defend the young and innocent. In the name of the Maid I charge you to protect all women ... [Martin, "The Hedge Knight" 518].

This vow is sworn by Brienne's ancestor, Ser Duncan the Tall, who (along with Brienne) is one of the few in Westeros to live by the knights' code of honor. Likewise, Beric Dondarrion makes his Brotherhood without Banners swear to "defend those who cannot defend themselves, to protect all women and children."

The code seems noble and a code that will protect women and non-combatants; however, it has several inherent flaws. One is the lack of knights who truly follow the code. Joffrey uses loopholes: His mother told him not to hit his wife, so he has Ser Boros and Ser Meryn of the Kingsguard do it. Those knights in turn protest that they are sworn to obey their king, even when he gives unchivalrous commands. Ser Jaime, Westeros's beloved champion, likewise protests that it's contradictory and too hard to follow: "So many vows ... they make you swear and swear. Defend the king. Obey the king. Keep his secrets. Do his bidding. Your life for his. But obey your father. Love your sister. Protect the innocent. Defend the weak. Respect the gods. Obey the laws. It's too much. No matter what you do, you're forsaking one vow or another" (II.796).

The Hound, Sandor Clegane, straightforwardly refuses to become a knight, as he knows his brother the knight has no apparent moral code at all. Tyrion thinks of Ser Gregor as an "unthinking brute who led with his rage" (II.686). Sandor tells a disbelieving Sansa, "There are no true knights, no more than there are gods. If you can't protect yourself, die and get out of the way of those who can. Sharp steel and strong arms rule this world, don't ever believe any different" (II.757).

The other problem with chivalry is that it lifts women onto a pedestal, as men must battle on their behalf and protect them from the world. However, this enforces the belief that women cannot protect themselves, and in fact teaches them not to learn self-reliance but instead to depend on the men around them. By treating women as children, it infantilizes them. "Chivalry exalts the sword that protects and (unconsciously) devalues the body that cannot protect itself, which leads to moral vulnerability" (Goguen 207).

Chivalry also dictates roles that too many characters cannot fit into. Sansa can be Jonquil, the heroine of romantic ballads, but Arya has no one to emulate in them. Likewise, no one tells Brienne of brave warrior women celebrated in song; they only label her as a "freak." The Black Brothers sing of "Brave Danny Flint" who disguises herself as a boy to join the Night's Watch, but this is a tragedy that ends with her gang rape and death; they have no ballads like "Mu Lan" or "The Famous Flower of Serving Men." Jon the bastard earns no knighthood but goes to the Wall to serve beside murderers and rapists. "Medieval chivalry was homophobic, sexist, classist, ableist, and probably racist too" (Goguen 214).

RELIGION

The Old Gods, the Heart Trees, are inherently feminine. Red and white, like purity and blood side by side, they suggest the power of nature. Trees are endless providers of food, like Mother Earth from which they spring. They represent the feminized Old Ways, gradually falling out of power as the modern religion takes hold. The associated Children of the Forest are shown as male and female, remnants from an older time. Wildlings worship the Heart Trees, with males and females as equals in their society.

The Seven New Gods of Westeros are Maiden, Mother, Crone, Father, Smith, Warrior, Stranger. Notably, the female gods are life stages, while only one of the male gods is. The Stranger is considered androgynous, "less and more than human, unknown and unknowable" (II.372), representing the outsider and sometimes death incarnate. Admittedly, this is a shade better than the Catholic trinity that the Seven are based on; its split of Father, Son, and Holy Ghost contains no woman at all, until one goes to Mother Mary and the female saints. These icons are problematic from a gender standpoint.

> Throughout history, Christianity has fixated on the masculine, sublimating, abandoning, or even condemning the feminine. In the Bible, Jesus grows and learns, teaches and tells stories. By contrast, Mary's actions are virginal and divine, without variation. She nurtures Jesus, protects him, and mourns his death. Thus, she is portrayed as an idealized mother rather than a person. While Jesus appears on the lap of his mother (often crowning her) or with female sinners at his feet, we never see him side by side with a female in equality. The diluted Western European image emphasized Mary's passive receptivity, as her virginity guided men toward spirituality without carnality—without, in fact, imperfect, real women [Frankel, *From Girl to Goddess* 265].

Most female Catholic saints are virgins, martyrs, widows, or celibate married women, all sexless maiden archetypes. Since women cannot give birth immaculately, they cannot imitate Mary, and are left with sexless paradigms they cannot live up to. "If she renounces the flesh, she is God's creature, redeemed by the savior, no less than is man," Simone de Beauvoir criticizes (170). Thus woman is forced to take oaths of chastity and self-denial to approach the divine. This is no feminine role model.

In Westeros, mothers and crones are as honored as the male deities. Certainly Maiden-Mother-Crone is a logical split, based on ancient folklore and archetype. The Maiden particularly is revered as an archetype of innocence and purity: "On Maiden's Day widows, mothers, and whores alike were barred from the septs, along with men, lest they profane the sacred songs of innocence" (IV.834). A feminist reading might regret the lack of a career woman goddess like Athena or warrior-huntress like Artemis, but these Westerosi gods are seen as the models for conformists like Catelyn and Sansa to follow. For someone like Arya, there is the terrible Stranger, the god of death she selects for herself. Catelyn also muses, "There was as much beauty in the Crone as in the Maiden, and the Mother could be fiercer than the Warrior" (II.497). Maiden and Mother are revered in Westeros, as are Lady Olenna and Old Nan, the wise old woman. The Crone as a figure of wisdom echoes back to older, more matriarchal sources. Even on patriarchal earth religions, "there were curious survivals in patriarchy of the wise Crone as a divinity essential to, and perhaps more powerful than, God-like Athene in her role of the wisdom of Zeus" or Sophia, the Judeo-Christian embodiment of wisdom (Walker 59).

In Pantheons, gods are personified archetypes, each representing part of the human experience. In fact, they are also voices inside ourselves: "Except for brief transcendent moments of unity, each one of us lives with inner plurality—plurality that is usually not even integrated" (Pearson 67). These inner voices pull us in different directions and teach us to be whole people. Daenerys surrounded by Jorah's caution, Doreah's femininity, Viserys's selfishness, Drogo's strength, is in training to become a queen.

Nonetheless, the Faith of the Seven is as gender-biased as medieval Catholicism is on earth, unsurprising as the Seven is inspired by Catholicism and the Trinity ("George R.R. Martin Interview"). One Septon notes, "The Father rules, the Warrior fights, the Smith labors, and together they perform all that is rightful for a man" (IV.527). Apparently, the lifecycle is "all that is rightful" for a woman.

The concept of sex only permitted for procreation appears in the Faith of the Seven, as it is said male and female were created different to "beget trueborn children" (IV.765). Likewise, prostitutes are reviled, as it is "base and sinful for women to sell their holy parts for coin" (IV.765), though at least they are called "holy parts" rather than "evil parts."

The High Septon (always male and equivalent to the pope) is a particularly sexist figure in book four. As he notes, "The wickedness of widows is well-known, and all women are wantons at heart, given to using their wiles and their beauty to work their wills on men" (V.723). Women in the clergy are allowed some power and autonomy: The Sparrows and Poor Fellows can be either gender. Likewise, the High Septon appoints a maiden, mother, and crone to be judges among their male counterparts, adding, "Who could be more suited to judge the wickedness of women?" (IV.931).

CLERGY

Men and women of Westeros who take holy orders have a few choices: Monastic orders of septons called "Brown Brothers" live in sep-

tries, monasteries of a sort, while independent septons wander the countryside with begging bowls, ministering to the poor. Up through the reign of Jaehaerys the Conciliator, the Faith had a strong military arm with the orders of the Faith Militant. The Faith had two fighting orders—the knights called the Warrior's Sons, and the humbler Poor Fellows, which admits men and women. They, however, are no shining knights, but cudgel-carrying wanderers who escort pilgrims between septs. Both orders were killed off and outlawed by Maegor the Cruel, that decree standing until the events of the fourth book.

During the War of the Five Kings, a group of holy men begin collecting the bones of those killed in septs and carrying them to King's Landing seeking justice. Men and women join them, calling themselves "sparrows" for the most common birds. The Sparrows and Poor Fellows represent crusaders, as men and women both journeyed on the Crusades as warriors for their faith.

In Westeros, women become septas—their white, gray or blue robes presumably correspond to rank and/or their service to maiden, mother, and crone. Some Septas are governesses to highborn girls, like Sansa's constant companion Septa Mordane (killed in the books along with the rest of the Stark household). Convents of septas are called "motherhouses," with a large one in Oldtown. High ranking septas judge in trials and aid in electing the High Septon. According to Ned Stark, a woman cannot be High Septon, much like the pope. In the five existing books, no female characters come from the clergy, aside from Septa Mordane. (Admittedly, few septons feature in the plot either.)

The Silent Sisters, sworn to be brides of the Stranger, are a chilling archetype. They cowl themselves in gray, leaving only their eyes showing, and never speak a word. They clean and remove the flesh from dead bodies, especially the noble dead, and carry the bodies across the country. Septon Meribald explains to Podrick Payne and Brienne, "A vow of silence is an act of contrition, a sacrifice by which we prove our devotion to the Seven Above" (IV.657). However, he, as a man, is not performing the contrition. As such, they appear to represent many veiled, voiceless women throughout the world, forced to serve others and forbidden to vote, write, or speak out.

The history and current politics of Westeros involve sending uppity or uncontrollable women into their ranks—Theon threatens to send his sister there and Sandor Clegane considers sending Arya, noting, "If I had any sense, I'd give you to the silent sisters. They cut the tongues out of girls who talk too much" (III.885). To get rid of Falyse Stokeworth and keep her from talking, Cersei suggests she join, before she changes her mind and sends her to be tortured and killed. Minor characters are condemned there as well: When King Aegon IV Targaryen promised his armsmaster Ser Quentyn Ball a place in the Kingsguard, Quentyn forced his wife to join, so he could be a celibate knight. A daughter of Ser Elys Waynwood loses her virginity and joins. Ser Wylis Manderly threatens to send his daughter to the silent sisters if she refuses to wed Walder Frey. Tyrion believes a female dwarf dwells among their number. All those whom society no longer wants, like widows, are encouraged to join and unceremoniously dumped in the place. The Silent Sisters are considered unlucky and disturbing, but that doesn't stop roving marauders from raping them. They are society's discards, like the series' many prostitutes.

Ned's religion hasn't shown any religious leaders of either gender, only private contemplation before a heart tree. By contrast, dhampirs of the Drowned God (from the Iron Islands) appear to be male—hardly surprising in their sexist culture. Red Priests and Priestesses can be either, though Melisandre's sex magic suggests the female acolytes receive a different sort of training from the men. The many gods of death, seen in Braavos, seem the most balanced among genders, albeit with a disturbing twist.

Men in the Gender Biased System

Men's comments are just as gender-biased, of course. Craster asks Jon if he's a girl, noting that he's pretty enough. Jaime smirks that King Robb hides behind his mother's skirts. "Are you training women here?" the Hound asks the Winterfell armsmaster Ser Rodrik when he refuses to let Joffrey and Robb fight with live steel (I.74). Ser Rodrik appears offended by the challenge. Upon hearing that he'll be a steward, Jon wonders if he'll have to sew doublets and churn butter like a girl. By contrast, Jon's joke to Robb that he'll keep Westeros safe "so he might as well take up needlework with the girls" is more lighthearted (I.212).

"Mothers. I think birthing does something to your minds. You are all mad," Jaime tells Circe (I.82)

Meanwhile, some men are confined in their gender roles just as women are. Pearson explains that men following traditional paths will be the seeker or warrior archetypes: leaders and questors who are action-oriented rather than relationship-oriented (260). Brienne's father, Yara's father, and Arya's father all acknowledge their daughters' talents and arrange for them to learn fighting and similar skills as they embark on men's traditional paths. By contrast, Sam's father is horrified by his non-traditional attitude: "Whatever pride his lord father might have felt at Samwell's birth vanished as the boy grew up plump, soft, and awkward.... His passions were books and kittens and dancing, clumsy as he was. But he grew ill at the sight of blood, and wept to see even a chicken slaughtered" (I.268).

One armsmaster makes Sam sleep in armor; another parades him around in his mother's gown to shame him. His cruel father, wielder of the sword Heartsbane (symbolic in itself), lets him choose between the Wall and death. Though Sam has many talents, fighting is the only one that matters. Up north, Ser Allister Thorne makes Jon "defend his lady love" and calls Sam "Lady Piggy" (I.261). To him as well, a man who cannot fight is nothing. To save him from Thorne, Jon suggests Sam's talents will be useful to Maester Aemon, but it's Sam's manly deed—slaying a weight—that earns him respect and admiration from the callous Night's Watch. Theon's father similarly rejects his son upon hearing he's been castrated and can't further the family name. Brent Hartinger comments in "A Different Kind of Other: The Role of Freaks and Outcasts in *A Song of Ice and Fire*":

> [O]f the series' fourteen major point-of-view characters to date—Tyrion, Arya, Jon, Daenerys, Bran, Samwell, Brienne, Catelyn, Jaime, Cersei, Eddard, Davos, Theon, and Sansa—at least the first seven violate major gender or social norms. [Jaime and Theon are soon maimed, and Catelyn and Sansa are transformed into shadows of their former selves.] Until just the last few decades, individuals such as these have typically been treated as objects of scorn, ridicule, or pity—not just in most literature, but in the Western civilization that this literature has reflected [154].

Martin makes these outcasts point-of-view characters and heroes: Bran learns to ride, but more importantly, opens his mind and becomes a greenseer and warg. Tyrion outwits his enemies on many occasions. "My brother, Jaime, has his swords and I have my mind," he explains (1.1). All use non-traditional approaches to succeed in their world. Even Barristan, a celebrated knight, turns flexible in his exile. When Daenerys threatens to demote Barristan to her cook as punishment for hiding his identity, he accepts with "quiet dignity," saying, "I can bake apples and boil beef as well as any man, and I've roasted many a duck over a campfire" (III.988).

In their society of chivalry and manliness, Tyrion and Bran are handicapped in ways that won't let them become warriors (though Tyrion tries at times). In battle, Tyrion uses his disability, pointing out that if he is a halfman, he's showing more bravery than the men refusing to leave the Red Keep. Tyrion's advice to Jon in the first episode defines him clearly for the audience:

> *Tyrion Lannister:* Let me tell you something, Bastard. Never forget what you are, the rest of the world will not. Wear it like armor and it can never be used to hurt you.
> *Jon Snow:* What the hell do you know about being a bastard?
> *Tyrion Lannister:* All dwarfs are bastards in their father's eyes.

Several characters, including King Robert, Joffrey, and the Winterfell bannermen, whisper that it would be most merciful to let Bran die; since he cannot be a knight or father, little remains that's worthwhile. Tyrion likewise reflects that many families would have killed him as a baby. Tywin adds, "The day that you were born. I wanted to carry you into the sea and let the waves wash you away. Instead, I let you live. And I brought you as my son. Because you're a Lannister" (3.10). Varys, unsurprisingly, takes a different view:

> *Lord Varys:* How is your son, my lord?
> *Eddard Stark:* He'll never walk again.
> *Lord Varys:* But his mind is sound?
> *Eddard Stark:* So they say.
> *Lord Varys:* A blessing, then. I suffered an early mutilation myself. Some doors close forever, others open in most unexpected places ["The Wolf and the Lion," 1.5].

In the third season, Varys reveals the story of his maiming. Though he tells it lightly, with a "happy ending" of becoming rich and powerful, even gaining revenge on the sorcerer, his experience was a trauma still affecting his actions. "Step by step, one distasteful task after another, I made my way from the slums of Myr to the small chamber," he explains. He is the true outsider of the story. As a eunuch and foreigner, he appears to have fewer personal motivations than everyone else at court. He has no family ties, love interests, or grudges in Westeros, unlike every other character. Several people comment that it's impossible to tell what he wants. "Why is it no one ever trusts the eunuch?" Varys asks (1.8). He mentions that King Robert, "such a manly man, has little love for sneaks and spies and eunuchs" (I.321). Nonetheless, Varys becomes a survivalist, lasting through Aerys and Robert as well as the Lannisters. As he puts it, "The storms come and go, the big fish eat the little fish and I keep on paddling" (2.2).

He often codes himself feminine or others do, as he notes, "I do so hate the sight of blood" (1.8) and courtiers mutter that poison is a woman's weapon ... or a eunuch's. He dresses in silks and velvet and smells of lilac, and he's never seen fighting. He's also a master of disguise, even wearing women's clothes on occasion.

> Eddard Stark: You watched my men being slaughtered and did nothing.
> Lord Varys: And would again, my lord. I was unarmed, unarmored, and surrounded by Lannister swords. When you look at me, do you see a hero? ["The Pointy End" 1.8].

Likewise, Tyrion reflects that if he fights on his own behalf, he'll die with "gales of laughter ringing in his ears" (III.899). In a world where those in power can appoint giant Gregor "The Mountain" Clegane as their champions, finding the dishonorable proxy Bronn, one who not only defends himself but uses laws of the street, becomes the only option. "The rules are rigged: they're set up by and for kings and princes with well-trained, well-armored champions. Tyrion and Varys might not fight fair, but it wasn't a fair fight to begin with. If they play the game the way it's intended to be played, the outcasts always lose" (Hartinger 162). Bran, Tyrion, and Varys fortify their minds instead of their bodies, but they are constantly reminded they are "cripples, bastards, and broken things"—less than men in their ableist world. As Hartinger adds:

> Varys is a fat, bald, effeminate eunuch. He's also a master of information, using his "little birds" to constantly spy on those around him, manipulating everyone, always for his own secretive ends. He'll do what needs to be done, even if it sometimes means betraying friends and allies. But how much of

Varys's paranoia and ruthlessness are the result of his own horrible powerlessness when, as a boy, he was forced to take a drug that paralyzed him—
but did not shield him from pain—so he could be involuntarily castrated?
Surely his perspective is also colored by the fact that as an adult, most people
see him as a freak, and he knows better than anyone exactly what kind of
justice a freak usually receives [160–61].

In modern gender scholarship, these characters are coded as queer—
this is not to say that Bran or Jojen is homosexual—and indeed, many
of these outcasts like Tyrion and Sam are clearly interested in women.
"Queer" in this context does not mean the opposite of heterosexual—it
is "an identity without essence" marking "whatever is at odds with the
normal, the legitimate, the dominant" (Halperin 62). They are queer
because they establish nonconformist lifestyles in the incredibly binary
medieval society of brawling men and dainty ladies.

Other male characters must struggle to conform in public. A man
crowns a woman queen of beauty in tournaments, so Loras tosses a rose
to Sansa, though Renly is the secret object of his affection. "Chivalry
dictates gender roles, and heterosexuality is woven throughout the
chivalric interpretation of gender," notes Stacy Goguen in her essay on
the series, "'There Are No True Knights': The Injustice of Chivalry." As
a king, Renly publicly marries Margaery, though in private he prefers
her brother and has trouble consummating the marriage. Likewise, Loras
is betrothed to Sansa and then Cersei because admitting publicly that
he will not marry a woman is unthinkable.

The series is filled with outcasts of other sorts: bastards, hostages,
exiles, and lowborn men include Jon Snow, Ramsay Snow, Littlefinger,
the Blackfish, Theon, Gendry, Bronn, Ser Jorah, Ser Barristan, and the
men of the Night's Watch—the ultimate outcasts. The Brotherhood
Without Banners are likewise a society of outcasts who have left the feudal system to defend the entire kingdom, and the Faceless Men too can
never be part of society. There are foreigners and minority religions,
including the fading Old Gods. Many characters, like Beric Dondarrion,
the Hound, and Shireen Baratheon are terribly scarred or maimed. "Even
Jaime Lannister finds himself with a new perspective when he becomes
an outcast of sorts after losing a hand to Vargo Hoat" (Hartinger 165).
Another outcast, the one-armed blacksmith Donal Noye, gives Jon a lesson on being an outsider. "They hate me because I'm better than they

are," Jon complains. "No," Donal responds. "They hate you because you act like you're better than they are" (I.182). His privileged training has not truly made him better than his brothers.

In the series, many outcasts make friendships or alliances. Jon, who grew up as the bastard of Winterfell, sympathizes instantly with Sam. Tyrion and Varys enjoy playing the political game in a way that physically powerful Robert and Ned never did. Tyrion falls for Shae and protects Ros. Tyrion and Sansa form an understanding:

> Tyrion Lannister: My lady, people have been laughing at me far longer than they've been laughing at you. I'm the Half-Man, the Demon-Monkey, the Imp.
> Sansa Stark: You're a Lannister. I am the disgraced daughter of the traitor, Ned Stark.
> Tyrion Lannister: The disgraced daughter and the demon monkey. We're perfect for each other ["Mhysa," 3.10].

Perhaps they are.

Women Despise Men by Despising Women

Several women put men down by calling them women. This speech trend emphasizes gender is a performance: Men can have feminine qualities, and women, masculine ones. In itself this is a positive step toward escaping rigid gender rules. However, these words also indicate the women's denigration of their own sex. Calling a weak man a woman means women are weak and undesirable. When Jaime bemoans losing his hand, Brienne retorts, "You have a taste, only a taste, of the real world where people have important things taken from them. And you whine and cry and quit. You sound like a bloody woman" (3.4).

Rhiannon notes that this exchange "suggests that there is some antifeminine sentiment going on in the writing of her character. Brienne, it seems, has somehow overcome the fact that she is a woman. She has transcended her femininity and become a warrior instead, and so she of course hates those *normal* women" ("*Game of Thrones*: Not the Women They Were Before"). Jaime in turn thinks to himself, "It was his right hand that made him a knight, his right hand that made him a man" (III.416). Manliness is about action in this system, and femininity about talking and quitting. If this is the case, it's no surprise Brienne performs masculinity.

Likewise, Ygritte teases Jon, noting that he was "a maid" (III.364). By contrast, she notes, "I am nineteen, and a spearwife, and kissed by fire. How could I be maiden?" (III.365). On the show she boasts of her relationship conquests, reversing the traditional gender roles. She is the "spearwife" of the relationship, while Jon is younger and more innocent. He seems a bit offended by the gender roles she casts them in, and in retaliation, he's quick to condescend when they reach Westeros, as he suggests she'll faint at the sight of a castle. In true warrior fashion, she's never even heard the word "faint" before.

When Prendahl of the Stormcrows calls Daenerys "woman," she quips, "Is that meant to insult me? I would return the slap, if I took you for a man" (III.576). While she specifically does not consider "woman" to be an insult, disputing his manliness suggests he too is a woman, a problematic bit of diction.

Cersei's anger at being stuck as a woman in a man's world appears many times in the books, especially in her own thoughts. She protects the castle's women in the Battle of Blackwater, but tells Sansa that none of the women are important—only their husbands. Most especially, she envies the men she thinks are doing a worse job with their entitlement than she would, like ill Lord Gyles. "The gods must have been mad to waste manhood on the likes of him," she thinks (II.848). On the show, she tells Tywin:

> Did it ever occur to you that I am the one that deserves your confidence and your trust? Not your sons. Not Jaime or Tyrion, but me. Years and years of lectures on family and legacy—the same lecture really, just with tiny tedious variations. Did it ever occur to you that your daughter might be the only one listening to them, living by them, that she might have the most to contribute? ["And Now His Watch Is Ended," 3.4].

He rebuffs her the way all the other patriarchs do. Cersei likewise mocks Robert: "What a jape the gods have made of us two. By all rights, you ought to be in skirts and me in mail" (I.429). She tells Jaime, "A pity Lord Tywin Lannister never had a son. I could have been the heir he wanted, but I lacked the cock" (III.1005). She is pleased about christening a new ship *Lord Tywin* because "she looked forward to hearing men speak of her father as 'she.'" By contrast, the ship *Sweet Cersei* will have a figurehead of her, with "mail and lion helm, with spear in hand," though she has never worn such things (IV.590). To Cersei, tears are "the woman's weapon, my mother used to call them" (II.845). Though she's obsessed with gender roles, she herself uses manipulation, poison, and seduction to play politics, rather than learning swordplay or other manly pursuits.

Yara's diction in "The Prince of Winterfell" (2.8) when she visits her brother Theon in the north is likewise gender-biased. Rhiannon comments:

> This episode had so many uses of the word c*nt that it's like they were trying to fulfill a particularly demanding quota—perhaps competing for the world record? (And yes, I will censor it here, because I cringe at the word on a gut-reaction level.) … [Yara] repeatedly called her little brother a c*nt, creating the weird set-up of a badass woman calling a man a misogynistic insult, because the ultimate sign of weakness and patheticness is to be a woman. And hey, perhaps Yara is misogynistic. Maybe she also believes she's "not like other girls" ["Are 'Most Women Stupid?'"].

In the fifth book, by contrast, Asha resents men for yelling that label at her on the battlefield, noting, "Cunt again? It was odd how men like Suggs used that word to demean women when it was the only part of a woman they valued" (V.349).

Arya likewise names two stupid bravos "camel cunts" (IV.549). Women who are so "strong" that they insult men by saying they have female body parts goes in the same category as Arya's "most girls are stupid" comment. By raising themselves up, these women denigrate all the other women of the world.

Men's Attitudes Toward Women

In this highly patriarchal world, all men are sexist to some degree. However, misogyny is often correlated with evil. Joffrey is a creep, and torturing women is just part of torturing everyone. King Robert screams, "You do not tell me what to do, woman" in public (I.300) and hits Cersei in private. He's likewise disturbed by leaving young Robert Arryn to be "raised by women," adding, "The boy is my namesake, did you know that? Robert Arryn. I am sworn to protect him. How can I do that if his mother steals him away?" (I.45). It's clear that Cersei's example, con-trasted against the powerful king's, has done little to teach their son.

Theon is dismissive of women, bedding and abandoning the cap-tain's unimpressive daughter as he sails for home. To him, his sister is an unfeminine freak who nonetheless will acquiesce to being married off. Meanwhile, Theon falls for her when they meet, for he believes female sailors get "a man's appetites" and admires Asha for her bold flirting (II.378). At the same time, he keeps pushing her to give in to him sexually despite her repeated refusals. Though her excuse that she's married and pregnant is a lie, Theon's harassment of a woman who keeps refusing him shows how little he cares for her beyond what he wants for himself. Once he realizes who she is, Theon calls his sister an "unnatural creature" and says she isn't fit for marriage (II.393). Theon likewise dismisses Osha, who tricks him back at Winterfell. By the fifth book, however, he becomes sympathetic to a young woman and saves her, indicating he's finally learned from his adventures.

Daenerys spends much of her time facing down the patriarchy. "The Copper King offers me a single ship on the condition that I lie with him for a night. Does he think I will whore myself for a boat?" she asks Xaro (2.6).

When Dany points out that she won't marry him because of his sweet words, Xaro says, "I have traveled very far in my life and met many women and none that are immune to flattery" (2.6). Though he manages to seduce her maid, Daenerys remains immune to his charms.

In the third season, the slaver of Astapor calls her a bitch and slut in each of their exchanges, confident that she doesn't speak his language. The sellswords battling Yunkai are just as vile: Mero, the "Titan's bastard," spanks Missandei and asks Daenerys to strip and sit on his lap. "If you please me, I might bring the second sons over to your side."

"If you bring the Second Sons over to my side, I might not have you gelded," she retorts (III.576). While she's offended by his behavior, she balances strength and diplomacy in their exchange. Only afterwards does she tell Ser Barristan to "kill that one first" ("Second Sons," 3.8). Daenerys also uses her knowledge of gender politics, noting, "A man who fights for gold can't afford to lose to a girl" (3.8).

While Ned Stark indulges Arya's desire for fencing lessons, he still expects her to have a traditional marriage.

> Arya cocked her head to one side. "Can I be a king's councilor and build castles and become the High Septon?"
>
> "You," Ned said, kissing her lightly on the brow, "will marry a king and rule his castle, and your sons will be knights and princes and lords and, yes, perhaps even a High Septon."
>
> Arya screwed up her face. "No," she said, "that's Sansa." She folded up her right leg and resumed her balancing. Ned sighed and left her there [I.256].

When he finds Needle, he says, "This is no weapon for a child, least of all for a girl" (I.220). As such, he presents himself as the establishment as well as a loving father; his understanding will only stretch to a point.

Outside the city, Thoros of Myr and Lord Tywin give Arya respect while they observe that she's a girl, though Tywin is certain she's hiding something. Tywin admires Arya on the show and comments that she reminds him of Cersei. He's clearly willing to deal with strong women like Lady Olenna, and he gives Arya a boy's tasks and listens to her thoughts. "You're a dangerous person. I like dangerous people," Thoros notes politely (3.2). Gendry too treats Arya as a friend and comrade.

Lord Tarly is as cruel to women breaking gender rules as he is to his son Sam. Tarly tells Brienne, "You never should have donned mail, nor buckled on a sword. You never should have left your father's home.... When you're raped, don't look to me for justice. You will have earned it with your folly" (IV.295–96).

Theon's father, Balon Greyjoy, seems more flexible. He only values manly strength, but he's happy to train his daughter to it, as his last remaining child. However, he has nothing but contempt for Theon, asking if Ned Stark was pleased "to garb you in velvets and silks and make you his own sweet daughter?" (II.183) and adding that while Asha has chosen the axe, Theon garbs himself in trinkets "like a whore" (II.184). When Theon is castrated and "cannot further the Greyjoy line," his father abandons him on the show (3.10).

Jaime Lannister begins as the establishment—not terribly misogynist, but used to men's and women's roles. He agonizes over how the mad king treats his wife and resents Robert for similar abuses. Jaime begins his association with Brienne making snide remarks about her gender, like "You move well ... for a great beast of a woman" (3.2). In the following episode, Brienne retorts that he was barely holding his own against a woman. However, he acts to save her from being raped and she in turn comforts him after the loss of his hand. He returns to haul her out of the bear pit and comes to respect her and her code of honor. His journey from misogyny to sympathy mirrors his growth toward morality and wisdom.

His change also comes with his transformation from insider to outsider—from the famous, popular Jaime Lannister to a crippled stranger who goes unrecognized when he returns to King's Landing. In the books, he beheads the soldier who has been repeatedly raping the servant girl Pia and then saves her by giving her a job. He shows talent with politics, arguing several lords into peaceful surrenders. He begins to discover who he is beyond talented swordfighter and accursed kingslayer.

Other outsiders also act sympathetically toward women, recognizing that all of them are demeaned by society. "Who is it that finally treats Brienne with kindness and is able to see beyond the limitations of his culture, recognizing her for what she is? It's Renly Baratheon, a closeted gay man secretly in love with the Knight of Flowers" (Hartinger 159). In his other dealings, Renly negotiates politely with Catelyn and proves himself flexible, in contrast with the hidebound Stannis.

Jon too shows the flexibility of an outsider: He gives Arya Needle and loves her the way she is. Beyond the Wall, Jon falls for Ygritte, another strong woman. When placed in command, Jon acknowledges that wildling women can fight as well as men, but segregates them for their protection. Jon is perceptive enough to identify girls trying to mix in among the black brothers' pages, and he forbids them, remembering the tragedy of a girl in a ballad who joined up. He proves wise and fair with the women under his command.

Fan Reactions

Many of the online posts focus on the controversies on the series, as fans discuss some of the more disturbing tropes. Nonetheless, the basic truth is that most people posting about the show, or writing books about it, are enthusiastic fans who wait for each episode with desperate anticipation. If a person hates a show, he or she will probably ignore it, not search online to discover posts about it and respond to those posts. Keeping this in mind, the posts seem to fall into two camps:

1. A woman writes that the show in unwatchable by women, mentioning the nudity and violence, and also referencing fantasy as a male fandom. Many fans, especially women, post hundreds of responses and quote the article in their own posts to contradict it. They point out that they are definite fantasy fans, and appear to resent a non-fantasy fan who happens to be female dictating what females should and shouldn't like.

2. A feminist site posts that the show is enjoyable despite the sex and

violence or that the show made a particular race or feminist mistake. These articles get mostly supportive comments and minor quibbles. Most of these articles describe Daenerys, Arya, and Brienne as wonderful characters, though responses to Catelyn, Sansa, and Cersei are divided. The myriad of female characters, some strong, some weak, is generally celebrated as is their fight against misogyny in Westeros.

To preserve a segment of fan culture and share the multitude of opinions, a selection of responses from magazines and blogs has been included below.

> George R.R. Martin is creepy.... He is creepy, primarily, because of his TWENTY THOUSAND MILLION GRATUITOUS RAPE AND/OR MOLESTATION AND/OR DOMESTIC VIOLENCE SCENES.
> —Sady Doyle, *Tiger Beatdown* (qtd. in Rosenberg 16)

> As well as being mightily entertaining, *Game of Thrones* is racist rape-culture Disneyland with Dragons. To say that this series is problematic in its handling of race and gender is a little like saying that Mitt Romney is rich: technically accurate, but an understatement so profound that it obscures more than it reveals. Take, for example, one single subplot: A very young princess, a blonde and beautiful thirteen-year-old virgin whose remarkable fairness of complexion is a motif of the series, is sold off as a child-bride by her unscrupulous brother, a man who likes to have sex whilst talking about dragons in the bath.
> The unfortunate girl's new husband is a dark-skinned, savage warlord from the Mystical East who, being a savage, is unable to conceive of any sex that isn't exclusively rape-based, and as such violently assaults the little princess every night. But it's all ok because a prostitute slave teaches the thirteen-year-old princess super sexy sex skills, and she proceeds to blow the warlord's mind so thoroughly that they fall in love. Later in the series she uses her magical blondness and a bunch of baby dragons to free all the slaves in the Mystical East. If the enormous teetering pile of ugly stereotypes here is not immediately obvious, see me after class and we'll go through it step by step.
> —Laurie Penny, *New Statesman*

> In my books, *Game of Thrones* is not feminist. There seems to be just too much gender-based violence, too much gratuitous girl-on-girl action (rather than actual lesbian desire) and too much of a nudity imbalance for *Game of Thrones* to be truly feminist. It is however, bloody entertaining and if we had to limit our consump-

tion of media to things that are 100 percent feminist we wouldn't be able to read or watch anything, ever. So proceed with caution and enjoy if you can.

—Elizabeth Mulhall, *Literatico*

The imagined historical universe of *Game of Thrones* gives license for unhindered bed-jumping—here sibling intimacy is hardly confined to emotional exchange. The true perversion, though, is the sense you get that all of this illicitness has been tossed in as a little something for the ladies, out of a justifiable fear, perhaps, that no woman alive would watch otherwise. While I do not doubt that there are women in the world who read books like Mr. Martin's, I can honestly say that I have never met a single woman who has stood up in indignation at her book club and refused to read the latest from Lorrie Moore unless everyone agreed to *The Hobbit* first. *Game of Thrones* is boy fiction patronizingly turned out to reach the population's other half.

—Ginia Bellafante, *The New York Times*

A Song of Ice and Fire seems determined to tell us that people cannot be easily categorized. The loving mother can also be a spiteful murderer. A man can kill a king for a good reason, and attempt to kill a boy for a terrible one. The sister who fights with a sword and the sister who fights with smiles both have their strengths and weaknesses, and both will work hard to survive. But when it comes to female characters, the show doesn't seem interested in all that. Much better to fit the characters into the categories they try to transcend, the "masculine" or the "feminine," the weak dreaming girl or the bold love interest who's not like those silly other things.

If the show existed on its own, these tropes would probably not even be noticeable. They are, after all, common tropes. But when the books present us with such rich characters, and the show decides to force them into those tropes anyway, it suddenly seems startlingly obvious. Why have these complexities, the show seems to say, when these basic tropes are more appealing?

—Rhiannon, "*Game of Thrones*: Not the Women They Were Before," *Feminist Fiction*

Seven Reasons Women Love *Game of Thrones*

3. One of *Game of Thrones*' major themes is love.
And speaking of lost love ... much of *Game of Thrones* is devoted to showing the damage it does to people's hearts to live in a turbulent feudal aristocracy where marriages are arranged purely for tactical reasons. On this show, love conquers Tyrion Lannister's sex

addiction, Robb Stark's need for an army, and death itself (well, almost). If that's not romantic, I don't know what is.

4. Another major theme? Female pleasure.

Sure, it's unrealistic that all those male virgins are so good at sex. But it still sends the message that men should want to be good at sex. That they should care about pleasing their women and not just rut on them like a bunch of wildling savages. That they should go down on their ladies for as long as the ladies like! Even though nobody showers in *Game of Thrones* world! If that's not commitment to the female orgasm, I don't know what is.

—Jamie Peck, *The Gloss*

If I were to identify the central theme of *Game of Thrones,* it would be power. Some characters have a lot of it; some don't. The show asks questions about what people are willing to do to acquire power, what they do with it once they get it, and how they handle themselves if they lose it. *Game of Thrones* is set in a highly patriarchal fantasy world, which means that society works to rob women of power. But instead of accepting this as a given, the show asks how women face up to their powerlessness in this world, and how they might empower themselves despite the strictures of the societies they live in. This doesn't always result in "strong ass-kicking badass women" (though sometimes it does)—more importantly, it results in some of the most three-dimensional and well-developed female characters in the whole fantasy genre.

—Luz Delfondo, *Disrupting Dinner
Parties: Feminism for Everyone*

Game of Thrones ranks somewhere on the Girl Dislike scale between NASCAR and that National Geographic show where the guy sticks his hand in a catfish's mouth. But why does she throw so much shade? If you just can't understand why we're intent on harshing your medieval buzz, here are some telltale clues.

• We hate gross things. Know what's gross? Screwing your sibling.

• It's hard to follow. Brilliantly developed storylines are great, but whipping out a dry erase board and Venn diagrams to figure it all out isn't our idea of a good time. Unless we're talking about soap operas. Those are perfectly fine.

• It reminds us of the kids that used to play magic cards in the cafeteria. And people who go to Renaissance festivals. Eating a giant drumstick and drinking out of a goblet is cool, just not every Sunday night for three months straight.

• It's all naked chicks. In addition to the actual ladies of the night on the show, there seem to be a lot of … unofficial ladies of the

night on the show. This is why guys love it, we get it, but we can do without seeing topless wenches in loin cloths.
- Dudes get their hands chopped off. And their nipples. And their balls. Really? How is it that you guys like this again?

—Renata Sellitti, Thrillist

Some women like *GoT* because it's simply a good show. Others like myself appreciate it not only because we appreciate good story-telling, but because we appreciate the nuances of gender relations within the story and the world in which it takes place. In a series that is arguably focused more heavily on women than men, it can't be said that this fandom belongs to men alone. Not only are women watching this so-called man's show, we take part in it. We love it, we analyze it, and we critique it. We make fan art, write fan fiction, cosplay, and go to conventions covered in dragon eggs. And to the dismay of sexists like those at *Thrillist,* we make it a feminist issue, because the politics of both the show and the books require that we do so.

—"Shocker (Not): Women Like Game
of Thrones," Persephone Magazine

Too often, TV shows lack a strong, relatable, and realistic female character. Thankfully, despite being "a show for boys," *Game of Thrones* is jam-packed with amazing female characters. Watching Daenerys transform from a weak noble pawn to a powerful leader is truly inspirational, and characters like Brienne and Ygritte are easy to root for. Hey, there's a reason Arya is one of the fastest-growing baby names in America, and that reason is simple. Men and women both love *Game of Thrones.*

—Tucker Cummings, Yahoo TV

When people talk about wanting to see "strong female characters," this is what we're talking about. Not an army of superhuman, you-go-girl ass-kickers with no complicating romantic lives or moral failings, but a glorious array of faceted, complex, problematic, not-sure-if-they-can-be-trusted human beings.... These ladies pass the Bechdel Test so fast they break the sound barrier.... What *GoT* has going for it is sheer numbers. Characters like Brienne and Arya and Olenna Tyrell and Melisandre [etc.] ... [T]hey are what more TV shows—and movies, for that matter—need to look like so that we don't have to look so assiduously for sparks of feminism in the ones that we have.

—Andi Zeisler, Bitch Magazine

Sexual violence is a disturbing theme in *A Song of Ice and Fire.* *Game of Thrones* actually tones it down, which will come as a surprise to anyone who has seen the show but not read the books. To me, though, it only slightly exaggerates the horrors women are subjected to in reality. Martin combats that violence by proving that even with such an oppressive framework, women are just as capable as men of rising to the challenge and manipulating the system in their favor. Perhaps even more so. The women of Westeros are not the delicate ladies or trophy wives they were raised to be. They kick ass, often and powerfully, and fight to the death (or beyond?) for what they want.

—Jenna Sackler, *Feminists at Large*

Game of Thrones persuasively demonstrates why some of us are always yammering on about the need for increased representation of women (and minorities) on television: Through the relatively simple process of upping the numbers, the burden on any individual woman magically lightens. No single character in *Game of Thrones* has to be the show's final word on womanhood, and that's a freeing prospect. I can find Melisandre a dinner-theater–esque take on the sorceress archetype; you can find Daenerys an appalling victim of untreated Stockholm syndrome. But it's OK. With the women of *Game of Thrones*, you don't have to put all your dragon eggs in one basket.

—Nina Rastogi, *Salon*

Obviously, fan reactions come down strongly on both sides as blogs, pop culture magazines, and even *The New York Times* weigh in. As the show stirs up ever-increasing debate, its popularity also soars. Even with its flaws, it's scoring millions of viewers from all races, classes, nationalities, and genders.

Conclusion

Since season one, the series has been heading in a better direction:

Season 3 reduced the amount of sex and nudity, at least in frequency. Where the first and second seasons featured sex and/or nudity in 10 out of 10 and 8 out of 10 episodes, respectively, the third season got sexually explicit in only 5 out of 10.... Of course, it wouldn't be *Game of Thrones* without also including a few trips to Lord Baelish's bordello, but on the whole, the sex this season felt more organic to the story than in the past (Noble).

With the naked women less often presented as objects, the genders are becoming more balanced. Conqueror Daenerys no longer lives to please her khal, but crushes the patriarchy in Slaver's Bay. Olenna and Margaery scheme in King's Landing, offering additional players beyond the selfish Cersei.

The difficulty appears when women are shown with two paths: masculinized women who hate their own sex and feminized women who are ineffectual and victimized. "A woman is handicapped by her sex, and handicaps society, either by slavishly copying the pattern of man's advance in the professions, or by refusing to compete with man at all," Friedan notes (509). The issue of male gaze is also a factor, and women are once again drawn away from female values and identity, and forced to comply with male ones. "The woman who identifies with a female character must adopt a passive or masochistic position, while identification with the active hero necessarily entails an acceptance of what Laura Mulvey refers to as a certain 'masculinization' of spectatorship" (Doane 5–6). Women shine as role models when they are allowed to utilize all their skills as warriors, intellectuals, mothers, lovers, and queens, and when they're allowed to identify with a sparkling, active heroine, not just the men as rulers of their society.

When the only female role model becomes one like Yara or Arya, powerful independent girls who think girls who enjoy painting, or gardening, or even sewing are "stupid," many girls devalue themselves and find they have no role model. One should be able to be a mother without becoming scheming Cersei, wimpy Gilly, or (on the show) irrational Catelyn. Readers interested in adult fantasy novels with clever women from all ages and backgrounds should seek out works by Marion Zimmer Bradley, Andre Norton, Juliet Marillier, Anne Bishop, and more.

Meanwhile, Martin's books continue, with two more to be published. With emerging female characters like the Sand Snakes, Arianne of Dorne, and Asha/Yara taking stronger roles, many intriguing arcs are coming. Daenerys must fulfill her destiny, but other women are rising as well: Sansa is gaining skill at dissembling and Margaery and Cersei have yet to resolve their conflict over King's Landing. Melisandre will wield her powers in the war of ice and fire, and Arya will choose her life path. Martin has also promised more of Osha and her quest to protect Rickon on an isle of monsters and magic. The story may have begun with Ned and Robert, but it will finish with the women.

An upcoming prequel novella, "The Princess and the Queen," is coming in 2013 with the epic battle of two Targaryen rulers, Rhaenyra and the Dowager Queen Alicent. As Queen Alicent puts her reluctant son Aegon forward for his half-sister's throne, a terrible civil war engulfs Westeros. This story will offer other impressive female characters, including Baela Targaryen, the teenage dragonrider called Nettles, and Alys Rivers, a seer. As an early review notes, "All are secondary characters, but they make quite an impression even in the midst of all the macho posturing, chest-thumping, limb-hacking, and throne-stealing" (McGovern). In 2014, *The World of Ice and Fire: The Official History of Westeros and the World of* A Game of Thrones by George R.R. Martin, Elio Garcia and Linda Antonsson will feature other heroines and queens from ancient days of Westeros. As the world expands, more dazzling she-wolves and swordswomen will appear.

So is the show problematic or empowering? Without question, it's both. Fans of both genders cheer when Arya mouths off once more or Daenerys rides proudly through the east in her short blue conqueror's gown, surrounded by her new army. Nonetheless, even the most devoted fans must remember that women are more than warriors, prostitutes, and damsels—they are people. And that's something the show too often leaves out.

Appendix 1: Cast

George R.R. Martin—Author
David Benioff, D.B. Weiss—Executive Producers

Starring

Aidan Gillen as Lord Petyr Baelish
Alfie Allen as Theon Greyjoy
Carice van Houten as Lady Melisandre
Charles Dance as Tywin Lannister
Emilia Clarke as Daenerys Targaryen
Gwendoline Christie as Brienne of Tarth
Harry Lloyd as Prince Viserys Targaryen
Iain Glen as Ser Jorah Mormont
Isaac Hempstead-Wright as Bran Stark
Jack Gleeson as Joffrey Baratheon
Jason Momoa as Khal Drogo
Joe Dempsie as Gendry
John Bradley as Samwell Tarly
Kit Harington as John Snow
Lena Headey as Queen Cersei Lannister
Liam Cunningham as Ser Davos Seaworth
Maisie Williams as Arya Stark
Mark Addy as King Robert Baratheon
Michelle Fairley as Catelyn Stark
Natalie Dormer as Margaery Tyrell
Nikolaj Coster-Waldau as Jaime Lannister
Oona Chaplin as Queen Talisa Stark
Peter Dinklage as Tyrion Lannister
Richard Madden as Robb Stark
Rory McCann as Sandor Clegane
Rose Leslie as Ygritte

Sean Bean as Lord Eddard Stark
Sophie Turner as Sansa Stark
Stephen Dillane as King Stannis Baratheon

Guest Starring

Aimee Richardson as Princess Myrcella Baratheon
Amrita Acharia as Irri
Anton Lesser as Qyburn
Art Parkinson as Rickon Stark
Ben Hawkey as Hot Pie
Callum Wharry as Prince Tommen Baratheon
Ciarán Hinds as Mance Rayder
Clive Russell as Ser Brynden Tully
Conleth Hill as Lord Varys
Daniel Portman as Podrick Payne
Diana Rigg as Lady Olenna Tyrell
Ed Skrein as Daario Naharis
Ellie Kendrick as Meera Reed
Esme Bianco as Ros
Finn Jones as Loras Tyrell
Gemma Whelan as Yara Greyjoy
Hannah Murray as Gilly
Jerome Flynn as Bronn
Ian McElhinney as Lord Commander Barristan Selmy
Iwan Rheon as Ramsay Snow
Jacob Anderson as Grey Worm
James Cosmo as Jeor Mormont
Julian Glover as Grand Maester Pycelle
Kate Dickie as Lady Lysa Arryn
Kristian Nairn as Hodor
Kristofer Hivju as Tormund Giantsbane
Mackenzie Crook as Orell
Maisie Dee as Daisy
Mia Soteriou as Mirri Maz Duur
Michael McElhatton as Lord Roose Bolton
Natalia Tena as Osha

Nathalie Emmanuel as Missandei
Noah Taylor as Locke
Paul Kaye as Thoros of Myr
Richard Dormer as Lord Beric Dondarrion
Ron Donachie as Ser Rodrik Cassel
Sibel Kekilli as Shae
Thomas Brodie-Sangster as Jojen Reed
Tobias Menzies as Lord Edmure Tully

Appendix 2: Episode List

		Episode Title	Director	Writers
Season One				
1	1	"Winter Is Coming"	Tim Van Patten	David Benioff & D. B. Weiss
2	2	"The Kingsroad"	Tim Van Patten	David Benioff & D. B. Weiss
3	3	"Lord Snow"	Brian Kirk	David Benioff & D. B. Weiss
4	4	"Cripples, Bastards, and Broken Things"	Brian Kirk	Bryan Cogman
5	5	"The Wolf and the Lion"	Brian Kirk	David Benioff & D. B. Weiss
6	6	"A Golden Crown"	Daniel Minahan	Jane Espenson, David Benioff & D. B. Weiss
7	7	"You Win or You Die"	Daniel Minahan	David Benioff & D. B. Weiss
8	8	"The Pointy End"	Daniel Minahan	George R. R. Martin
9	9	"Baelor"	Alan Taylor	David Benioff & D. B. Weiss
10	10	"Fire and Blood"	Alan Taylor	David Benioff & D. B. Weiss
Season Two				
11	1	"The North Remembers"	Alan Taylor	David Benioff & D. B. Weiss
12	2	"The Night Lands"	Alan Taylor	David Benioff & D. B. Weiss
13	3	"What Is Dead May Never Die"	Alik Sakharov	Alik Sakharov
14	4	"Garden of Bones"	David Petrarca	Vanessa Taylor
15	5	"The Ghost of Harrenhal"	David Petrarca	David Benioff & D. B. Weiss
16	6	"The Old Gods and the New"	David Nutter	Vanessa Taylor
17	7	"A Man Without Honor"	David Nutter	David Benioff & D. B. Weiss

		Episode Title	Director	Writers
18	8	"The Prince of Winterfell"	Alan Taylor	David Benioff & D. B. Weiss
19	9	"Blackwater"	Neil Marshall	George R. R. Martin
20	10	"Valar Morghulis"	Alan Taylor	David Benioff & D. B. Weiss

Season Three

21	1	"Valar Dohaeris"	Daniel Minahan	David Benioff & D. B. Weiss
22	2	"Dark Wings, Dark Words"	Daniel Minahan	Vanessa Taylor
23	3	"Walk of Punishment"	David Benioff	David Benioff & D. B. Weiss
24	4	"And Now His Watch Is Ended"	Alex Graves	David Benioff & D. B. Weiss
25	5	"Kissed by Fire"	Alex Graves	Bryan Cogman
26	6	"The Climb"	Alik Sakharov	David Benioff & D. B. Weiss
27	7	"The Bear and the Maiden Fair"	Michelle MacLaren	George R. R. Martin
28	8	"Second Sons"	Michelle MacLaren	David Benioff & D. B. Weiss
29	9	"The Rains of Castamere"	David Nutter	David Benioff & D. B. Weiss
30	10	"Mhysa"	David Nutter	David Benioff & D. B. Weiss

Appendix 3: Archetypes

Anima—A man's inner female, the feminine presence that guides and completes him with emotion and spirituality.

Animus—A woman's inner male, the masculine side that offers rationality and order.

Caregiver—The generally feminized relative or other guardian whose entire motivation focuses on another person.

Crone—The elderly woman or grandmother. Freed from the demands of children, she may be a stateswoman, leader, or guide to the ancient wisdom.

Destroyer—Ender of the world and enemy of life but also catalyst for new growth.

Divine Child—One's blossoming creative side, the young demigod that bridges mystical heaven with common earth.

False Seer—Liar and distorter of the future.

Femininity—Traditionally behaviors and qualities such as dependency, submission, politeness, niceness, emotion, beauty, sensuality, gentleness, goodness, motherliness, sensitivity, permissiveness, softness, modesty, mystery, compassion, empathy, deference, conformity, and cooperation. These qualities can be performed by either gender.

Femme Fatale—The destructive lover as seductress and occasionally murderess.

Good Mother—Endless source of love and caring, vulnerable angelic side of the self.

Great Goddess—The creator, protector, and sometimes destroyer of the world, queen of life and death.

Hero/Heroine/Chosen One—The independent rule-breaker who changes the world while growing to adulthood and enlightenment, the metaphor for the Self.

Inner Child—An immature, unloved self desperate for affection and belonging.

Innocent—A person who believes the world will protect her if she behaves well enough. Among the Greek goddesses, she is a Persephone figure, kidnapped as a pawn for more powerful gods.

Lover/Hetaera—A character who allows love and devotion for another to dominate his or her personality. An Aphrodite woman in the spectrum of Greek gods.

Masculinity—Traditionally behaviors and qualities such as physical strength, power, aggression, authority, decisiveness, dominance, forcefulness, individualism, self-reliance, adventurousness, leadership, intellect, stoicism, rebelliousness, anger, sexual aggression, honor, toughness, ambition, boldness, competitiveness, assertiveness, and independence. These qualities can be performed by either gender.

Medium/Seer—The truth teller and predictor of the future who receives divine insights.

Mentor—Trains the hero or heroine in qualities needed for adulthood. Crones and Mediums frequently take this role.

Monster—The ultimate outsider. Female monsters are generally an outlet for female rage that's forbidden in society.

Mystery Woman—A woman whose motivations and origin are hidden from other characters. This role emphasizes women's status as Other rather than the norm.

Orphan—Suspicious and abandoned by protectors, this character grows into self-sufficient power.

Other/Outsider—The outcast rejected by society. Freed from social norms, this character often finds unusual approaches and sympathizes with society's downtrodden.

Patriarchy—The force of authority and conformity, the restrictive father. The king or father god usually embodies this archetype as the voice of society and its laws.

Persona—One's superficial self presented to others.

Predator—Greedy destroyer of other parts of the Self.

Self—The total personality, encompassing many archetypes, including those undiscovered.

Shadow/Alter-Ego—One's dark side—everything a person buries and refuses to acknowledge in herself.

Strong Woman—While a powerful character and often a warrior, the "strong woman" often lacks a more nuanced personality.

Terrible Mother—The killer of the innocent as wicked witch and traditional antagonist for the heroine or occasionally the hero.

Trickster—The playful rule-breaker and reverser, usually an outsider of a sort.

Warrior-Anima—The warrior woman in love (generally with a feminized man). In extreme examples, she is mostly anima, existing only to further the man's story.

Warrior Woman/Amazon—The powerful, masculinized woman who often disguises as a boy and operates in a man's world. The Career Woman is often considered a modern example of this trope.

Works Cited

Primary Sources

Anders, Charlie Jane. "George R.R. Martin: The Complete Unedited Interview." *IO9*, 23 July 2013. http://observationdeck.io9.com/george-r-r-martin-the-complete-unedited-interview-886117845.

Ashmole, Elias. *The Institutions, Laws, & Ceremonies of the Most Noble Order of the Garter.* Whitefish, MT: Kessinger, 1997.

Benioff, David. "A Real Sense of Purpose." "Kissed by Fire." *HBO Go*, 2013. Online Television. http://www.hbogo.com.

_____. "Unflappable." "Second Sons." *HBO Go*, 2013. Online Television. http://www.hbogo.com.

Cogman, Bryan. "Season 3 Interview: Bryan Cogman." *Game of Thrones Features*, 30 April 2013. http://www.westeros.org/GoT/Features/Entry/Season_3_Interview_Bryan_Cogman

De Graeve, Nikki. "Game of Thrones—Comic-Con Panel 2013." *Entertainment Outlook*, 20 July 2013. http://www.entertainmentoutlook.com/2013/07/20/game-of-thrones-comic-con-2013.

Eleanor of Aquitaine. "Third Letter." *Medieval and Renaissance Women's Voices.* Ed. Ulrike Böhm. USA: Project Hamlet, 2009. http://www.project-hamlet.info/womens-writings/eleanor.html.

Game of Thrones: The Complete First Season. HBO Home Entertainment, 2012. DVD.

Game of Thrones: The Complete Second Season. HBO Home Entertainment, 2013. DVD.

Game of Thrones: The Complete Third Season. HBO Go, 2013. Online Television. http://www.hbogo.com.

Ghahremani, Tanya. "Interview: 'Game of Thrones' Actress Sibel Kekilli Talks Working with Peter Dinklage and Who Should Win the Iron Throne." *Complex Magazine*, 26 May 2013. http://www.complex.com/pop-culture/2013/05/interview-sibel-kekilli-game-of-thrones.

"George R.R. Martin Interview." The World Science Fiction and Fantasy Convention. Chicago, IL. 29 Aug.–3 Sept. 2012.

Harte, Bryant. "An Interview with George R. R. Martin, Part I." *Indigo.ca*, 12 July 2011. http://blog.indigo.ca/fiction/item/512-an-interview-with-george-r-r-martin-part-one.html.

Hibberd, James. "EW Interview: George R.R. Martin Talks 'A Dance With Dragons,'" *EW*, 12 July 2011. http://shelf-life.ew.com/2011/07/12/george-martin-talks-a-dance-with-dragons.

_____. "'Game of Thrones' Michelle Fairley Explains Catelyn's Murderous Decision." *EWwww*, 3 Jun 2013. http://insidetv.ew.com/2013/06/03/catelyn-red-wedding.

Lacob, Jace. "Game of Thrones' Creative Gurus." *The Daily Beast*, 29 Aug 2011. http://www.thedailybeast.com/articles/2011/08/29/david-benioff-d-b-weiss-discuss-game-of-thrones-season-2-more.html.

_____. "'Game of Thrones': Esmé Bianco Talks About Ros, Sexposition, Nudity, and More." *The Daily Beast*, 18 May 2012. http://www.thedailybeast.com/

articles/2012/05/18/game-of-thrones-esm-bianco-talks-about-ros-sex position-nudity-and-more.html.

Martin, George R.R. "Arianne: Excerpt from *The Winds of Winter*." *Not a Blog*, 27 Jan 2013. http://www.georgerr martin.com/excerpt-from-the-winds-of-winter.

_____. "Chicon 7 Reading." *Westeros: The Song of Ice and Fire Domain*, 2 Sept 2012. http://www.westeros.org/Citadel/SSM/Category/C92.

_____. *A Clash of Kings*. New York: Bantam Books, 1999.

_____. Correspondence with Fans." *Westeros: The Song of Ice and Fire Domain*, 12 Feb 2001. http://www.westeros.org/Citadel/SSM/Category/C91/P120.

_____. "Correspondence with Fans." *Westeros: The Song of Ice and Fire Domain*, 15 Aug 2001. http://www.westeros.org/Citadel/SSM/Category/C91/P90.

_____. *A Dance with Dragons*. New York: Bantam Books, 2011.

_____. *A Feast for Crows*. New York: Bantam Books, 2005.

_____. *A Game of Thrones*. New York: Bantam Books, 1996.

_____. "The Hedge Knight." *Legends*. Ed. Robert Silverberg. New York: Tor, 1998. 451–534.

_____. "Interview in Barcelona." Asshai-www, July 28, 2012. http://www.westeros.org/Citadel/SSM/Entry/Asshai.com_Interview_in_Barcelona.

_____. "The Mystery Knight." *Warriors*. Ed. George R.R. Martin and Gardner Dozois. New York: Tor, 2010. 649–736.

_____. *A Storm of Swords*. New York: Bantam Books, 2000.

_____. "You Guys Are Scary Good, the Sequel." *Not a Blog*, 21 July 2011. http://grrm.livejournal.com/168824.html.

Martin, Michael. "Anna Paquin." *Interview Magazine*, 2013. http://www.interviewmagazine.com/film/anna-paquin-true-blood.

Mitchell, Elvis, with David Benioff and D.B. Weiss. "UpClose: Game of Thrones with David Benioff and D.B. Weiss." *KCRW's UpClose*, May 2013. https://soundcloud.com/kcrw/upclose-game-of-thrones-with.

Nguyen, Hanh. "*Game of Thrones*' Sophie Turner: Sansa Has Been Manipulated by Joffrey." *TV Guide*, 9 June 2011 http://www.tvguide.com/News/Game-Thrones-Sophie-Turner-1034079.aspx

Nicholson, Helen, ed. and trans. *Histoire des Ducs de Normandie et des Rois d'Angleterre*, ed. Francisque Michel. Paris: Renouard, 1840. http://freespace.virgin.net/nigel.nicholson/wom5.htm.

Parker, Melissa. "Sibel Kekilli Interview: 'Game of Thrones' Star Says, 'Shae Would Be the Perfect Queen.'" *Smashing Interviews*, 16 May 2013. http://smashinginterviews.com/interviews/actors/sibel-kekilli-interview-game-of-thrones-star-says-shae-would-be-the-perfect-queen.

Pasick, Adam. "George R.R. Martin on His Favorite *Game of Thrones* Actors and the Butterfly Effect of TV Adaptations." *Vulture*, 20 Oct 2011. http://www.vulture.com/2011/10/george_rr_martin_on_his_favori.html.

Pizan, Christine de. *Le Livre des Trois Vertus*. Trans. Garay and Jeay. Paris: H. Champion, 1989. http://mw.mcmaster.ca/scriptorium/links.html.

Roberts, Josh. "'Game of Thrones' Exclusive! George R.R. Martin Talks Season Two, 'The Winds of Winter,' and Real-World Influences for 'A Song of Ice and Fire.'" *Smarter Travel*, 1 Apr. 2012. http://www.smartertravel.com/blogs/today-in-travel/game-of-thrones-exclusive-george-martin-talks-season-the-winds-of-winter-and-real-world-influences-for-song-of-ice-and-fire.html?id=10593041.

Ryan, Mike. "*Game of Thrones*' Emilia Clarke on Eating Fake Horse Heart, Nude Scenes, and Ned's Fate." *Vulture*, 17 June 2011. http://www.vulture.com/2011/06/emilia_clarke.html.

Salter, Jessica. "Game of Thrones's George RR Martin: 'I'm a Feminist at Heart.'" *The Telegraph*, 1 Apr. 2013. http://www.telegraph.co.uk/women/womens-life/9959063/Game-of-Throness-George-RR-Martin-Im-a-feminist.html.

"Stars Turn Out for Game of Thrones Series 3 Premiere." *The Telegraph*, 27 Mar 2013 http://www.telegraph.co.uk/culture/tvandradio/9956322/Stars-turn-out-for-Game-of-Thrones-series-3-premiere.html.

"A Very Long Interview with George R.R. Martin." *Oh No They Didn't.com*, 10 Oct 2012. http://ohnotheydidnt.livejournal.com/72570529.html.

Vineyard, Jennifer. "*Game of Thrones*' Natalie Dormer on Power Plays and the Margaery-Joffrey Dynamic." *Vulture*, 22 Apr. 2013. http://www.vulture.com/2013/04/game-of-thrones-margaery-natalie-dormer-interview.html

Wieselman, Jarett. "Natalie Dormer: 'Thrones' Finale Will Traumatize." *ET Online*, 31 May 2013. http://www.etonline.com/tv/134654_Natalie_Dormer_Game_of_Thrones_Interview_Season_Three_Finale/index.html.

Secondary Sources

Alexander, Priscilla. "Prostitution: A Difficult Issue for Feminists." *A Gender and Culture Reader*. Ed. Sue Scott and Stevi Jackson. Edinburgh: Edinburgh University Press, 1996. 342–357.

Armstrong, Jennifer. "'Game of Thrones': Feminist or Not?" *Popwatch*, 18 Apr. 2011. http://popwatch.ew.com/2011/04/18/game-of-thrones-feminist-or-not.

Arthur, Kate. "9 Ways *Game Of Thrones* Is Actually Feminist." *Buzzfeed*, 17 Apr. 2013. http://www.buzzfeed.com/kateaurthur/9-ways-game-of-thrones-is-actually-feminist.

Baldick, Robert. *The Duel*. New York: Clarkson N. Potter, 1965.

Bellafante, Ginia. "A Fantasy World of Strange Feuding Kingdoms." *New York Times*, 14 April 2011 http://tv.nytimes.com/2011/04/15/arts/television/game-of-thrones-begins-sunday-on-hbo-review.html?_r=0.

Birmingham, John. "A Conversation with Game of Thrones Author George RR Martin." *Sydney Morning Herald*, 1 Aug. 2011. http://www.smh.com.au/technology/blogs/the-geek/a-conversation-with-game-of-thrones-author-george-rr-martin-20110801-1i6wj.html.

Blair, Casey. "Making Society Uncomfortable: Why Monsters Matter." *Sirens: Collected Papers 2009–2011*. Ed. Hallie Tibbetts. USA: Narrate Conferences, 2012. 117–134.

Bolen, Jean Shinoda. *Goddesses in Everywoman*. New York: Quill, 2004.

Booker, M. Keith, ed. "Feminism." *Encyclopedia of Comic Books and Graphic Novels. Volume 1*. Westport, CT: Greenwood, 2010.

Bornstein, Diane. *The Lady in the Tower: Medieval Courtesy Literature for Women*. Hamden, CT; Archon Books, 1983.

Carpenter, Jennifer, and Sally-Beth MacLean, eds. *Power of the Weak: Studies on Medieval Women*. Chicago: University of Illinois Press, 1995.

Castor, Helen. *She-Wolves: The Women Who Ruled England Before Elizabeth*. New York: Harper, 2011.

Chocano, Carina. "Tough, Cold, Terse, Taciturn and Prone to Not Saying Goodbye When They Hang Up the Phone." *New York Times*, 1 July 2011. http://www.nytimes.com/2011/07/03/magazine/a-plague-of-strong-female-characters.html?_r=0.

Clover, Carol J. "Her Body, Himself: Gender in the Slasher Film." *Feminist Film Theory*. Ed. Sue Thornham. Edinburgh: Edinburgh University Press, 1999, 234–250.

Cogman, Bryan. *Inside HBO's Game of*

Thrones. San Francisco: Chronicle Books, 2012.

Cole, Myke. "Art Imitates War: Post-Traumatic Stress Disorder in A Song of Ice and Fire." *Beyond the Wall: Exploring George R. R. Martin's* A Song of Ice and Fire. Ed. James Lowder. Dallas: BenBella Books, 2012, 73–87.

Cummings, Tucker. "From Gunsmoke to Game of Thrones: A Brief History of Prostitution on TV." *Sex Is Social*, 29 Feb. 2012. http://www.edenfantasys.com/sexis/sex-and-society/history-prostitution-television-0229121.

_____. "Thrillist Is Wrong: Women Love 'Game of Thrones,' and Here's Why!" *Yahoo TV*, May 16, 2013. http://tv.yahoo.com/news/thrillist-wrong-women-love-game-thrones-heres-why-173800210.html.

de Beauvoir, Simone. *The Second Sex*. Trans. Constance Borde and Shiela Malovany-Chevallier. New York: Knopf, 2009.

Delfondo, Luz. "Why More Feminists Should Watch Game of Thrones." *Disrupting Dinner Parties: Feminism for Everyone*, 14 June 2013. http://disruptingdinnerparties.com/2013/06/14/why-more-feminists-should-watch-game-of-thrones.

Doane, Mary Ann. *Femme Fatales: Feminism, Film Theory, Psychoanalysis*. New York: Routledge, 1991.

Downing, Christine. "Sisters and Brothers." *Mirrors of the Self: Archetypal Images That Shape Your Life*. New York: St. Martin's Press, 1991, 110–17.

Estés, Clarissa Pinkola. *Women Who Run with the Wolves*. New York: Ballantine, 1992.

Frankel, Valerie Estelle. *From Girl to Goddess: The Heroine's Journey through Myth and Legend*. Jefferson, NC: McFarland, 2010.

_____. *Winning the Game of Thrones: The Host of Characters and Their Agendas*. USA: LitCrit Press, 2013.

_____. *Winter Is Coming: Symbols and Hidden Meanings in* A Game of Thrones. Brooklyn, NY: Thought Catalogue, 2013.

Friedan, Betty. *The Feminine Mystique*. New York: W.W. Norton and Co., 1963.

"*Game of Thrones*: A Feminist Episode, a Gay Episode, or a Dull Episode? The *Game of Thrones* Roundtable." *The Atlantic*, 7 Apr. 2013. http://www.theatlantic.com/entertainment/archive/2013/04/-i-game-of-thrones-i-a-feminist-episode-a-gay-episode-or-a-dull-episode/274734/.

"Game of Thrones and Violence Against Women of Color." *Feminist TV*, http://feministtv.tumblr.com/post/52154773960/game-of-thrones-and-violence-against-women-of-color.

George, Demetra. *Mysteries of the Dark Moon: The Healing Power of the Dark Goddess*. New York: HarperCollins, 1992.

Glynn, Basil. "The Conquests of Henry VIII: Masculinity, Sex, and the National Past in The Tudors." *Television, Sex, and Society: Analyzing Contemporary Representations*. Eds. Basil Glynn, James Aston, and Beth Johnson. New York: Continuum, 2012, 157–173.

Goguen, Stacy. "'There Are No True Knights': The Injustice of Chivalry." *Game of Thrones and Philosophy: Logic Cuts Deeper Than Swords*. Ed. Henry Jacoby. New York: John Wiley & Sons, 2012, 205–219.

Halperin, David. *Saint Foucault: Towards a Gay Hagiography*. Oxford: Oxford University Press, 1995.

Hartinger, Brent. "A Different Kind of Other: The Role of Freaks and Outcasts in *A Song of Ice and Fire*." *Beyond the Wall: Exploring George R. R. Martin's* A Song of Ice and Fire. Ed. James Lowder. Dallas: BenBella Books, 2012, 153–168.

Haskell, Ann S. "The Paston Women on Marriage in Fifteenth-Century England." *Viator*, Vol. 4 (1973): 459–471.

Hill, Logan. "Inside the New Season of 'Game of Thrones,' TV's Sexiest Blood-Soaked Epic." *Rolling Stone*, 29 Mar. 2013. http://www.rollingstone.com/movies/news/inside-the-new-season-of-game-of-thrones-tvs-sexiest-blood-soaked-epic-20130329#ixzz2Ow7Lkjlz.

Hughes, Wind. "Maiden, Mother, Queen and Crone." *Sowell Magazine*, 2000.

Huneycutt, Lois L. "Intercession and the High-Medieval Queen: The Esther Topos." *Power of the Weak: Studies on Medieval Women*. Eds. Jennifer Carpenter and Sally-Beth MacLean. Chicago: University of Illinois Press, 1995, 126–146.

"In Defense of Cersei Lannister." *Feminist TV*, http://feministtv.tumblr.com/post/51697770740/in-defense-of-cersei-lannister.

Jacoby, Henry, ed. *Game of Thrones and Philosophy: Logic Cuts Deeper Than Swords*. New York: John Wiley & Sons, 2012.

Jones, David E. *Women Warriors: A History*. Washington: Brassey's, 1997.

Jung, Carl. *Collected Works 13: Alchemical Studies*. Trans. R. F. C. Hull. Princeton: Princeton University Press, 1967.

Jurich, Marilyn. *Scheherazade's Sisters: Trickster Heroines and Their Stories in World Literature*. Westport, CT: Greenwood, 1998.

Keveney, Bill. "In Game of Thrones, the Women Are." *USA Today*, 29 Mar. 2012.

Lowder, James, ed. *Beyond the Wall: Exploring George R. R. Martin's A Song of Ice and Fire*. Dallas: BenBella Books, 2012.

"Martial and Physical Arts." *The Oxford Encyclopedia of Women in World History*. Ed. Bonnie G. Smith. Oxford: Oxford University Press, 2012. http://www.oxfordreference.com.rpa.santaclaracountylib.org.

McDougall, Sophia. "I Hate Strong Female Characters." *New Statesman*, 15 Aug 2013. http://www.newstatesman.com/culture/2013/08/i-hate-strong-female-characters.

McGovern, Bridget. "Valyrian Roots: A Non-Spoiler Review of George R. R. Martin's 'The Princess and The Queen, Or, The Blacks and The Greens.'" Tor-www, 30 July 2013. http://www.tor.com/blogs/2013/07/story-review-george-r-r-martin-the-princess-and-the-queen-or-the-blacks-and-the-greens.

McNamara, Mary. "HBO, You're Busted." *Los Angeles Times*, 3 July 2013. http://articles.latimes.com/2011/jul/03/entertainment/la-ca-hbo-breasts-20110703.

McNutt, Myles. "Game of Thrones—'You Win or You Die.'" *Cultural Learnings*, 29 May 2011. http://cultural-learnings.com/2011/05/29/game-of-thrones-you-win-or-you-die.

Meslow, Scott. "*Game of Thrones* Finale: The Powerful Women of Westeros." *The Atlantic*, 20 June 2011. http://www.theatlantic.com/entertainment/archive/2011/06/game-of-thrones-finale-the-powerful-women-of-westeros/240686.

_____. "*Game of Thrones*: Making Sense of All the Sex." *The Atlantic*, 25 Apr. 2011. http://www.theatlantic.com/entertainment/archive/2011/04/game-of-thrones-making-sense-of-all-the-sex/237759.

Molton, Mary Dian, and Lucy Anne Sikes. *Four Eternal Women: Toni Wolff Revisited—A Study in Opposites*. Carmel, CA: Fisher King Press, 2011.

Mulhall, Elizabeth. "The Fans Doth Protest Too Much, Methinks: Is Game of Thrones Truly Feminist?" *Literatico*, 22 Apr. 2013. http://literatico.com/features-and-opinion/the-gender-card/the-fans-doth-protest-too-much-methinks-is-game-of-thrones-truly-feminist.

Mulvey, Laura. "Visual Pleasure and Narrative Cinema." *Screen*, 16.3 (Autumn 1975): 6–18. http://www.scribd. com/doc/7758866/laura-mulvey-visual-pleasure-and-narrative-cinema.

Murdock, Maureen. *The Heroine's Journey*. Boston: Shambhala Publications, 1990.

Newark, Tim. *Women Warriors*. New York: Sterling Publishing Co., 1991.

Noble, Oliver. "Game of Thrones' Sex Scenes and Nudity: The Complete Third Season." *The Huffington Post*, 10 June 2013. http://www.huffingtonpost. com/2013/06/10/game-of-thrones-sex-scenes-nudity_n_3417008.html.

Parsons, John Carmi. "The Queen's Intercession in Thirteenth-Century England." *Power of the Weak: Studies on Medieval Women*. Eds. Jennifer Carpenter and Sally-Beth MacLean. Chicago: University of Illinois Press, 1995, 147–177.

Pearson, Carol S. *Awakening the Heroes Within*. San Francisco: Harper San Francisco, 1991.

Peck, Jamie "Seven Reasons Women Love *Game Of Thrones*." *The Gloss*, 17 May 2013. http://www.thegloss.com/ 2013/05/17/culture/women-love-game-of-thrones.

Penny, Laurie. "Game of Thrones and the Good Ruler Complex." *New Statesman*, 4 June 2012. http://www.new statesman.com/blogs/laurie-penny/ 2012/06/game-thrones-and-good-ruler-complex.

Prioleau, Betsy. *Seductress: Women Who Ravished the World and Their Lost Art of Love*. New York: Penguin, 2003.

Rastogi, Nina Shen. "TV's Best Show about Women." *Salon*, 8 Apr. 2012. http://www.salon.com/2012/04/08/ tvs_best_show_about_women.

Rhiannon. "Are 'Most Women Stupid' in Game of Thrones: The Prince of Winterfell?" *Feminist Fiction*, 22 May 2012 http://feministfiction.com/2012/05/22/ do-most-women-suck-in-game-of-thrones-the-prince-of-winterfell.

_____. "Game of Thrones: Not the Women They Were Before." *Feminist Fiction*, 23 May 2013. http://feminist fiction.com/2013/05/23/game-of-thrones-not-the-women-they-were-before.

_____. "Sansa Stark Does Not Kneel." *Feminist Fiction*, 21 May 2013. http:// feministfiction.com/2013/05/21/sansa-stark-does-not-kneel.

_____. "Sexposition and Exploitation in HBO'S Game of Thrones." *Feminist Fiction*, 2 May 2012. http://feminist fiction.com/2012/05/02/sexposition-and-exploitation-in-hbos-game-of-thrones.

Rich, Adrienne. *Of Woman Born: Motherhood as Experience and Institution*. New York: Norton, 1976.

Rosenberg, Alyssa. "Men and Monsters: Rape, Myth-Making, and the Rise and Fall of Nations in A Song of Ice and Fire." *Beyond the Wall: Exploring George R. R. Martin's A Song of Ice and Fire*. Ed. James Lowder. Dallas: BenBella Books, 15–28.

Ruberg, Bonnie. "Women Monsters and Monstrous Women." *Escapist Magazine*, 1 Nov 2005. http://www.escapist magazine.com/articles/view/issues/ issue_17/105-Women-Monsters-and-Monstrous-Women.3.

Sackler, Jenna. "Women of Westeros: An Introduction to Feminism in Game of Thrones/A Song of Ice and Fire." *Feminists At Large*, 14 Mar 2013. http:// feministsatlarge.wordpress.com/2013/ 03/14/women-of-westeros-an-intro duction-to-feminism-in-game-of-thronesa-song-of-ice-and-fire.

Salmonson, Jessica Amanda. *The Encyclopedia of Amazons*. New York: Paragon House, 1991.

Sellitti, Renata. "The Reasons She Throws Shade on Your Medieval Man Show." *Thrillist*, 6 May 2013. http://www. thrillist.com/entertainment/nation/ why-girls-hate-game-of-thrones.

"Shocker (Not): Women Like Game of Thrones." *Persephone Magazine*, 7 June

2013. http://persephonemagazine.com/2013/06/07/shocker-not-women-like-game-of-thrones.

Silverman, Eric J. "Winter Is Coming: The Bleak Quest for Happiness in Westeros." *Game of Thrones and Philosophy: Logic Cuts Deeper Than Swords*. Ed. Henry Jacoby. New York: John Wiley & Sons, 2012, 63–74.

Smelik, Anneke. *And the Mirror Cracked: Feminist Cinema and Film Theory*. New York: St. Martin's Press, 1998.

Spector, Caroline. "Power and Feminism in Westeros." *Beyond the Wall: Exploring George R. R. Martin's A Song of Ice and Fire*. Ed. James Lowder. Dallas: BenBella Books, 169–187.

Stewart, Sara. "Dames of Thrones." *New York Post*, 26 March 2013. http://www.nypost.com/p/entertainment/dame_of_thrones.

Thornham, Sue. *Feminist Film Theory*. Edinburgh: Edinburgh University Press, 1999.

Walker, Barbara G. *The Crone*. San Francisco: Harper San Francisco, 1985.

Zeisler, Andi. "Does It Matter Whether Game of Thrones is Feminist?" *Bitch Magazine*, 7 June 2013. http://bitchmagazine.org/post/does-it-matter-whether-game-of-thrones-is-feminist.

Index

Index